Early Cambridge theatres

The excavations of the Rose and the Globe theatres have created renewed scholarly controversy about the reconstruction of English Renaissance theatres. This book engages with this debate by attempting a reconstruction of early Cambridge theatres in the context of the professional theatres of Renaissance London. Cambridge provides a rich source of material: most of the college halls and chapels in which scaffold-theatres were constructed still stand, while records of the Cambridge theatres and the plays performed in them survive in hitherto unrecognized abundance. The Queens' College theatre (1546–9) is reconstructed and illustrated in minute detail. The stage for Trinity College hall (built by Nevile c. 1605), which was the site of numerous royal visits involving plays, is also reconstructed, while the college's tiring chamber, comedy room, and acting chamber are the subject of close detective work. The book includes a full survey of some dozen Cambridge colleges, the university's commencement stage, and extramural theatrical sites used by travelling professional companies, which leads to useful comparisons with the theatres of London. The author concludes with a plea for greater attention to documentary evidence in reconstructing English Renaissance theatres.

This book will be of interest to historians of English Renaissance theatre, as well as to those working on the history of university drama, and the history of the university of Cambridge.

Frontispiece Trinity College hall, constructed c. 1605, looking toward upper end. Door in upper-end wall on left (west) is functional; door on right (east) is currently blocked.

Early Cambridge theatres

college, university, and town stages,
1464–1720

Alan H. Nelson

Professor of English, University of California, Berkeley

CAMBRIDGE
UNIVERSITY PRESS

792.0942
N42e

Published by the Press Syndicate of the University of Cambridge
The Pitt Building, Trumpington Street, Cambridge, CB2 1RP
40 West 20th Street, New York, NY 10011-4211, USA
10 Stamford Road, Oakleigh, Melbourne 3166, Australia

© Cambridge University Press 1994

First published 1994

Printed in Great Britain at the University Press, Cambridge

A catalogue record for this book is available from the British Library

Library of Congress cataloguing in publication data

Nelson, Alan H.
Early Cambridge theatres: college, university, and town stages, 1464–1720 / Alan H.
Nelson.
    p.   cm.
Includes bibliographical references and index.
ISBN 0 521 43177 8
1. Theatres – England – Cambridge – History – 16th century.
2. Theatres – England – Cambridge – History – 17th century.   I. Title.
PN2596.C3N45   1994
792′.09426′59–dc20   93-31690   CIP

ISBN 0 521 43177 8 hardback

TAG

Early Cambridge theatres

college, university, and town stages, 1464–1720

Alan H. Nelson

Professor of English, University of California, Berkeley

CAMBRIDGE
UNIVERSITY PRESS

792.0942
N42e

Published by the Press Syndicate of the University of Cambridge
The Pitt Building, Trumpington Street, Cambridge, CB2 1RP
40 West 20th Street, New York, NY 10011-4211, USA
10 Stamford Road, Oakleigh, Melbourne 3166, Australia

© Cambridge University Press 1994

First published 1994

Printed in Great Britain at the University Press, Cambridge

A catalogue record for this book is available from the British Library

Library of Congress cataloguing in publication data

Nelson, Alan H.
Early Cambridge theatres: college, university, and town stages, 1464–1720 / Alan H.
Nelson.
  p. cm.
Includes bibliographical references and index.
ISBN 0 521 43177 8
1. Theatres – England – Cambridge – History – 16th century.
2. Theatres – England – Cambridge – History – 17th century. I. Title.
PN2596.C3N45   1994
792′.09426′59–dc20   93-31690   CIP

ISBN 0 521 43177 8 hardback

TAG

To the memory of Sam Wanamaker, 1919–1993

Contents

List of illustrations   *page* viii
Preface   ix
Acknowledgements   xi
List of abbreviations   xii
Note on sources   xiv

1   Introduction: London to Cambridge   1
2   Queens' College   16
3   Trinity College from 1605   38
4   Other colleges   61
5   The university commencement stage, 1464–1720   77
6   Secular playing sites   88
7   Cambridge staging practices   102
8   Postscript: Cambridge to London   118

Appendixes

1   Matthew Stokys on extraordinary commencement, 1564   127
2   Nicholas Robinson on extraordinary commencement, 1564   129
3   Queens' College stage inventory, 1640   131
4   Comments on Queens' College stage inventory, 1640   137
5   Security plans for royal visit, March 1615.   140
6   Records of Trinity College drama, 1661–96   142
7   Tabor's search for the university theatre, c. 1620   153
8   University graces for a theatre, 1673–5   154
9   Commencement stage timber dimensions, 1528–1668   156
10 Records of the university proctors' booth, 1597–1638   158

Notes   161
Select bibliography   178
Index   180

Illustrations

	Trinity College hall.	frontispiece ii
1.	Cambridge, c. 1615.	*page* 4
2.	Plan of shopkeeper's house, Moxon, *Mechanick Exercises.*	6
3.	Elevation of shopkeeper's house, Moxon, *Mechanick Exercises.*	8
4.	Demountable stage construction.	9
5.	King's College Chapel, 1564 stage superimposed.	11
6.	Commencement stage, royal visit of August 1564.	12
7.	Queens' College hall, stage superimposed.	17
8.	Queens' College stage, great gallery, first face.	19
9.	Queens' College stage, great gallery, second face.	20
10.	Queens' College stage, great gallery, third face.	21
11.	Queens' College stage, great gallery.	22
12.	Queens' College stage, east side and screens galleries.	23
13.	Queens' College stage, west tiring house.	25
14.	Queens' College stage, stage platform.	26
15.	Queens' College stage, east addition.	27
16.	Queens' College stage, west addition.	27
17.	Queens' College stage, west addition with doorway.	28
18.	Queens' College stage, horizontal timbers.	30
19.	Queens' College stage, perspective view.	31
20.	Trinity College hall, stage superimposed.	41
21.	Trinity College hall stage, schematic reconstruction.	42
22.	Loggan print of Trinity College, 1688 (detail).	44
23.	Trinity College hall, from behind upper-end wall.	45
24.	Trinity College, 1555, plan.	46
25.	Trinity College master's lodge, groundplan.	47
26.	Trinity College, 1920, back of upper-end wall of hall, east side.	49
27.	Trinity College, 1920, back of upper-end wall of hall, west side.	50
28.	Jesus College, plan showing chapel and great hall.	72
29.	Commencement stage, 1613.	80
30.	Commencement stage, 1615.	81
31.	Cambridge Guildhall, 1781, upper level.	90
32.	Custance Map of Cambridge, 1798, Guildhall and innyards.	93
33.	Falcon Inn yard, 1883.	94
34.	Falcon Inn yard, c. 1860.	95
35.	Falcon Inn, c. 1820, gallery detail.	96
36.	Wandlebury Round, Gog Magog Hills.	101

Preface

My aim is to reconstruct as many early Cambridge theatres as evidence permits, both for their own sakes and for comparison with professional theatres of Renaissance London. The total bulk of surviving evidence is so enormous that to have printed all relevant documents between the covers of this book would have been out of the question, and even to have supplied full citations to every piece of evidence adduced would have increased its size unconscionably. In composing my text and notes, therefore, I have tried to keep in mind a general reader willing to take my word for places and dates, and for the accuracy of my transcriptions. The specialist or the constitutionally sceptical reader who wishes to track down and verify individual pieces of evidence will, I trust, consult not only standard reference works, but two specialized reference works, both of which I have myself edited: the two-volume *Cambridge* collection in the Records of Early English Drama series (1989), here cited as REED; and the unpublished 'The Cambridge University Commencement Stage, 1464–1720', here cited as CUCS, housed in the Manuscripts Room of the Cambridge University Library.

In the course of assembling these documents and arguments, I have encountered numerous instances of generosity, above all from Dr Elisabeth Leedham-Green, Deputy Keeper of the Cambridge University Archives. Dr Leedham-Green is one of many who not only showered me with information, advice, and other forms of assistance, but in fact saved me from a multitude of errors and embarrassments, and in vain strove to save me from yet more. My many other advisors include Richard Beadle, Herbert Berry, Susan Cerasano, John Cotton, Creighton Don, Elizabeth Freidberg, R. H. Glauert, Michael Heaney, William Lepowsky, David McKitterick, Michael J. Petty, Conrad Russell, L. G. Salingar, Clare Sargent, John Twigg, Iain Wright, Abigail Young, and several anonymous readers for the Press. I am grateful to Sarah Stanton of Cambridge University Press for her continuing support from the time this project was little more than an outline on the back of an envelope, and to Rosemary Morris for catching and correcting errors and inconsistencies of style and orthography.

My work has been made possible by the access I have been granted to the libraries and archives of the University of Cambridge and of Queens' College and Trinity College; the Cambridge County Record Office, Shire Hall, Cambridge; the Cambridgeshire Collection, Central Library, Cambridge; the Library of All Souls

College, Oxford (by correspondence); the British Library, Senate House Library, Institute of Historical Research, and Public Record Office in London; the library of the University of California, Berkeley; and the Huntington Library in San Marino, California.

The University of California, Berkeley, has been an important source of support. Its Committee on Research provided me with funds for the hardware and AutoCad software which created my line drawings. The staff of the Berkeley Department of Architecture initiated me into the mysteries of CAD, and allowed me access to the plotter which created the final drawings. The Education Abroad Program of the University of California provided me with the opportunity to spend two years on an administrative appointment within easy reach of Cambridge. Finally, I am grateful to Judith Nelson for putting up with my long periods of absence and abstraction.

News of the death of Sam Wanamaker on 18 December 1993 reached me as I was reading page proofs. Sam Wanamaker lived to see the new Globe's first theatrical performance on 23 April 1993, and though the timber polygon was not complete by the time of his death, he saw his project through to the point where its eventual and even imminent completion was assured. I dedicate this book to his memory.

Acknowledgements

I am grateful to the following for permission to reproduce illustrations and cite documents:

John Bethell Photography, St Albans: Frontispiece.

The British Library: Figs. 31, 35.

The Director of the Cambridge University Archives: all citations from the University Archives.

The Syndics of Cambridge University Library: Figs. 22, 24, 25, 28, 32, 36.

Cambridgeshire Collection, Cambridgeshire Libraries: Fig. 34.

Ordnance Survey: Fig. 36.

The Folger Shakespeare Library: Appendix 2

The Huntington Library: Figs. 2, 3.

Records of Early English Drama: Figs. 1, 5, 7, 20; Appendix 3.

Royal Commission on Historical Monuments, England: Figs. 5, 7, 20, 28 (Crown Copyright).

The Master and Fellows of Trinity College: Figs. 26–7; Appendix 5.

Abstract

Abbreviations

Atkinson — Thomas Dinham Atkinson, *Cambridge Described and Illustrated: Being a Short History of the Town and University* (London, 1897).

Chambers, *ES* — Edmund K. Chambers, *The Elizabethan Stage*, 4 vols. (Oxford, 1923).

Cooper — Charles Henry Cooper, *Annals of Cambridge*, 5 vols. (vol. V ed. John Williams Cooper) (Cambridge, 1842–1908).

CUCS — 'The Cambridge University Commencement Stage, 1464–1720', ed. Alan H. Nelson. Housed in Manuscripts Room, Cambridge University Library.

DNB — *Dictionary of National Biography*, ed. Leslie Stephen and Sidney Lee, 21 vols. (London, 1921–2).

Mullinger — James Bass Mullinger, *The University of Cambridge*, 3 vols. (Cambridge, 1873–1911).

OED — *Oxford English Dictionary*, 13 vols. First edn (Oxford, 1933).

Orrell, *HS* — John Orrell, *The Human Stage: English Theatre Design, 1567–1640* (Cambridge, 1988).

RCHM — Royal Commission on Historical Monuments, England, *An Inventory of the Historical Monuments in the City of Cambridge*, 2 parts with accompanying box of plans (London, 1959).

REED — *Cambridge*, 2 vols., ed. Alan H. Nelson, Records of Early English Drama (Toronto, 1989).

Smith, *CP* — George Charles Moore Smith, *College Plays Performed in the University of Cambridge* (Cambridge, 1923).

Smith, 'Academic' — George Charles Moore Smith, 'The Academic Drama at Cambridge: Extracts from College Records,' *Collections*, vol. II, pt 2, Malone Society (Oxford, 1923), pp. 150–231.

STC — *A Short-Title Catalogue of Books Printed in England, Scotland, and Ireland, and of English Books Printed Abroad, 1475–1640*, comp. A. W. Pollard and G. R. Redgrave; 2nd edn Katharine F. Pantzer, 3 vols. (London, 1976–91).

VCH	The Victoria History of the Counties of England, *History of the County of Cambridge and the Isle of Ely*, vol. III: *The City and University of Cambridge*, ed. J. P. C. Roach (London, 1959).
Venn	John Venn and J. A. Venn, compilers, *Alumni Cantabrigienses*, Part 1: *From the Earliest Times to 1751*, 4 vols. (Cambridge, 1922–7).
W&C	Robert Willis and John Willis Clark, *The Architectural History of the University of Cambridge and of the Colleges of Cambridge and Eton*, 4 vols. (Cambridge, 1886; vols. I–III rpt 1988).
Wing	*A Short-Title Catalogue of Books Printed in England, Scotland, Ireland, and British America, and of English Books Printed in Other Countries, 1641–1700*, comp. Donald Wing, 2nd edn, 3 vols. (New York, 1972–88).

Note on sources

Cambridge dramatic records up to 1642 are cited from REED (by academic year and institution). An endnote is supplied when a citation is buried in a document several printed pages or more in length, or occurs elsewhere than under the expected year.

Trinity College records from 1661–2 to 1695–6 are cited from Appendix 6 (by academic year).

Cambridge commencement records from 1463–4 to 1719–20 are cited from CUCS (by academic year), a transcription of and guide to records in the Cambridge University Archives, including Grace Books to 1543–4, and MSS U.Ac.1(1–6), U.Ac.2(1–2), and VCV.1–12. An endnote is supplied when a citation occurs elsewhere than under the expected year.

Dating is usually by academic year (e.g. 1563–4), reflecting the standard organization of original documents and published transcriptions. Since most dramatic and degree-granting activity occurred after 1 January in any year, the calendar reference should normally be understood as referring to the *latter* part of the year (here, 1564).

Text and notes: I follow printed sources (including my own appendixes), except that I always substitute 'th' for thorn; I expand abbreviations silently; I overlook scribal deletions; I include scribal corrections and insertions silently except where the original text is positively ambiguous.

Appendixes: I follow rules outlined in REED, pp. 813–16, except that I substitute 'th' for thorn. Appendix 3 is a photographic reproduction of the 1640 Queens' College inventory as printed in REED, pp. 688–93.

1

Introduction: London to Cambridge

31 January 1989. Bankside, Southwark. Workmen excavating for an office complex near Southwark Bridge on the South Bank of the Thames strike an ancient chalk foundation. Archaeologists from the Museum of London order a temporary halt to the excavation. The world is amazed as newspapers and television report the discovery of the Rose theatre. For all the joy at finding the remains of an original English Renaissance theatre, however, academic experts are perplexed, even dismayed. The Rose, as it emerges from the mud, is not what they had thought it must be.

Also in 1989, under the leadership of the actor and visionary Sam Wanamaker, scholars are nearing the fulfilment of another life's dream: the reconstruction of Shakespeare's First Globe theatre in near-perfect detail. Theatre historians have consulted among themselves, academic conferences have been convened, books have been written, architects have been hired, and a funding drive is well under way. With the discovery of the Rose, however, doubts begin to creep in: fundamental principles of the reconstruction are thrown into question; confidence in architectural drawings wanes; funds which might have reconstructed the First Globe are diverted to saving the foundations of the Rose.[1]

In several respects the experts were vindicated by the Rose excavation. If it is possible to generalize from one playhouse to all playhouses, then Elizabethan and early Jacobean public theatres were not round, as they are shown in many contemporary drawings, but polygonal, as they are shown in other drawings. The polygonal shell, moreover, contained galleries in its sides, and the stage was located against one side of the interior yard.

In respect to certain general principles and numerous small details, by contrast, the experts had indeed erred. The theatrical polygon, many had argued and most agreed, had to have sides in multiples of four, probably a total of sixteen or twenty-four; but the Rose evidently had fourteen sides, or perhaps only thirteen. The polygon had to be completely regular, its sectors highly uniform; but the sides of the Rose were far from uniform, and reconstruction within a decade of its first construction turned an irregular 'O' into a mis-shaped 'D'. The internal dimensions must have been established by the medieval *ad quadratum* geometrical method; but no unequivocal geometrical or mathematical relationships are discernible in the foundations as uncovered. The stage had to reach from the inside of the polygon to near the centre of the yard; but this stage was shallow and reached only about half way to the centre. The stage platform must be rectangular and large; but the stage platform of the Rose was not only shallow, but narrowed toward the front in the manner of a trapezoid or squashed hexagon.[2]

This was the Rose, of course, and not the Globe, but more was known about many other theatres than about either the First or the Second Globe, which meant that the Globe had to be reconstructed not so much from physical, pictorial, or archival evidence as by hypothesis. Since the foundations of the Globe have now been discovered in part, it is possible that evidence necessary to a faithful reconstruction will yet surface; in any case, Sam Wanamaker's dream is now being realized as the Globe rises bay by bay on Bankside.[3] Clearly, however, reconstruction of Renaissance theatres by resort to abstract geometrical principles has suffered a hard knock.[4]

I propose to try an approach to English Renaissance theatre design which avoids appeals to abstract principles, and is as close as possible in nature to the excavations on the south bank of the Thames. Herbert Berry has already done something of this sort for the Boar's Head playhouse.[5] For my part, I propose to look at buildings which are known to have been used for plays and which for the most part survive intact; I propose to look at archival records and contemporary descriptions for evidence of construction of particular theatres; and I propose to devote my attention in the first instance to Cambridge rather than London. Cambridge – I hope – will shed new light on murky London territory, and test claims for priority on behalf of the capital.

Cambridge is not the only provincial town available for study, but it is a logical one at the moment, first because the extensive records of early Cambridge drama have recently been published, secondly because I myself am the editor of the records and am thus pretty familiar with them, thirdly because there is yet more to be learned than is contained in the records volumes, and fourthly because Cambridge has a vital connection with London drama, having supplied Christopher Marlowe, Thomas Nashe, and Robert Green (among many others) to the London stage.[6]

Marlowe, Nashe, and Green, being playwrights and not stagewrights, could well have supplied literary texts without making a concomitant impression on London stagecraft or playhouse construction. Furthermore, whereas Cambridge hall theatres provide a natural antecedent for indoor London theatres like Blackfriars, the connection to London's open-air amphitheatres is less obvious. I believe, nevertheless, that stage construction in Cambridge may tell us something about playhouse construction in London, particularly if I am right in my further belief that theatres in both locations were designed not by architects under the influence of classical and Italian models, but by carpenters applying century-old techniques of construction in timber.

Cambridge: an overview

Most of the historic town of Cambridge (fig. 1) lies within a bend of the river Cam: if the river's bend is imagined as an arc lying to the north-west, the market and the principal church, Great St Mary's, may be imagined as lying near the point from which the arc is swung. Backing on to the river or very near it lie all but one of the colleges which will concern us. Clockwise from the south-west, these are Peterhouse, Pembroke and Corpus Christi (both away from the river), Queens', King's, Clare, the college of Gonville and Caius (away from the river), Trinity Hall (which we shall largely overlook), Trinity, St John's, and Jesus. This leaves out only Christ's, south-east of the market near the suburb of Barnwell. Also inland but nearer the market are the Guildhall and (formerly) the Falcon Inn. Several miles down-river to the north-east are Chesterton on the left bank and the grounds of Sturbridge Fair on the right. Some three miles to the south-east lies Wandlebury Round, an Iron Age hill fort in the Gog Magog Hills.[7]

With one major exception, all the institutions relevant to my investigation were in place by 1520: the university itself, established in the early thirteenth century (and by 1520 beginning to rival Oxford); most of the early colleges, including St John's (the most recent), founded in 1511; the church of Great St Mary's, reconstruction essentially complete by 1520; the Guildhall, built in the fourteenth century; and the Falcon Inn, established by the early sixteenth century. The exception is Trinity College, which arose in 1546 from an amalgamation of three earlier institutions, including King's Hall, but which quickly established itself as the most active of play-producing colleges.[8]

Thanks to the active creation and preservation of records as well as to a flourishing tradition of drama, more performances and more general dramatic activity are recorded for Cambridge through the 1560s than for any other town or city in England, including London.[9] Professional players sometimes made use of venues such as the Guildhall and the Falcon, though information about the plays they performed is wanting. Some 300 individual college performances are known or can be inferred before 1576: beginning in 1456–7, burgeoning in the 1520s and 1530s, and reaching a veritable frenzy in the 1550s, with at least one and as many as five plays a year at Christ's, Corpus, King's, Queens', St John's, and Trinity.[10] The construction of stages, merely implied in late fifteenth-century records, is fully verifiable from the 1530s, while abundant details are available from the 1540s and 1550s. Later records give even more of the picture, down to 1640, the date of an elaborate stage inventory from Queens' College, and to 1671–2 at Trinity College, the final year of the pre-modern college playing tradition at Cambridge.[11]

Some sixty original Cambridge play texts survive from about 1540 onward (REED, Appendix 6): these include imitations of classical tragedies and comedies; translations of Italian comedy (usually into Latin but occasionally into English); farce, including the still-admired *Gammer Gurton's Needle* (c. 1551); and thoroughly domesticated satire, including the *Parnassus* trilogy (c. 1600–3), which includes important allusions

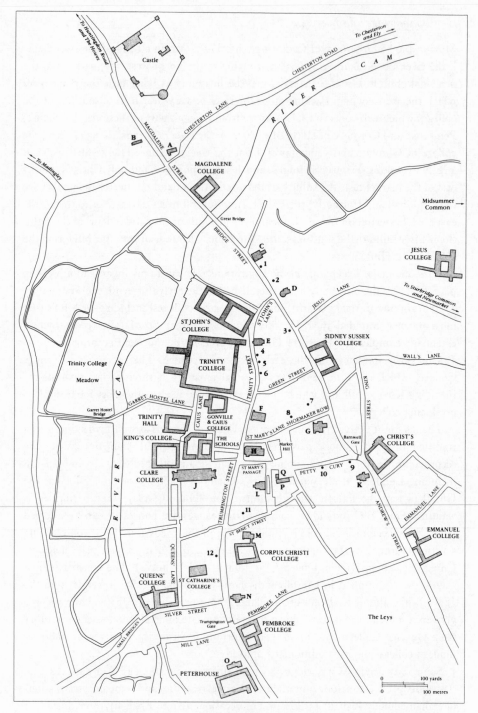

Fig. 1.   Cambridge, c. 1615. H: Great St Mary's Church; J: King's College Chapel; P: Guild Hall; 2: Elephant (conjectural); 7: Bear; 10: Falcon; 11: Eagle. (Full key in REED, p. 838.)

to Shakespeare and Ben Jonson (REED, p. xiv). Taking a warning from scholars who have experienced qualified success at best in using play texts as evidence of London theatre construction, however, I have mostly (though not entirely) shunned texts as evidence of production techniques, trusting instead that documentary evidence will serve more successfully to shed eventual light on the texts.

The halls in which most college plays were performed were of a fairly uniform plan (see frontispiece, figs. 7, 20). All were substantial rectangular rooms with distinctive upper and lower ends.[12] In general, doors to the outside were provided at the lower end on both sides of the hall. These doors were often separated from the body of the hall by a light wooden wall called 'the screens', normally in three panels defining two openings. When the screens passage was covered, as was usually the case, the natural result was a gallery above, overlooking the hall. (Sometimes romantically styled 'minstrels' galleries' in modern times, such structures played a negligible role in early play productions.)[13] At the upper end of the hall was generally a single door through which persons of higher standing entered the hall, and a wooden platform – the dais – raised perhaps a foot above the hall floor. Upon the dais stood in normal circumstances the table for the master of the college, senior fellows, fellow commoners, and important guests. As a consequence of the hierarchical ordering of persons dining in the hall, the upper end came to be regarded as superior under all circumstances. Yet another feature of many college halls was an oriel, or large bow window, generally in the side wall at or near the upper end, intended to increase the amount of daylight entering the hall, and also perhaps to afford additional floor-space.

Moxon's 'Mechanick Exercises'

As a handbook for my investigation of the timber stage structures built in college halls and other Cambridge venues, I have chosen *Mechanick Exercises, or, The Doctrine of Handy-works*, written and published in parts beginning in 1678 by Joseph Moxon.[14] Parts I to III are devoted to 'Smithing'; Parts IV to VI to 'The Art of Joynery', or fine carpentry; Parts VII to IX to 'The Art of House-Carpentry'. The first English manual for the building trades, *Mechanick Exercises* was not superseded until 1733.[15]

Moxon's modern reputation rests almost exclusively on his second volume, *Mechanick Exercises, or, The Doctrine of Handy-works. Applied to the Art of Printing*, published in 1683.[16] The relative neglect of the first volume is to be regretted, for Moxon bears approximately the same relation to the carpenters who built Renaissance English theatres as to the printers who issued Renaissance English plays.

As historians of printing have long appreciated, Moxon is a model of descriptive clarity. His use of specialist terminology, rather than being obscurantist, lends an air of sturdy eloquence to his prose:

> At the heighth of the first story in this Principal Post, must be made two Mortesses, one to receive the Tennant at the end of the Bressummer that lies in the Front, and the other

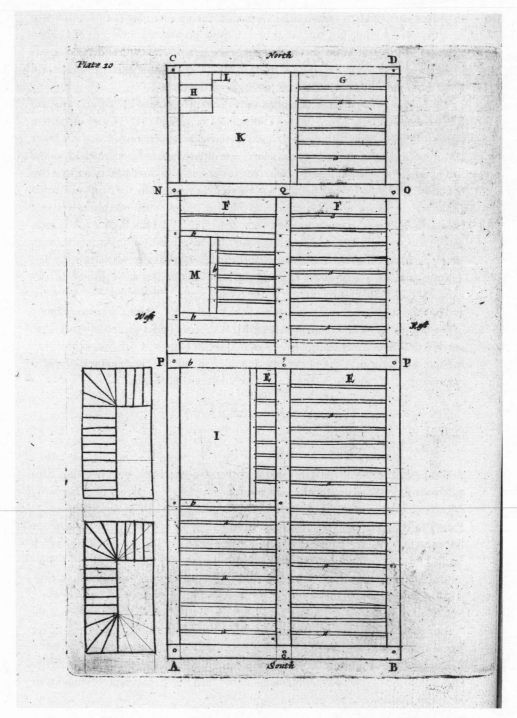

Fig. 2.   Plan of shopkeeper's house, from Joseph Moxon, *Mechanick Exercises* (Wing, M3013), plate 10.

to entertain the Tennant at the end of the Bressummer that lies in the Return side. (p. 138)

Typical is Moxon's use of 'entertain' as a delightful double for the more literal-minded 'receive': here as elsewhere, he conducts his parallel constructions like a skilled rhetorician, and varies his language like a poet.

Moxon is fully a man of his time and place in his equivocal attitude toward design:

> Being now come to exercise upon the Carpenters Trade, it may be expected by some that I should insist upon Architecture, it being so absolutely necessary for Builders to be acquainted with: But my answer to them is, that there are so many Books of Architecture extant, and in them the Rules so well, so copiously, and so completely handled, that it is needless for me to say anything of that Science: Nor do I think any man that should, can do more than collect out of their Books, and perhaps deliver their meanings in his own words. Besides, Architecture is a Mathematical Science, and therefore different from my present undertakings, which are (as by my Title) Mechanick Exercises: yet because Books of Architecture are as necessary for a Builder to understand as the use of Tools; and lest some Builder should not know how to enquire for them, I shall at the latter end of Carpentry give you the Names of some Authors, especially such as are printed in the English Tongue. (p. 119)

At the close of his third and final part on carpentry, proving as good as his word, Moxon names seven 'Titles of some Books of Architecture':

> *Sebastion Seirlio*, in Folio.
> *Hans Bloom's* Five Collumns, Folio.
> *Vignola*, in Folio.
> *Vignola*, Or the *Compleat Architect*, in Octavo
> *Scamotzi*, Quarto.
> *Palladio*, Quarto.
> Sir *Henry Wotton's* Elements of Architecture, Quarto.
>
> These Books are all Printed in English: But there are many others extant in several other Languages, of which *Vitruvius* is the chief: For from his Book the rest are generally derived; as *Philip Le Orm, Ditterlin, Marlois*, and many others, which being difficult to be had among Book-sellers, and these sufficient for information, I shall omit till another opportunity. (p. 162)

More eloquent of Moxon's true attitude toward design is his shopkeeper's house (figs. 2–3), which owes nothing to books on architecture, and everything to centuries-old north European traditions of construction in timber. With a full knowledge of Vitruvius, Serlio, and Palladio, and having himself published *Vignola, Or the Compleat Architect*,[17] Moxon in practice limits his application of architectural principles to an occasional surface feature, like wainscoting.[18] Like the designers of English Renaissance theatres – Inigo Jones is the classic exception – Moxon was concerned not with architecture, but with carpentry.[19]

Moxon will serve in the first instance as a guide to contemporary nomenclature. He provides, in an alphabetical list cross-referenced to his illustrations of the shopkeeper's

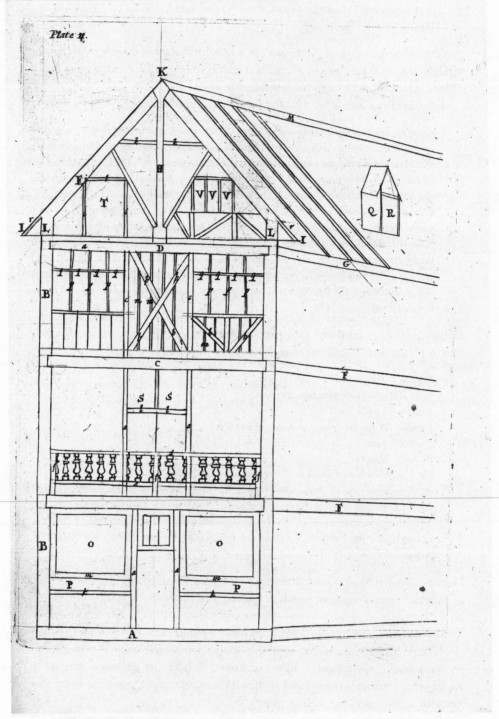

Fig. 3. Elevation of shopkeeper's house, from Joseph Moxon, *Mechanick Exercises* (Wing, M3013), plate 11.

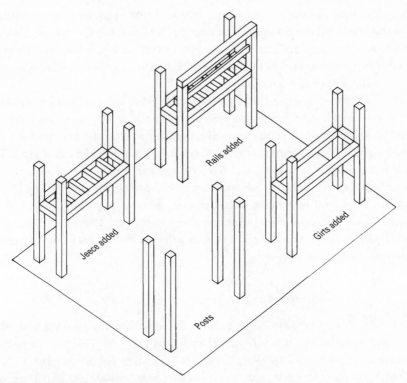

Fig. 4.   Demountable stage construction, typical disposition of essential timbers.

house, 'An Explanation of Terms used in Carpentery' (pp. 163–73): thus we learn that a 'Carcass, is (as it were) the Skelleton of an House, before it is Lath'd and Plaistered', and that 'Principal-Posts' are 'The Corner Posts of a Carcass'.

Moxon also explains the relative disposition of each sort of timber:

> It is to be remembered that the Bressummers and Girders are laid flat upon one of their broadest sides, with their two narrowest sides perpendicular to the Ground-Plot; but the Joysts are to be laid contrary: for they are framed so as to lie with one of their narrowest sides upwards, with their two broadest sides perpendicular to the Ground-Plot. The reason is, because the Stuff of the Bressummers and Girders are less weakened by cutting the Mortesses in them in this position, than in the other position; for as the Tennants for those Mortesses are cut between the top and bottom sides, and the flat of the Tennants are no broader than the flat of the narrowest side of the Joysts; so the Mortesses they are to fit into, need be no broader than the breadth of the Tennant, and the Tennants are not to be above an inch thick, and consequently the Mortesses are to be made with an Inch Mortess-Chissel ... for great care must be taken that the Bressummers and Girders be not weakened more than needs, least the whole Floor dance. (p. 139)

This information will prove highly useful to us, particularly the observation that joists (Cambridge: 'jeece') are traditionally mortised into the girders (Cambridge: 'girts'), rather than lying over them as in modern frame construction.[20]

The inventory of Queens' College stage in 1640 – the single most important document which we shall be analyzing – tells us virtually nothing about the scantlings (= cross-sectional dimensions) of the stage timbers, but we may rely on Moxon as a guide to carpenters' practice.[21] The inventory tells us where but little about how timbers were joined: as we have just witnessed, Moxon describes standard conventions for cutting mortise-and-tenon joints.

In the timber-frame construction described by Moxon, as it applies to Cambridge stage construction, the primary verticals at the corners and junctions are called posts (see fig. 4); intermediate verticals may also be called posts but are more properly called studs. The primary horizontals at the level of a raised floor are called girts. These horizontal timbers carry jeece, which intersect at right angles. The jeece carry floorboards (not shown in fig. 4, but easily imagined). Stability is provided by braces of various kinds, and by binding-jeece (lying in the same plane as regular jeece, but mortised into vertical timbers). Running from post to post above the level of a floor were rails, serving to protect against falls, as well as to provide additional strength and integrity to the structure.

Royal Cambridge: Elizabeth's visit of August 1564

Late July 1564. Cambridge. Lewis Stocket, Surveyor from the royal Office of Works, arriving in advance of a royal visit scheduled to begin on 6 August, inspects two academic stages erected by town carpenters. The stage for college plays in King's College hall fails to impress: although it has long suited private college performances, it will not do for a royal visit. Not only is the stage too lightly built for the anticipated crush, the hall itself is too small. Fortunately, the college has a suitable space: the western bays or antechapel of its capacious Chapel, built by the grandfather and father of the queen. Stocket orders the dismantling of the hall stage and construction of a new stage in King's College Chapel at the expense of the royal treasury (REED, pp. 233–4).

The second of the two stages annually transforms Great St Mary's, then as now known as the University Church, into an auditorium for the granting of M.A. and higher academic degrees. This stage passes muster; it will, however, be supplemented by galleries over the side aisles, and by a raised enclosure within the chancel to carry a throne for the queen (Appendix 1).

The visit of Queen Elizabeth in 1564 was a landmark in the history of Cambridge University. Not since 1522 had a monarch paid a formal visit to the university and town.[22] During the forty-two year interval the university had been caught up in the first stirrings of the reformation; the divorce controversy which cost the life of John Fisher, instrumental in refounding Christ's College and in founding St John's, and a leading officer of the university in various capacities from 1501 to 1535; the disestablishment of the religious houses which nearly resulted in the disestablishment of the colleges and thus of the university itself; the reforming reign of Edward VI; the reign of Catholic Mary with the consequent martyrdom of several members of the university; and the accession of Elizabeth in 1558.[23]

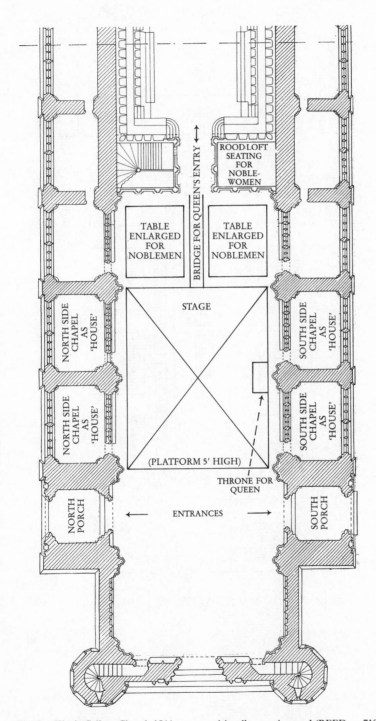

Fig. 5.   King's College Chapel, 1564 stage provisionally superimposed (REED, p. 718).

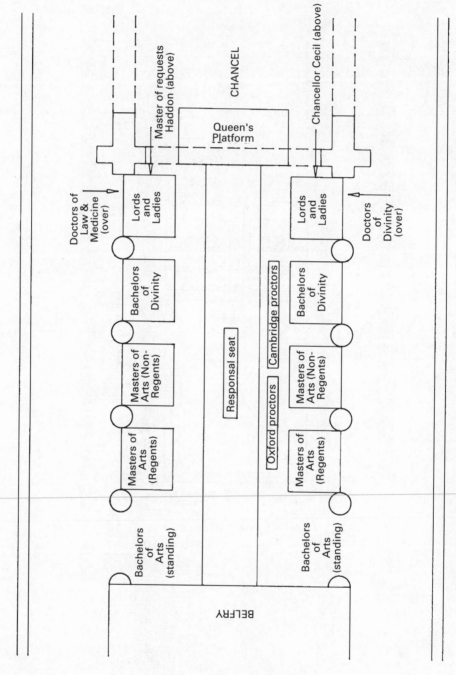

Fig. 6. Commencement stage in Great St Mary's church arranged for royal visit of August 1564, schematic plan.

Elizabeth came to Cambridge on Sunday, 6 August, and departed the morning of Thursday the 10th.[24] M.A. ceremonies were held a month after the traditional first Tuesday in July;[25] college plays, normally scheduled between Christmas and Lent, were organized for each night of the queen's sojourn. University officials looked forward eagerly to welcoming this learned monarch, notoriously fluent in Latin, 'adorned with all kinde of good literature, which is rare & mervelous in a woman, & well able to judge of all owre doyngs' (REED, p. 228).

King's College Chapel was the most capacious building in Cambridge, with a width of 40′ and a length of 120′ in the antechapel alone (from the west door to the screen), yielding a floor area there of 4800 sq. ft.[26] The stage erected in this space (fig. 5) is described in more or less comprehensive detail in at least four contemporary accounts of the royal visit.[27] The stage platform spanned the whole width of the antechapel and ran the length of two side chapels. The Chapel survives unchanged in its principal dimensions, of course, so it is possible to establish the size of the platform, though the imagination staggers at the thought of a playing platform 40′ wide by nearly 50′ deep. Of its width there can be no doubt, since Matthew Stokys says explicitly that it contained 'the breadth of the churche from thone syde vnto thother' (REED, p. 234); its depth (distance from front to back) is almost as certain, since Stokys reports that 'In lenght it ranne twoe of the Loer chapels full with the pillers.'[28] The height of the stage is given by Nicholas Robinson as 5′ (REED, p. 236); we may infer from Abraham Hartwell's description that the stage was constructed of oak (REED, p. 238: *nodoso robore*).

Stokys explains that the stage spanned the whole width of the antechapel 'that the chapels myght serve for howses' (REED, p. 234). Stagehouses were a standard feature of Cambridge college theatres, as we shall see; they were invariably situated not at the back of the stage, as we might imagine for Roman comedy, but at the sides, facing each other across the stage platform. It is not clear whether the stage was built right up against the doors of the side chapels, or whether there was a gap defined by the projection of the pillars beyond the side walls of the antechapel. Either arrangement would have been possible, thanks to the 10′ height of the side-chapel doors.[29]

The queen entered from the eastern or high-altar end of the Chapel, through the central opening of the rood screen which still divides King's College Chapel into two essentially equal halves, and along a raised 'bridge' leading to the stage. (A door to the outside had been made in the side chapel on the north at the eastern end of the building in anticipation of the queen's visit.)[30] A throne for the queen was placed on the stage against the side wall of the antechapel on the south.

Between the stage platform and the rood screen, on either side of the bridge, were two platforms made by widening large tables: on these platforms sat various noblemen. The seating platforms were apparently the height of standard tables, 2′ 6″; by the same token they were apparently 2′ 6″ lower than the 5′ stage. High atop the rood screen further seating was erected for noble women. Doubtless these seats were reached by means of the stair leading to the organ which perched on top of the screen.

William Cecil and Robert Dudley, both Cambridge graduates, held books of the play on the stage (REED, pp. 230–1): probably they sat near the queen, and certainly they 'would not suffre eny to stande vpon the stage savying a veraye fewe vpon the north syde'. Along the front and rear edges of the stage, on the ground, stood the queen's guard, holding torches.

Several theatre historians have attempted to reconstruct the 1564 King's College Chapel stage. Glynne Wickham and Richard Leacroft follow E. K. Chambers in backing the dramatic action against the north wall, with only the two north side chapels serving for houses; Leslie Hotson shows stage houses on both sides, but situates the throne among the platforms reserved for the male nobility.[31]

Hotson is probably correct in insisting that chapels on both sides of the stage were used for houses, for Stokys makes no distinction between the two sides; Wickham and Leacroft are doubtless correct in placing the throne on the stage platform. The action of the play was apparently oriented along an east–west axis. This may seem to have left Elizabeth to view the action from the side, but of course she could still have made perfect sense of it, and in addition it was the duty and probably the desire of the monarch not so much to see, as to be seen.[32]

As plays in King's College Chapel were the chief event of Elizabeth's Cambridge evenings, academic ceremonies in Great St Mary's Church were the chief event of her Cambridge days. The usual commencement stage was erected in the capacious nave of the church, which was 25′ wide by 75′ in length from the belfry to the chancel, giving a floor area of 1875 sq. ft. (fig. 6).[33] The side aisles more than doubled the floor area available in the nave alone, while the slender pillars scarcely obstructed the view.

Stokys, who characterizes this commencement stage as a 'theatre', notes that there was first provided 'for disputacions a great and ample stage / from the ... wall of the belfrye hard vnto the chauncell'. At the east end of the church, perhaps just within the opening of the chancel, was 'a spacious and hie Rome for the quenes maiestie which was by her owne servauntes Richelye hanged with arras and clothe of state and all other necessaries with a quoyshen to leane vpon' (Appendix 1). Robinson gives the height of this raised platform as 8′, though if he is correct this must have been the height not from the ground, but from the stage (Appendix 2).

Because the queen's throne was in the chancel to the east, 'All the disputacions were dryven to that ende of the stage.' This arrangement suited the four Masters of Arts who stood upon the main stage 'nere vnto her stage and lokyng westward'. One of these four was Thomas Preston, who may later have written *Cambyses*, possibly one of the first fruits of Cambridge influence upon London drama; as a token of her admiration, Elizabeth dubbed Preston 'her own scholar' and gave him an annuity of 20s, recognition recorded many years later in Preston's funeral brass in the entrance to Trinity Hall Chapel.[34]

The same physical arrangements proved quite unsatisfactory for a disputation among three doctors (Appendix 1):

> by cause their voices weare smalle and not audible her maiestie first sayed vnto them loquimini altius [= speak louder!] / and when that would not helpe she lefte her seate / and came to the stage over their headdes but by cause their voices were loe / and that she should not well heare theim her grace made not muche of that disputacion ...

Thanks to academic shyness, a vivid picture is preserved for us of the queen advancing to the fore edge of her raised platform and peering over the rails[35] to gain a better account of events occurring on the stage platform directly below.

In detail, other seats and structures distributed around the church included the following:

— On both sides of the church toward the chancel sat lords and ladies, in the places usually reserved for the doctors.

— The doctors sat in elevated galleries, specially built for this occasion directly over their usual forms. These raised galleries were affixed to the pillars of the church, above the heads of the lords and ladies below, but 'loer then the rayls of the hier stages'. The doctors of divinity sat on the south side next to the queen's stage, with the Chancellor William Cecil seated closest to the queen, 'before hym the vsuall clothe and a longe velvet quoishen'. Opposite the divines in the north side gallery sat the doctors of law and medicine; opposite the Chancellor, also in a place of honour, sat Dr Walter Haddon as Master of the Requests.

— In the middle of the church stood the responsal seat, facing east.

— On both sides of the church, below the doctors but above the responsal seat, sat the bachelors of divinity.

— Below the bachelors of divinity, on both sides of the church, sat the non-regent and regent masters, probably on low platforms rather than in elevated galleries.

— At the far west end of the church stood the bachelors of arts.

— The proctor's stall stood on the one side of the nave, not far from the responsal seat, below the doctors of divinity.

— Immediately below the proctors of Cambridge sat the proctors of Oxford (as guests of Cambridge University).

The complex commencement stage in Great St Mary's was not technically theatrical, and so has not been the subject of sustained investigation by modern theatre historians.[36] It was, however, in the eyes of its contemporaries, a theatre, and thus bears further analysis. I will return to the commencement stage after we have had an opportunity to look at genuine theatrical stages in the several colleges.

2

Queens' College

Ash Wednesday, 18 February 1640. The President and fellows of Queens' College have ordered a town carpenter to make a detailed inventory of their college stage. Over the years, each piece of timber has been signed with one or more carpenters' marks; furthermore, timbers belonging to each separate structure have been marked in the same colour for easy identification: great gallery at the upper end, red; stage platform, all structures on the east side, and screens gallery, black; all structures on the west, light (or whitish) russet. The master carpenter, with the assistance of fellow carpenters, now carefully notes down the colour, kind, and marks of each timber making up the stage platform, tiring houses, and spectator galleries. He takes particular pains to note how and where timbers attach to other timbers or to the fabric of the hall.

The college stage has been set up and taken down again annually for nearly a century without the need for an inventory, but with each passing year in these unsettled times the prospect that the stage will be used again in the near future seems increasingly remote. The college has just recently completed a purpose-built storehouse – called 'the Stagehouse' – to store the stage timbers outside the college walls. The inventory will serve as a set of instructions for re-assembling the stage on the much-to-be-wished-for chance that these wooden bones will some day live again.[1]

The Queens' College stage inventory of 1640 (Appendix 3) offers one of the most detailed insights into any English theatre before the Restoration,[2] yet only one attempt has hitherto been made at an imaginative reconstruction. Leslie Hotson, in *Shakespeare's Wooden O*, provides a set of three reasonably accurate drawings. The influence of these drawings, however, has been limited because of Hotson's failure to provide an accompanying discursive analysis, and by his mistaken assertion that this was a theatre first constructed in 1638,[3] a date too late to be of much interest to Shakespeareans and too early for historians of the Restoration Drama. In fact, construction on Queens' College stage began in 1546, some thirty years before James Burbage's Theatre in Shoreditch, and the stage was in continuous use right through the most active decades of Elizabethan and Jacobean theatre.[4]

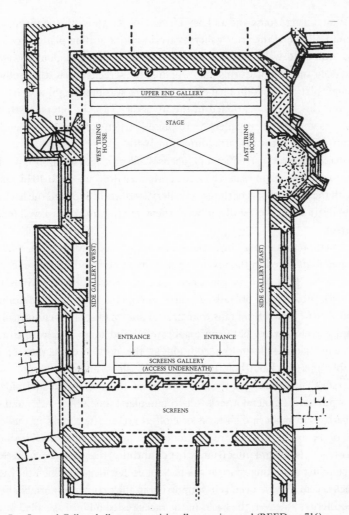

Fig. 7.   Queens' College hall, stage provisionally superimposed (REED, p. 716).

The hall which accommodated the stage (fig. 7) is about 27′ wide by 44′ from the upper end wall to the screens, with a floor area of approximately 1200 sq. ft. The hall has five bays, four approximately 11′ deep and a shallower bay at the screens end. The side walls are interrupted by a small door at the north-west corner of the hall, an oriel in the second bay from the upper end on the east, and a fireplace on the west side, in the middlemost bay. The oriel leaves a break of approximately 11′ in the east wall. The height to the bottom sills of the side windows, relevant to an eventual determination of the height of the side galleries, is approximately 9′. After successive campaigns of redecoration and restoration, the hall for all practical purposes remains essentially as it was in 1546.[5]

The 1640 inventory reveals that the stage platform stood near the upper end of the hall, opposite the screens. On the flanks of the platform, backed against the side walls, stood a West Tiring House and an East Tiring House. Above the platform, against the upper-end wall, stood the great gallery, carrying three seating platforms. Against the east and west side walls at the lower end of the hall stood double-galleries, one platform deep and two platforms high. Against the screens stood still another gallery, with a single platform. (Additional elevated seating was presumably available over the screens, but this is not mentioned in the inventory.) In the interstices between the tiring houses and the great gallery were poised structures installed recently enough that they were still identified as additions in 1640.

The imaginative reconstruction of Queens' College stage (see fig. 19, p. 31) is made easier by the orderly manner in which the craftsmen drew up the 1640 inventory: they began with the forward part of the great gallery, and worked toward the back; they also tended to begin at the west wall and work their way toward the east wall (occasionally the reverse).

The structural function of the posts, studs, girts, jeece, boards, rails, binding-jeece, braces, and studs listed in the inventory may be understood by reference to Moxon (see figs. 2–4). Rails used in the stage were of several different kinds (some are unspecified). 'Board rails' or 'rails of board' were presumably made of timber an inch thick and 4″ to 6″ broad. Stud rails were presumably made of timber normally used for studs and therefore were both more substantial and more nearly square in cross-section. The 'slope-rail' in the addition at the north-west corner of the stage presumably offered a hand-hold to the user of a 'slope-board' or ramp.

The 'racks' mentioned in the description of the upper-end and side galleries present a puzzle. In general a rack is a rectangular frame filled with parallel, evenly spaced bars, as in modern dish racks or clothes racks. Since racks in the lower back platform of the upper gallery were positioned behind 'Matted formes' (= benches) in the lower front platform, I infer (somewhat doubtfully) that they provided elevated (or raked)[6] standing or seating space at the back of each gallery in which they were used. Some racks seem to have been self-supporting in the manner of portable benches; in the side galleries, however, the backs of the racks rested on boards nailed into window openings.

The great gallery

The great gallery at the upper end of the hall consisted of three vertical planes – called 'faces' – carrying three horizontal platforms. The foremost platform was apparently carried by the first and second faces, while a rear platform at the same level and an upper platform were apparently both carried by the second and third faces. The absence of rails at the backs of these two platforms suggests that the third face backed directly on to the upper-end wall.

The first face (fig. 8) included two principal posts, marked A1 and B1. (A1 and B1 were echoed by A2 and B2 in the second face and by A3 and B3 in the third.) A secondary post stood somewhere between the west wall and A1, while between B1 and the east wall stood another secondary post. The fore edge of the forward platform was

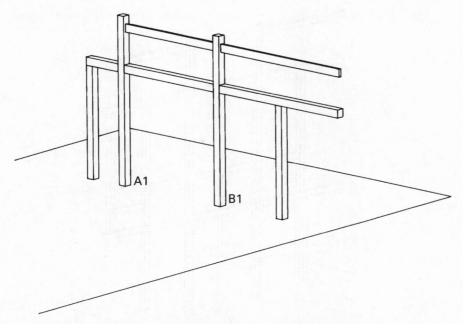

Fig. 8.   Queens' College stage, great gallery, first face. End of girt and rail on right supported by east side wall.

carried by a sequence of three girts, going from the western secondary post into A1; from A1 to B1; and from B1 over the eastern secondary post into the east wall.

The second face (fig. 9) consisted of principal posts A2 and B2 and two sets of girts, one above the other. The back edge of the forward platform and the fore edge of the lower rear platform were carried by a set of three girts going from the west wall to A2, from A2 to B2, and from B2 into the east wall; the fore edge of the upper platform was carried by an upper set of three similar girts. Standing on the floor and rising to the lower girts in the interstices between post and wall or post and post stood three short posts; against the first of these (between the west wall and A2) was 'Another stud with a staple fastened in it' – the role of this supernumerary stud is unclear. Standing on the lower girt were four posts or studs, marked in succession K (between the wall and A2), L (between A2 and B2), and M and N (standing in order between B2 and the east wall). (For markings K, L, M, etc., see Appendixes 3 and 4.)

Posts A3 and B3 in the third face (fig. 10) stood on ground-pieces; each post was stabilized by a brace. The two principal posts stopped at a single long lower girt which spanned the hall from wall to wall. This girt carried the back of the lower rear platform. On this girt stood two posts (presumably directly over A3 and B3) supporting a single long upper girt which carried the back of the upper platform.

Granted the rather drastic expedient of cutting holes in masonry walls for the sake of the theatre (first recorded at Queens' in 1546–7),[7] how was it possible to manoeuvre full-length girts into the holes? One end of each girt was probably tipped into a hole cut extra deep on one side of the hall, then the other end was lifted into its hole, then

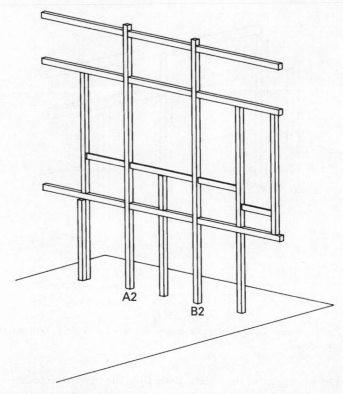

A2

B2

Fig. 9.   Queens' College stage, great gallery, second face. Ends of girts and upper rails supported by side walls.

the girt was centred so that an equal portion remained in each hole. Packing at one or both ends would lock the girt in place and prevent sideways movement.

Floorboards on the forward platform were carried by fourteen jeece; on the lower rear platform by nineteen jeece and two binding-jeece; on the upper platform by seventeen jeece. Seating on the forward platform consisted of padded benches – called 'forms'. Seating or elevated standing on the lower rear platform was accommodated by eight racks; on the upper platform, by seven racks.

Posts in the first face carried a two-part rail, possibly from principal post A1 to B1, and from B1 to the wall on the east. The foremost platform was apparently separated from the lower rear platform by a 'board rail' in the second face, in four parts: first from K to A2; second from A2 to B2 (presumably supported in the middle by L); third from B2 to M; fourth from M to N. For once, explicit dimensions are given: all these board rails were inserted a yard above the girts except for the one between M and N, which was inserted 16″ lower, or 20″ above its corresponding girt.

Rails at the top of the second face are listed redundantly (as I believe), first as 'Vpper Railes', and then as '3 Railes for the vpper scaffold' marked F, G, and H: those described as 'vpper Railes' are said to go (from west wall) to post, from post to post, and from post to east wall.

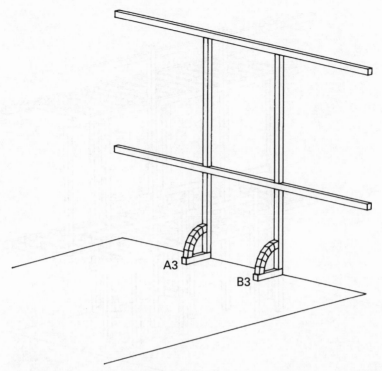

A3

B3

Fig. 10.   Queens' College stage, great gallery, third face. Ends of girts supported by side walls.

The fully integrated great gallery (fig. 11) was given stability by three pairs of principal posts; by secondary posts and studs, especially in the second face; by girts fixed into principal posts and the masonry walls; by normal jeece and binding-jeece mortised and pegged into the opposing girts and posts; and perhaps in a small way by its elaborate series of rails.

The side and screens galleries

Only the east side gallery is described in the inventory, but since the west side gallery was a mirror image, one description could serve for both. Because the two side galleries each shared a corner post with the screens gallery, it seems logical to consider side and screen structures together (fig. 12).

Each side gallery carried two platforms, one directly over the other, while the screens gallery carried but one platform. The footprint of each side gallery was defined by two fore corner posts (A and B) rising to the top, and by two corresponding short back corner posts. A single fore girt spanned the distance between the fore corner posts, supported in the middle by a short fore middle post. The inventory specifies a short back middle post, but not a back girt, a problem to which we shall return; for safety's sake I have inserted a single long back girt in its logical place.

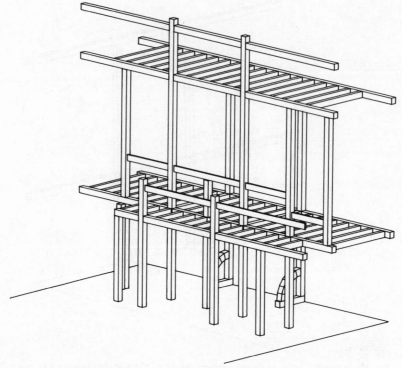

Fig. 11.   Queens' College stage, great gallery. Ends of girts and rails supported by side walls.

Directly over each short post stood another post at the first platform level. At the back of the upper platform, the three short upper posts carried an undivided rear girt. The upper middle fore post was substantially longer than those three, since it carried both the upper fore girt, which was in two sections, and the rail at the top of the platform.

The principal fore posts (B) at the screens end of the side galleries doubled as principal fore posts of the screens gallery, carrying between them a fore girt supported in the middle by a single fore post. Directly over this lower fore post stood an upper fore post. Projecting from the lower fore post was a 'spur' upon which stood a 'little stud': possibly this appendage served to stabilize the upper fore post. The screens gallery is said to have had *two* back girts:

> A Girt ouer this [fore] post marked 10.O.17 *a back girt to it L. A back girt on the South side before the screene marked F.*

Since the screens gallery is given two back girts and the side gallery none, I assume the inventory is in error. Since L belongs to the same alphabetic and numeric sequences as other parts of the screens gallery, the girt marked F presumably belonged to the side gallery.

Associated with the screens gallery is 'Another vpright post standing next the west

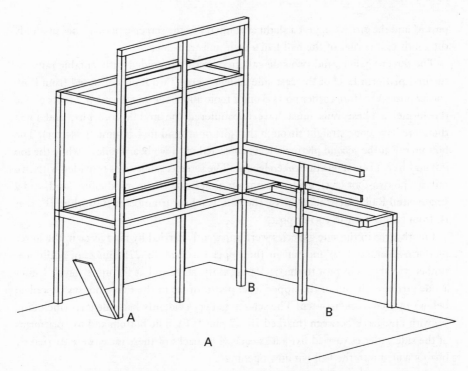

Fig. 12.   Queens' College stage, east side gallery and screens gallery. Placement of slope board leading to stage is conjectural.

scaffold of the hall marked M', while associated with the first level fore girt of the east side gallery is 'Another girt from it to the end against the staires of the trap dore which doth serue also for a Ieece marked on the side N'.

One clue to post M and girt-jeece N may be their alphabetic association with back girt L: perhaps L was carried by M and N much as the top girt 10 in the third face of the great gallery was carried by posts 11 and 12. (No other elements in the inventory seem available to carry the back girt of the screens gallery.) It seems reasonable that M, called a post, should carry the back girt, but what about N, which is called both a girt and a jeece? And what about the trap-door and its associated stair?

The trap-door is one of the more puzzling features of the stage complex, for it is situated not in the stage platform, but at the lower end of the hall, and in fact seems to have been a feature of the hall itself. Moreover, since N came against the stair somewhere in the upper reaches of the intersection of the east side gallery and screens gallery, it seems that the stair must have led to the permanent gallery above the screens. As a tentative solution to this puzzle, I have imagined that a stair rose from the floor of the hall up into the screens, and that the trap-door was situated in the floor over the screens.[8] This configuration assumes either a screens-gallery floor projecting from the screens into the hall, or a steep stair cutting through the face of the screen.

In any case, the stair itself seems to have carried the south end of girt N, which may somehow have served to carry the east end of the back girt L of the screens gallery. The post M and the girt N suggest a slight asymmetry in the screens, perhaps because only the south-east corner of the hall had a stair and trap-door.

The screens gallery and two side galleries were all provided with suitable rails. At the first platform level of the east side gallery were 'Two Railes of board from [fore corner post] A to [fore corner post] B one 2 foote aboue the girt the other 2 foote aboue the former'. These rails must have encountered the middle fore girt, and must therefore have gone straight through that girt or around it (I assume the latter). The bottom rail at the second platform level consisted of 'Two board railes', while the top rail may have been of one unbroken length. The screens gallery was provided with two rails at the two-foot level, evidently one on either side of the middle fore stud, and a single 'stud Raile ouer them Crosse the hall, reaching from black B to white B', that is, from corner post to corner post.

Floorboards in the side galleries were apparently carried by nine jeece in the lower platform (marked 1–9) and ten in the upper (marked 18–27). Since an additional timber tied the front post to the back post at the stage end at the upper level, I infer a side girt at each end of the upper-level platform (as in the tiring houses described below) and ten jeece between. The screens gallery evidently had side girts (including N) with nine jeece between (marked 10–17 plus 'O'). The bottom and top platforms of the side galleries carried five racks each. The backs of these racks were carried by boards nailed into the hall window openings.

The construction of the side and screens galleries with common principal posts afforded considerable stability to all three galleries; perhaps all the fore corner posts as well as the upper fore middle posts were lashed at the top to the side walls. The long girts of the side and screens galleries (except for the back girt of the screens gallery) were all supported in the middle by posts.

The tiring houses

The east tiring house is inventoried in detail; the west tiring house, a mirror image, is described by inference. The east tiring house was situated over the bible-clerks' table: this piece of information, however, is more useful for locating the bible-clerks' table than for establishing the precise location of the tiring house. The tiring houses were straightforward three-storey structures, closer than any other element of the college stage to the house described by Moxon (figs. 2–3).

'Four maine posts' rising full height stood at the four corners of the tiring-house carcass (fig. 13). The fore girt at the first platform level was supported by four fore studs, the back by a single 'middle back stud'.

The flooring of the first-level platform, doubtless at the same level as the stage platform, was carried by seven jeece, along with side girts which tied the fore principal posts to the back principal posts. At the front, upon the fore girt, stood two fore middle studs, conceivably dividing the face of the tiring house into three equal parts with the possibility of one, two, or three doorways. Another two studs stood at the back.

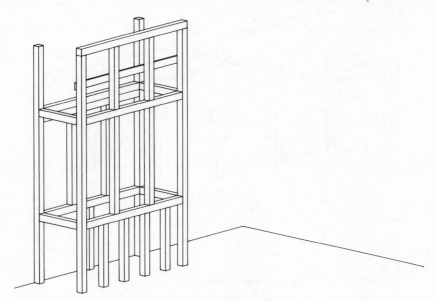

Fig. 13.   Queens' College stage, west tiring house (mirror image of east tiring house). Placement of rails is conjectural.

Carried by the corner posts and the two fore studs was one fore girt, answered by a puzzling *two* girts at the back.

The upper platform had the same characteristics as the lower: at its front stood two fore middle studs, evidently directly over the two below. Two rails were placed here, probably one above the other, or possibly one rail in two parts.

The tiring houses were designed to withstand vertical loads, being supported not only by the main corner posts but by four front studs at the first platform level and by two at the second level, as well as by studs and evidently by a double girt at the upper back. Possibly the fore corner posts were lashed back against the side walls: the lashings may also have served as side rails at the upper level.

The stage platform

The stage platform or 'frame' (fig. 14) was a simple rectangle carried by three rows of five studs each. Over each row of studs lay a long raising – in this case, two lengths of timber joined to make one horizontal timber running the whole width of the platform. The floorboards were carried by fourteen jeece.

The studs were 'mortised in' to the raisings. The jeece are described as 'lying Crosse' (rather than being mortised into) the three raisings. Since even the mortising of the studs into the raisings would have provided little in the way of inherent stability, the stage platform was presumably stabilized by the flanking houses. It may also have been stabilized by at least one 'slope board next the stage like a brace'.[9]

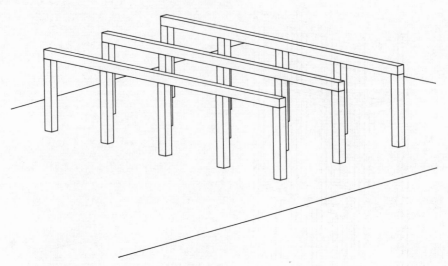

Fig. 14.   Queens' College stage, stage platform.

Additions to the tiring houses

The 'additions' to the tiring houses were apparently alike in being affixed to the north principal posts of the tiring houses and to elevated posts in the second face, in particular to post K on the west and posts M and N on the east. Not being exact mirror images, however, the two additions are separately described. Their asymmetry may explain, or perhaps be explained by, the asymmetry in the first and second faces of the great gallery.

The east addition (fig. 15) consisted essentially of a fore girt running from the fore corner post of the tiring house to post M, with an answering back girt at the same level connecting the back corner post to N, with these two girts matched by a similar pair above. In addition, 18″ above the lower fore girt was a board rail; 18″ above this was a stud rail.

The inventory in fact describes the four girts in the following illogical sequence: (1) upper back girt connected to N; (2) answering fore girt (presumably joined to M); (3) fore girt above connected to M; (4) answering back girt (presumably joined to N). The illogic can be corrected by emending (1) to lower back girt.

Problematic record (1) and unproblematic record (3) characterize upper girts as going 'upon the top of' posts N and M respectively. I have not accepted this wording quite at face value, since in the interest of stability I have imagined that M and N should be mortised at their top ends into the girts above. I have mortised the four girts and two rails into the principal posts of the tiring house at their far ends because those seem the logical vertical timbers to carry them. This decision in turn dictates that the depth of the east addition from west to east is exactly equal to the depth of the tiring house. Curiously, no rail is indicated for the top platform, nor are jeece indicated for either platform.

The west addition (fig. 16) seems to have had an altogether different structure.

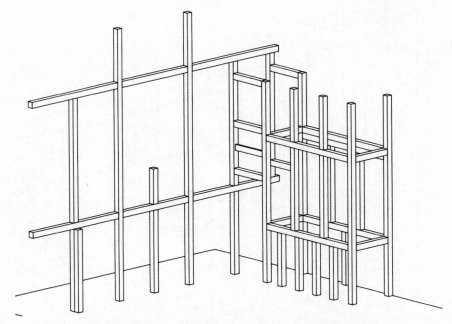

Fig. 15.   Queens' College stage, showing addition between east tiring house and second face of great gallery. Platform heights are conjectural.

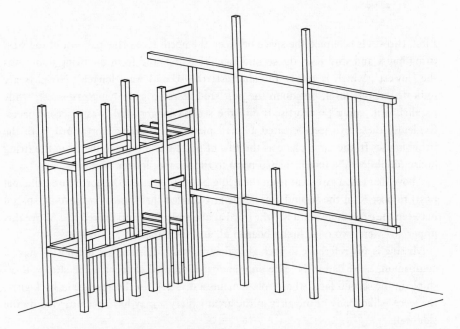

Fig. 16.   Queens' College stage, showing addition between west tiring house and second face of great gallery. Platform heights are conjectural.

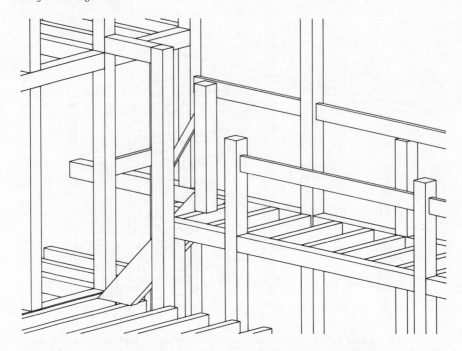

Fig. 17.   Queens' College stage, showing west addition as in Fig. 16, with door, slope board, and rail added.

First, two studs occupied the space between the north fore principal post of the west tiring house and stud K in the second face. The first stud from the tiring house was the 'lowest', which is to say the shortest; the second was 'longer'. No girts are indicated at this level, but upon the first stud rested a jeece lying east–west, while parallel to it, going (= mortised) into the second longer stud, was a second jeece. Evidently these two jeece created a small platform extending northward from the tiring house. In the same plane as the row of posts was a rail coming from the tiring house (doubtless the fore principal post) to the second, longer post.

Above that rail, a girt went from the tiring house (doubtless the north fore principal post) to post K in the second face. This girt carried three jeece, two evenly spaced between the tiring house and K, 'the third at one end going into the red K'. Above this upper girt were two rails, first a board rail, and then another rail over it.

Missing is any reference to back girts for this west addition; nor did post K have a companion, as M had in N. The only known additional element is the stud-with-a-staple in the second face, whose role remains a mystery. In the absence of back girts, the jeece – like many of the girts in the great gallery – may have been carried by the side wall.

For want of further information, I wager a guess that the west addition provided platforms to expand the floor-space of the west tiring house in the direction of the great gallery.

The west addition had itself an addition (fig. 17):

A Post Comming from the ground close by the stage side and making with the corner
of the Tyring house a dore way from of[f] the stage to the Doctors Gallery ...
Another against it grounded upon that little fore gallery ...
A slope board raile betweene them ...
Another stud Raile ouer it ...

Evidently 'the Doctors Gallery' is the same as 'that little fore gallery' or lower seating
platform, which was indeed small relative to either the rear or the upper seating
platform. The doorway must have served either for the actors or the doctors to
communicate between the gallery and the stage.

From the 'slope board rail' I infer a 'slope board'. I have imagined – though
without solid evidence – that the board sloped upward rather than downward from the
stage to the little gallery. I have also imagined that the slope board bridged an open
space between the stage and the second face, and that it was necessary to step sideways
from the top of the slope board to enter the gallery. Absent this supposition, I am at
a loss to find a logical role for the post 'grounded upon that little fore gallery' and for
the slope-board rail and associated stud rail.

Estimating dimensions

Of all the timbers which made up the Queens' College stage, the common jeece with
their associated binding jeece or girts are the most open to direct numerical analysis:

Great gallery, fore platform	14	
Great gallery, rear platform	19 + 2 = 21	(8 racks)
Great gallery, upper platform	17	(7 racks)
Tiring house platforms	7 + 2 = 9	
Stage platform	14	
Side galleries, lower platform	9 + 2 = 11	(5 racks)
Side galleries, upper platform	10 + 2 = 12	(5 racks)
Screens gallery	9 + 2 = 11	

(The rear platform of the great gallery contained nineteen numbered jeece plus two
'binding jeece'. With varying evidence, I add side girts and/or binding jeece to the
tiring houses, side and screens galleries, and great gallery.)

It is in the very character of jeece that their spacing is highly regular.[10] In the second
platform of the great gallery, twenty-one jeece spanned the hall, a distance of 27':
assuming that the two outermost jeece came right up against the side walls, this means
that the jeece must have been spaced almost exactly 16″ on centre.[11]

Assuming 16″ spacing throughout the entire stage structure (fig. 18), the stage
platform had a width of 17′ 4″, the tiring houses a width of 11′ 2″. Assuming that the
stage was essentially as deep as the tiring houses were wide, the stage had a depth of
10′ 2″. Assuming that stage platform plus tiring houses spanned the entire 27′ width
of the hall, the tiring houses each had a depth of 4′ 8″.

Another hypothesis which may be attempted for the stage platform is that its posts

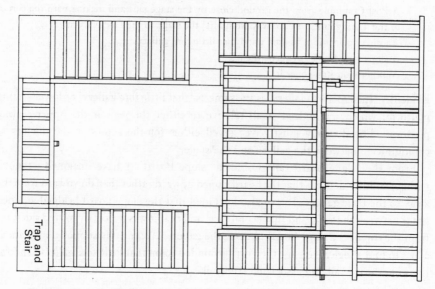

Fig. 18.   Queens' College stage, showing disposition of horizontal timbers on the assumption that all jeece and side girts are spaced 16" on centre.

were set out in squares. At five posts in width by three in depth, given a width of 17′ 4″ the depth of the stage platform would have been about 10′ 4″. Yet another hypothesis is that the tiring houses (whose width matched the depth of the stage) were as wide as the 11′ oriel bay. The three very different hypotheses yield relatively consistent estimates of 11′ 2″, 11′ 4″ (stage-width plus two 6″ post widths) and 11′ respectively for the depth of the stage.

No jeece are named for the east addition, but in the west addition one jeece went into stud K while two more lay between K and the tiring house. At 16″ on centre, the distance from the fore principal post of the tiring house to stud K would have been 42″,[12] which in turn suggests a limit to the depth of the lower fore platform.

Since the great gallery girts were fixed into the side walls of the hall, including the east girt in the first face, all its platforms must have been confined within the 11′ depth of the upper-end bay. Accepting a depth of 3′ 6″ for the fore platform, the back platforms together with the timbers of the second and third faces must have spanned the remaining 7′ 6″.

The 16″-on-centre hypothesis works less compellingly for the galleries at the lower end. Even assuming side girts in addition to the documented nine jeece, the screens gallery at this spacing seems somewhat too narrow, or rather – and more to the point – the side galleries seem too deep, so deep as to jeopardize sight-lines for those standing at the back corners. Similarly, even assuming side girts in addition to the documented ten jeece in the upper platform(s), the side galleries at this spacing fail to come as close as they otherwise might to the tiring houses. In favour of the 16″-on-centre hypothesis for the lower-end seating galleries is the argument that slope boards reached like braces from the side galleries to the stage: this would apparently work best

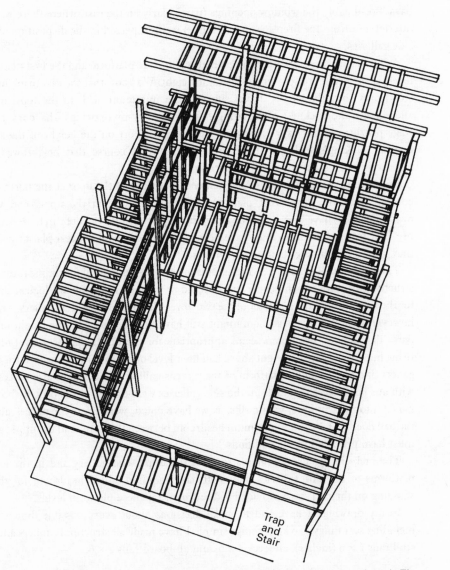

Trap
and
Stair

Fig. 19.   Queens' College stage, perspective view. Horizontal dimensions are those shown in Fig. 18. Platform heights are based on the following assumptions: stage platform and tiring house first-platform level, 5′; gallery first-platform levels and tiring house upper-platform levels, 7′ under (offering headroom beneath); upper gallery levels, 9′ under (offering headroom for persons standing on racks).

if the side galleries projected further from the side walls than the tiring houses, and with a substantial gap (figs. 18, 19). A greater depth in the side galleries than in the screens gallery also seems to be implied by the fact that the side galleries alone carried racks. Since the backs of the racks were carried by boards nailed into the side windows, the side galleries may have been centred on the boundary between the corresponding bays. Presumably the window openings (particularly on the east, where there was no interference from the fireplace and chimney) were respected in the disposition of the side galleries.

As for vertical measurements, presumably the stage platform and the first platform levels of the tiring houses were at the same height. We know that the east tiring house stood over the bible-clerks' table, suggesting a minimum of 3′ to the top surface allowing for the thickness of the tiring-house jeece. In my drawings I have taken the stage platform height as 5′, following Robinson's report on the height of the stage erected in King's College Chapel in 1564,[13] but of course that height was not necessarily sacrosanct for all of Cambridge.

Entrance to the upper end of the hall was by means of the door at the north-east corner. Since the lower rear platform evidently backed on the upper-end wall, headroom must have been available beneath the platform for the door to have been of use. The forward platform must have been at the same level as the rear platform since they shared the same girts in the second face.

The minimum height of 7′, which seems to have been universal for simple theatrical structures beneath which people had to stand or move,[14] seems to be a logical choice for the height above the hall floor of the two lower platforms in the great gallery – note, however, that effective headroom might still have been reduced by the height of the dais. The same 7′ headroom seems appropriate for the upper platform level of the tiring houses and for the height above hall floor level of the lower platforms of the side gallery and for the single platform of the screens gallery. (This height also sorts well with our knowledge that racks in the side galleries were carried at the back by boards nailed into the windows, whose sills, as we have noted, were approximately 9′ above the hall floor.) The same 7′ minimum headroom between the lower and the upper girts must have prevailed in the additions.

The racks in the lower rear platform of the upper-end gallery and in the lower platforms of the side galleries may well have required added headroom for those standing on them: I have provided 9′ headroom for these platform levels.

In my drawings I have had to make decisions about every possible dimension, including scantlings. To keep things simple I have made all structural timbers and all stud rails 6 × 6 (inches), all jeece 4 × 6, and all board rails 2 × 6.

The original stage

The designation of parts of Queens' College stage as additions prompts me to ask, What were the additions added to? Can we, in other words, find our way back to a form of the stage a decade or more earlier than 1640?

Although post K in the second face has a mirroring counterpart in M, post N (east) has no counterpart unless we infer a lost I/J (west); further, rail P going from K to A2 has no predecessor O going from I/J to K, so O was perhaps discarded along with I/J. With putative I/J and O restored, an unbroken alphabetic sequence runs through much of the great gallery:

A–B: principal posts
C–E: upper girts in the second face
F–H: upper rails in the second face
I/J–N: upper secondary posts in the second face
O–S: lower rails in the second face[15]

Possibly all three faces of the great gallery were at first individually symmetrical; when the westernmost girt in the first face was subsequently cut short, perhaps to clear the way for the west addition and doorway, it had then to be carried by a post rather than by the west wall.

Archival evidence

Having ransacked if not exhausted the 1640 inventory, I will now turn to more extensive but also more diffuse documentary evidence. The earliest records for a dramatic performance in Queens' College are from 1522–3, when Richard Robyns received 3d for various carpenters' tasks, and also for his work when a comedy of Plautus was performed, while John Keyle, another carpenter, received 2d. It would be logical to assume that these carpenters built a stage.[16] The college purchased candles and torches along with tenterhooks 'with which the decorations of the houses were attached in the same comedy': tenterhooks imply a stretched fabric as infill for light timber-framed houses.

Records of play activity fall silent for almost two decades, but begin to speak volumes in 1540–1 when John Dowsey, a carpenter with whom we will become well acquainted, spent five days with two assistants setting up the stage in the hall (= 15 man-days). Nicholas Ott, a blacksmith, supplied five spikes for attaching steps to the stage. A wooden shrine required nails and straps as well as soutage, a canvas-like fabric[17] provided evidently by Joan Mere wife of John Mere, Esquire Bedell to the university.[18] The shrine was painted by one Thomas. Nails and straps were used to make a candlestick, while thirty-eight candlesticks of iron and silver-plate were procured. John Dowsey worked one day when the comedies were actually being performed; he and one assistant then spent two days each (= 4 man-days) taking the stage down and placing it in the store-room (*lignarium*).

Candles were purchased again in 1541–2. In 1543–4 one Atkinson was paid for taking away costumes, cleaning them, and returning them to the college tower. In 1545–6 the college purchased two lamps, wood for a fire (for rehearsals?), several oil-lamps nine pounds by weight, and rope 'for putting up the houses' for a comedy.

At the beginning of the next academic year, on 9 October 1546, the college mandated the annual public performance of comedies or tragedies: it was conceivably this mandate which set off a flurry of new construction over the next three years.

In 1546–7 John Dowsey, one of his sons, and William Hardewicke (another carpenter) took five and a half days to build the stage (= 16.5 man-days); the same three built a scaffold for the stage, and later took the entire structure down again.

Martin Avesse, John Gayttes, and Margaret Vetule carried boards from Corpus and St John's, returning them after the plays; wood was purchased outright for the construction of tripods. The college spent 8d 'for the finishing of two holes in the wall in order for the scaffold to be built': the ongoing use of such holes in the side walls is confirmed by the inventory of 1640. Playing garments were brought up into the tower this year; window-glass broken in the hall was repaired.

Payments for stage construction in 1547–8 are intermixed with payments for the hall screen. The carpenter John Frost worked on the stage and 'bench' for four days, while Christopher Whyrte worked one day on the stage. John Dowsey and his son worked eight days on the screen and stage, and three days on the stage alone. John Mere provided 350 boards for screen and stage; St Catharine's College was reimbursed for 59′ of planking ruined by cutting (presumably undamaged boards were returned at no charge). A smith, evidently George Ray, provided two hooks on which costumes were to be hung during the performance of comedies. The college also purchased two lamps, candles, and six bushels of coal. John Burwell provided a large chest for the comic clothes, while John Frost and John Graves were paid for transporting the chest to the college.[19]

In 1548–9 John Frost and Thomas Barber spent six days each on the stage and on spreading sand in a college garden (= 12 man-days), while John Dowsey and his two sons spent three and a half days each setting up the stage and taking it down again (= 10.5 man-days). Lawrence Tayler and John Popler spent a day and a half each on the benches upon the screen. Wooden planks for the tragedy were secured from Steeple Bumpstead (the site of a college property) by John Frost; carriage required three waggons. Lath and pasteboard along with nine ells (approximately $11\frac{1}{4}$ yards) of coarse cloth or canvas may suggest a lightly-framed structure like the shrine of 1540–1; 'hooks for the play' are reminiscent of the hooks for costumes of 1547–8. Torches were provided – three on one occasion and nine on another – as well as oil-lamps. Glass was repaired both in the hall and elsewhere.

Wood purchased for use in the parlour and in the master's chamber above the parlour 'while *Hypocrisis* was being put on' together with the purchase of string 'for the stage in the Master's chamber near the fireplace' may suggest a private performance. This inference is strengthened by the accounts of 1560–1 which reveal that the college purchased edibles 'when the show was put on in the President's chamber'. Conceivably Queens' College had a tradition of private performances in the chamber of the President.

Still in 1548–9, 'Mother' Lewyn was compensated 'for the furbishing of the chamber above the actors[?] room and of the store-room below' (*cubiculi supra conclaue theatriorum et promptuarij inferius*): the latter may have been the *lignarium* mentioned in 1540, while the apparent actors' room may have been a fore-runner of an acting chamber recorded from 1637–8 onward.

Candles were purchased in 1550–1. Expenditures of 1551–2 suggest that the Queens' College stage had reached a pinnacle of sophistication, for John Pople and the servant of King spent three days each before the plays 'building the frame for the heaven' and one day each 'putting up the heaven' (= 8 man-days): evidently this heaven (*coelum*) was a machine (*machina*) for descents. John Dowsey and his two sons spent six days each (= 18 man-days) putting the stage up, taking it down, and mending broken tables. Nails and faggots (probably for a fire) were purchased, Mother Lewyn was paid for sweeping, and items were taken from the tower before the plays and returned a month later. Repairs were made to the hall and to its glass.

The balance of the 1550s saw similar expenses, though never again in such detail. In 1552–3, for two 'public' plays, John Dowsey and three of his sons set the stage up and took it down again; John Frost put in two days, Graves and Botman one day each. Garments were taken from and returned to the tower. In 1553–4 John Dowsey and two of his sons (John and William) were reimbursed for work on an altar and for putting up the stage and taking it down. Garments or props were taken from and returned to the tower this year, as well as in 1554–5 (also a temple of Venus) and 1557–8. In 1558–9 the mandate of 1546 was renewed, requiring both private and public performances of college plays.

In 1561–2 the college spent money on a double padlock, on a hasp of the chest where costumes were kept, and on lamps for the shows. In 1572–3 an unnamed carpenter spent a day and a half on the plays while four labourers devoted five days each to planting trees and about the comedies; candles were also purchased this year. The accounts of 1576–7 mention a 'playe in our hale'; those of 1593–4 a payment to a carpenter for work at the comedy. In 1594–5 Queens' was visited by a bevy of noblemen who attended an early afternoon performance of *Laelia*, 'the day being turned into nyght'. Following the performance the hall fabric and the hall windows required repair.

Again a long silence occurs, until 1627–8 when payments are recorded for 'the comedy stage', for 'torches for comoedye stage', for sixteen pounds of candles, and for two dozen links (a variety of torch). Four dozen torches were purchased in 1633–4 along with four pounds of wax lights; an expense was incurred for 'layinge the stage in the storehouse'. The maintenance of costumes in the treasury is recorded in 1636–7, 1637–8, and 1638–9.

A detailed account of play expenses survives from 1637–8, almost certainly in connection with William Johnson's *Valetudinarium*, performed 6 February 1638 (REED, pp. 925–6, 961–2). Thomas Pestill, who assisted with the play, stabled his horse for twenty-seven nights, whence we may infer that rehearsals began around 11 January and lasted four weeks. The considerable sum of £2–2–0 was spent on 'the Painter for the Stage', and a workman was paid 'for mending the candlesticks'.

The accounts for 1637–8 refer to the college acting chamber and to the new construction of a stagehouse. In 1639–40 a lock and key were provided for the 'chamber for acting cloathes'; in 1640–1 the college constructed a 'press for the Acting cloaths' and mended 'walls over the Acting Chamber'.

Although historians of Cambridge architecture, drama, and printing have assumed that the Queens' College stagehouse of 1637–8 was a free-standing theatre, in fact it was an extramural storehouse for the timbers which made up the stage. The acting chamber was a room within the college walls set aside apparently for rehearsals and for storage of props and less valuable costumes. The more valuable costumes were stored in the treasury, where the 'press for the Acting cloaths' was installed in 1640–1.[20]

The acting chamber retained its name until at least 1665, reserved for general college use rather than being let to a fellow. Beginning in 1665–6, doubtless having been cleared of stage timber, the stagehouse was hired out as a general storehouse, then for the storage of printing supplies, and finally in 1696 it was pulled down to be replaced by the university's New Printing House.[21] The 'press for the Acting cloaths' evidently survived into the early twentieth century.[22] With the possible exception of a single play in 1661–2 (REED, p. 714), there is no evidence, however, of a revival of the play performances which were so much a part of life in Queens' College before the Civil War.

Coordinating the performance

Organization of play performances at Queens' College evidently began with rehearsals in the acting chamber approximately a month before the scheduled performance. The fellow in charge checked the costumes stored in the press in the tower and in the acting chamber itself (costumes not available in the college had to be borrowed, or ordered from a tailor.)

Perhaps a week before the performance Cambridge carpenters began constructing the stage in the college hall. Hall benches could be pressed into use as seating for spectators, but dining tables were cleared out or hidden beneath scaffolding. The timbers which made up the stage complex were carried in from the storehouse; the carpenters set to work guided by the colours and marks on the timbers, locking the joints with pegs. Flooring boards were distributed over the timber jeece as seemed best each year; cut to length and secured with nails rather than pegs, they tended to suffer damage and needed frequent replacement. Special structures were sometimes provided, as in 1551–2 when John Pople and his men spent three days fabricating a 'heaven'. Night watchmen were hired to prevent damage to the hall and to the stage, and to protect against theft.

Costumes brought from the tower were given out only against a signature; those from the acting chamber were perhaps treated more casually. Since the acting chamber was physically remote from the stage in the hall, all costumes and props had to be pre-positioned in one of the two tiring houses, some being hung on pegs.

The audience coming to the plays was in two parts. The President of the college, visiting noblemen, doctors, and other social or academic dignitaries evidently entered through the door in the north-west corner at the upper end and took their seats as appropriate, those of higher dignity in the 'Doctors' Gallery' on matted forms, those of lesser dignity behind and above on wooden racks. Other members of the college, students from other colleges, and townsmen entered the hall through the screens. Some sat on benches or racks in the raised galleries or perhaps over the screens; the rest sat on benches on the ground, or stood if they could find no seat.

Actors must have remained in the hall for the duration of the play, since the door at the upper end was somewhat inconvenient to the stage. Most actors probably walked on to the stage platform from the tiring houses, which doubled as house fronts, though occasional use might be made of the doorway leading from the doctors' gallery. An actor might speak his lines from the stage platform, from within one of the houses, or from the raised areas over the tiring-house enclosures; if he had to move behind the scenes from the house on the east to the house on the west, he would find plenty of space to do so beneath the upper-end gallery, though he would have to be on guard against running into a post or a girt in the dark.

Once the play was finished, costumes and props were returned to their proper places, whether the acting chamber or the tower: if the tower, the original signature was crossed through to show that the borrower had discharged his responsibility. The carpenters dismantled the stage and returned it to the storehouse. The hall was swept, and the tables and benches were returned to their normal position for dining.

3

Trinity College from 1605

Thursday, 9 March 1615. Evening. The great dining hall, Trinity College. Outside the weather is dreadful, for this is 'sharp Winter', 'all the world ... nothing but Aire and Snow'. Inside, by contrast, all is warmth and good humour. For the third night running King James I, Prince Charles, and a host of courtiers have joined forces with the university to watch a play. (A fourth play is in prospect for Friday night, and a fifth on Saturday night; but by Saturday the king will have reached the limit of his endurance.)[1] The play this night is *Albumazar*, written by Thomas Tomkis in imitation of Giambattista della Porta's *L'Astrologo*.[2] Tomkis's adaptation is never so self-conscious as when the trickster Ronca invites the gullible Pandolfo to peer into a 'perspective glass':

> *Ron.* For triall sir: where are you now?
> *Pan.*   In London.
> *Ron.* Ha you found the glasse within that chamber?
> *Pan.*   Yes.
> *Ron.* What see you?
> *Pan.*   Wonders, wonders: I see as in a Land-shappe
> An honorable throng of noble persons,
> As cleare as I were under the same roofe.
> Seemes by their gracious browes, and courteous lookes
> Something they see, which if t b'indifferent
> They'l fav'rably accept: if otherwise
> They'll pardon: who, or what they be, I know not.
> *Ron.* Why that's the court at Cambridge forty miles hence, what else?
> *Pan.* A Hall thrust full of bare-heads, some bald, some busht,
> Some bravely branch't.
> *Ron.*   That's th'University
> Larded with Townes-men. ...

Pandolfo has turned his telescope on the very audience of the play, whence he sees the throng of nobility and the hall full of academics mixed with townspeople: in this self-referential manner, Tomkis calls attention to Trinity College hall itself, fitted up as a theatre.

By any standard, Trinity College hall (see frontispiece and figs. 20, 22) must be considered the jewel in the crown of Thomas Nevile, respected Master from 1593 to 1615 and the college's greatest personal benefactor. Begun in 1602, roofed in 1605, and completed about 1608,[3] the hall survives today in a state of nearly perfect preservation. To the extent that Trinity College hall was consciously built for theatrical use, it must be reckoned as a rare survivor from the English Renaissance, older by several years than the vanished Second Globe of 1609 and older by more than a decade than Inigo Jones's Banqueting House, which still stands in Whitehall.

Of course Trinity College hall in the first instance is not a theatre but a college hall. Nevertheless, just as the Hope contract of 1613 specifies a multiple-purpose structure which could be used for games including bearbaiting or – by the introduction of a demountable stage and tiring house – for plays,[4] so Trinity College hall was designed for dining or – by the introduction of a demountable stage and galleries – for plays.

I am fully aware that my claim for the theatrical character of Trinity College hall risks dismissal as mere hyperbole. Imagine, however, that Blackfriars, with its upper dorter intact, still stood in London.[5] Would this building not be venerated today as Shakespeare's Blackfriars Theatre? Yet Trinity College hall has an even greater claim to be considered a Renaissance theatre, since it was not merely adapted for plays centuries after its original construction, but was intended for theatrical use from the beginning.

My arguments supporting the claim that theatrical use was integral to the original purpose of Trinity College hall are threefold: first, that a substantial area behind the upper-end wall was reserved from the beginning for a theatrical tiring chamber; second, that a trap-door associated with the fabric of the hall served as a supplementary entrance when the hall was used for plays; and third, that for some dozen royal visits from 1613 to 1642 – that is to say, for its optimal use – the hall was set up not for dining, but for plays.

Of these three arguments, the first, concerning the tiring chamber behind the upper-end wall, is based as nearly as may be on plain fact, while the second is admittedly speculative. The third argument, concerning optimal use, is also speculative, but highly probable in a more broadly historical sense.

Although both Cambridge and Oxford universities had been the object of royal visits as far back as anyone in the early seventeenth century could remember, the tradition of entertaining visiting royalty with both disputations and plays was established at Cambridge in August 1564. Since that important event, however, only Oxford had experienced the privilege of royal visits, in 1566, 1592, and 1605. At each of these three visits, the monarch had been entertained with plays in Christ Church hall. The best Cambridge had been able to manage during the same period was a royal visit to Audley End in 1578, when the university had been forced to transport its plays and academic ceremonies to the queen.[6]

In Christ Church hall, Oxford had a suitable place to entertain royalty with plays, whereas Cambridge had nothing comparable. King's College antechapel was not really suitable for plays, and had only been pressed into service at the last moment in 1564 after the college's hall was rejected by the queen's surveyor as inadequate. Although we do not have a detailed record of what went on in Thomas Nevile's mind, he must certainly have intended his new hall as Cambridge's answer to Oxford's Christ Church hall, in particular as a theatre suitable for royal visits. When, once the Trinity College hall was built, royal visitors did come, they did not dine in the hall, but rather watched plays there. The first two such occasions were in 1613 and 1615, during Nevile's lifetime. Between Nevile's death and the Civil War, royal visitors came to Cambridge in 1615 (a second visit), 1623, 1624, 1628, 1632, 1636, and 1642. On every one of these occasions except 1624, when the ageing James I fell unexpectedly ill, Trinity College hall was set up for plays, not for dining. During this same thirty-year period, royal visitors came to Oxford only once, in 1636, when the monarch again witnessed plays in Christ Church hall.[7]

Trinity College stage

When the Chancellor of the university and several foreign ambassadors visited Cambridge on 23 September 1629, they were treated like royal visitors. As was usual for royal visits, the university took steps to control the conduct of students and townspeople by publishing formal orders, with the following clauses included for the plays in Trinity College hall:[8]

> 8. At the Comoedy, that noe Scholler vnder a Master of Arts doe presume to take any place aboue the lower rayle, or barr, either vppon the ground, or the side scaffolds. The space aboue the said barr vnto the stage with the scaffolds one [= on] both sides, to be for the Regents in their caps, hoods, & habits, & for the ffellow commoners; The space vppon the ground beyond the stage, & the scaffold aboue at the end of the hall, for non Regents, & Knights eldest sonnes. yet soe, that they allsoe leaue the lowest seat of the said scaffold, at the end of the hall, with both the side scaffolds, which reach to the stage, for the doctors, & for such Courtiers, as shall not sit with the Chancellor, & the Embassador.
> 9. That noe graduate, or any other student beneath the condicion of a doctor, or of a publike officer of the Vniversitie (vnles he be personally cal'd for, or beinge of Trinity Colledge, be particularly imploid by the Master of the Colledge, or about the Comody) doe come into the Masters lodginge at Trinity Colledge, dureing our Chancellors abode there, nor doe seeke to passe through any dore of the said lodginge, or through the tyringe house into the hall, to the Comoedy.
> 10. That noe tobacco be taken in the hall, nor any where else publikely: & that neither at their standing on the Regent walke before named, nor before the Comoedy begin, nor all the tyme thereof, any rude, and immodest exclamations be made, nor anye humminge, hakeinge, whistlinge, hisseinge, or laughinge be vsed, nor any stampinge, or knockinge, nor any other such vncivill, or vnschollerlike, and boyish demeanor vppon any occasion: nor that any clapping of hands be had, vntill the Plaudite at the end of the Comoedy,

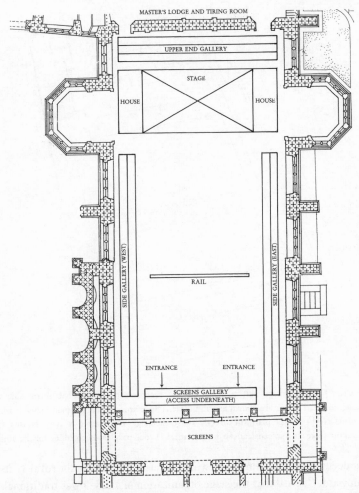

Fig. 20.   Trinity College hall of 1605, stage provisionally superimposed (REED, p. 716).

except the Chancellor, or the Embassador, & the best of quality there, doe apparantly begin the same.

These orders reveal that Trinity College's stage platform (probably including side houses) formed a barrier across the hall near the upper end (figs. 20–1). Beyond the stage stood a seating scaffold, whose lowest part (nearest the stage) was reserved for doctors. This scaffold and the above-stage side scaffolds both reached to the stage platform. Some floor-space above the stage was reserved for non-regents and for knights' eldest sons, all of whom evidently sat on forms.[9] Finally, as we shall see, it is likely that those of highest dignity sat on the stage itself. Below the stage, toward the lower end of the hall, seating scaffolds stood against both side walls, while the open floor between was subdivided into upper and lower halves by a rail or bar. Entrance to the hall at the upper end was through the master's lodge or through a tiring house; entrance at the lower end was through the screens.

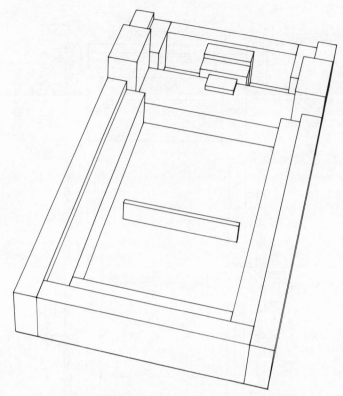

Fig. 21. Trinity College hall stage, schematic reconstruction. Stage platform, side houses, galleries, and rail or bar are shown as solid blocks. Spectators probably stood beneath all seating platforms except for the platform directly above the stage. Disposition of stage houses, galleries beyond the stage, and screens gallery is conjectural. A foot-pace has been added for the king's seat.

Various documents, including somewhat less elaborate orders for royal visits from 1612–13 onward,[10] reveal that the stage organization of 1628–9 was traditional. On 6 February 1611 John Scarlett of Pembroke College and one Perrin of Christ's entered the hall: 'Scarlett...sayeth that he satt nere mr Smyth with mr Perrin vppon a syde Scaffold at the first Comedye...' (REED, p. 465). Stagehouses are mentioned explicitly in a bill of 1612–13, and were reproduced in a 1615–16 college performance at Royston, where the king's workmen were paid for 'fytting and setting vp a stage with particions on the sides'. Both the king and the Vice-Chancellor (Samuel Harsnett) sat on the stage in 1614–15 (REED, pp. 872–3).

Trinity College's stage bears such an obvious similarity to the stage of Queens' College that I have felt secure in using some information derived from the 1640 Queens' inventory in its reconstruction. The Trinity stage, however, was more elaborate in several respects: side scaffolds and floor-space were provided above as well as below the stage; a bar or rail regulated the below-stage audience; and the tiring house was immediately outside the hall rather than incorporated into the flanking stagehouses.

The exact disposition of the seating scaffolds above the stage presents particular uncertainties. Was the upper-end floor-space (for non-regents and for knights' eldest sons) beneath or between the raised scaffolds? Did the seating in the side scaffolds run parallel to the upper-end wall or parallel to the side walls? Forced to make a choice in my drawing (fig. 21), I have opted for open floor-space between the main and side scaffolds, and for side scaffolds running parallel to the side walls.[11] I have also installed a gallery in front of the screens on the model of Queens' College, though without documentary warrant. Lacking details of construction, I have drawn the stage platform, side houses, scaffolds, and bar as undifferentiated blocks rather than as complex timberwork.

The relative complexity of the Trinity College stage is consistent with the vast scale of Trinity College hall, which measures 40′ in width by 85′ in length to the screens, making for an area of 3400 sq. ft., nearly three times larger than Queens'. John Chamberlain reports that for the performances before James I in 1615, the hall accommodated 2,000 spectators (REED, p. 540).

The tiring chamber

That Trinity College reserved a room behind the upper-end wall of its magnificent hall for use as a tiring chamber is attested by numerous documents. The university order of 1628–9 restricts entry 'through the tyringe house into the hall, to the Comoedy', a prohibition which was repeated nearly verbatim in 1631–2 and 1635–6. College and university records refer to such a room at least seven times from 1613–14 to 1635–6 (REED page and line numbers in parentheses):

repeating Chamber	1613–14	(519/41)
attyring chamber	1614–15	(527/32)
tyreing house	1614–15	(528/6)
tyringe chamber	1619–20	(569/32)
tyringe house	1628–9	(620/35)
tyringe howse	1631–2	(636/39)
attiringe howse	1635–6	(666/34)

From these appellations it seems that the principal use of the chamber was for attiring actors before and during play performances, but if the 1613–14 entry refers to the same site, it was also used for rehearsals.

Willis and Clark (II, p. 625) propose that the tiring chamber was located on the ground floor of the bay immediately behind the upper-end wall of the hall. Since the hall is built on a kind of pedestal, the level of the hall is higher by about six feet than the level of the ground chamber. This offset is clearly visible in the Loggan print of 1688 (fig. 22), which also shows the entrance door to the ground chamber from the Great Court.

Today a door at the north-west corner of the hall (see frontispiece, figs. 20, 23, 25) opens on to a stair leading down to ground level. Although the companion door at the north-east corner is now blank, Willis and Clark propose that a companion stair once

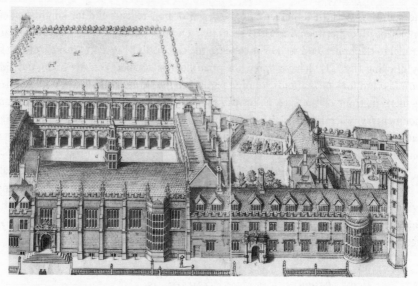

Fig. 22.   Loggan print of Trinity College, 1688, detail showing ornamental entrances to hall (left) and to master's lodge (centre right), and prominent bow window of putative 'comedy room' (far right, ground level). Note unadorned entrance to bay behind upper end of hall (centre), and difference in level between this bay and the elevated hall. The far end of the range behind the master's lodge (prominent gable) is designated as the comedy room by Willis and Clark.

led from a formerly functional doorway here also down to ground level, that is, down to the tiring chamber.

That the upper end of the hall originally had two functional doors is confirmed by an entry in the 1614–15 Junior Bursar's book for '2 keayes and a lock for a doare coming out of the masters Lodging into the Hall', and another for 'a locke for a dore going out of the tyreing house into the Hall'. A payment of 1619–20 'ffor a bolt for the doore that cometh out of the tyringe chamber into the Masters lodginge'[12] shows that the tiring chamber also communicated with the master's lodge, thus affording indirect passage from the lodge to the hall.

The security plan of 1615: the trap-door

A 'security plan' drawn up for the royal visit of March 1615 (Appendix 5) reveals that guards were posted at four points around the hall during the time of the comedies: at the 'hall dore'; at the 'doore entringe the Hall at the screene'; at the 'doctors seates'; and at the 'Trapp doore'. Of these four sites, the first two are easy enough to interpret as the Great-Court entrance to the screens passage (figs. 20, 22), and an entrance through the screens into the hall. The third site, leading to the doctors' seats, may be tentatively identified as the door at the north-west corner of the hall leading from the master's lodge. (James Tabor, the university Registrary, responsible for watching this door, was personally familiar with virtually all university personnel who would have had occasion to enter through the master's lodge.)

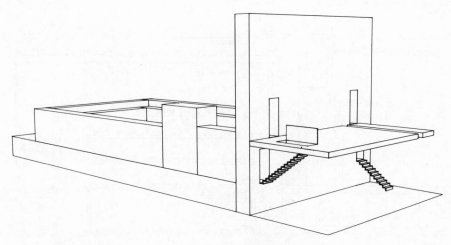

Fig. 23.   Trinity College hall, from behind the upper-end wall, conjectural reconstruction. Two openings are shown at dais level, with two more above. A trap-door in its conjectural location opens on to a stair which leads from the upper level behind the upper-end wall (tiring chamber?) down to the dais via the east dais door. The narrow passage leading from the upper-level opening on the right to the upper level of the master's lodge is conjectural. A wall from the 1550s construction period with a fireplace at the upper level should be visualized rising through the gap between the two upper-level floors.

Absent the specific reference to a trap-door, one would certainly have surmised that the fourth point of entrance was the door in the north-east corner of the dais leading from the tiring chamber, particularly as one of its three guards was Thomas Cecill, author of *Æmelia*, St John's College's contribution to the March 1615 comedies (REED, pp. 534, 538, 928), for it would make sense for Cecill to be at a door intended to be used by those involved in plays, perhaps to the exclusion of the general public. But where would a trap-door have been situated?

If the trap-door guarded by Cecill were in the stage platform, it makes little sense for it to have been guarded by a playwright if it needed to be guarded at all. As for a trap-door in the floor of the hall leading down to the cellar beneath,[13] there is no evidence that such a door existed, and is difficult to imagine that anyone needed to enter the hall from the cellar. A more reasonable speculative possibility is that a trap-door in the dais opened on to a stair angling down through the foundation of the upper-end wall to ground level in the room behind; but the area directly beneath the dais remains undeveloped to this day, and the foundation wall shows no evidence of any opening consonant with this hypothesis.[14]

A final hypothesis is that Thomas Cecill guarded a trap-door in the *upper* storey behind the upper-end wall, opening on to a stair which led downward to the door at the north-east corner of the hall (fig. 23). If so, then this upper-storey room may have been the site of the tiring chamber. It would be logical for a trap-door in such a location to be guarded by a playwright, since he would be familiar with anyone involved in a play production, and properly suspicious of anyone whom he did not recognize.

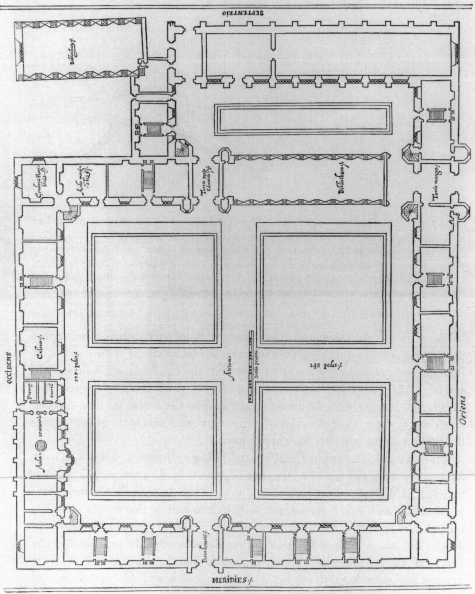

Fig. 24. Plan of Trinity College, 1555, showing walls in the west range (near the *Conclave magistri*) which were incorporated into the 1605 reconstruction of the bays behind the upper-end wall of the hall (see fig. 25). Also shown is the *Aula communis* inherited from Michaelhouse, which served as the principal college hall from c. 1546 to c. 1605. (Reprinted from Willis and Clark, II, pp. 464–5.)

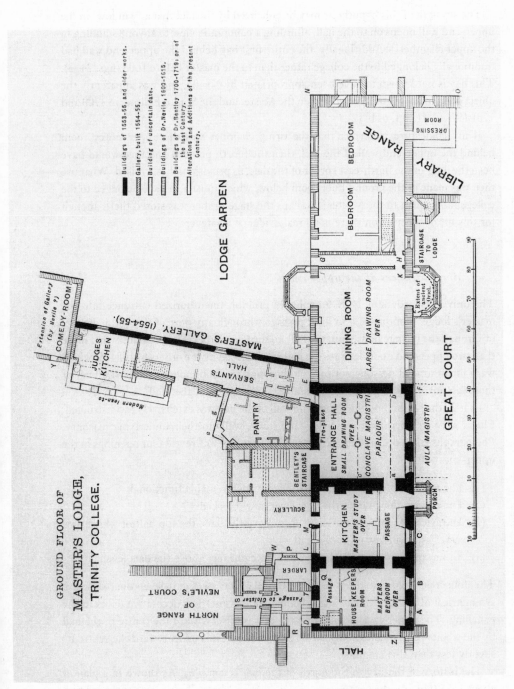

GROUND FLOOR OF
MASTER'S LODGE,
TRINITY COLLEGE.

Buildings of 1553-55, and older works.
Gallery, built 1554-55.
Building of uncertain date.
Buildings of Dr. Nevile, 1600-1615.
Buildings of Dr. Bentley 1700-1719; or of the last Century.
Alterations and Additions of the present Century.

LODGE GARDEN

Extension of Gallery (by Nevile ?) COMEDY-ROOM.

JUDGES KITCHEN

MASTER'S GALLERY (1554-55)

Modern lean-to

SERVANTS HALL

PANTRY

BENTLEY'S STAIRCASE

Fire-place

ENTRANCE HALL
SMALL DRAWING ROOM OVER

CONCLAVE MAGISTRI
PARLOUR

DINING ROOM
LARGE DRAWING ROOM OVER

AULA MAGISTRI

GREAT COURT

PORCH

PASSAGE

SCULLERY

KITCHEN
MASTER'S STUDY OVER

LARDER

HOUSE KEEPERS ROOM

MASTERS BEDROOM OVER

Passage

Passage to Cloister

NORTH RANGE OF NEVILE'S COURT

HALL

BEDROOM

BEDROOM

LIBRARY RANGE

DRESSING ROOM

STAIRCASE TO LODGE

Extent of ancient Oriel.

Fig. 25.   Groundplan of Trinity College master's lodge by Willis and Clark (II, p. 605). The upper-end wall of the 1605 hall is at the far left.
The comedy room is shown at the far end of the master's gallery (top of drawing); but the ground-level 'Dining Room' with the bow windows
may be a better candidate for the comedy room (? *alias* acting room).

The strength of this hypothesis may be enhanced by the fact that a 'window' in the upper-end wall opens on to the hall, affording a panoramic view to anyone standing in the upper chamber.[15] Additionally, the entire first bay behind the upper-end wall had traditionally belonged to the college rather than to the master before 1605 (figs. 24–5). This bay is not known to have been appropriated by Nevile, and was apparently the object of financial negotiations between the Master and the Senior Fellows in 1700 and 1701 (W&C, II, pp. 611–12).

If my conjecture is correct that the tiring chamber was the upper-storey room behind the upper-end wall of the hall, then the fourth point of entrance would have been the door in the north-east corner of the dais, as provisionally surmised. What use then was made of the ground floor room below, which must also have belonged to the college rather than to the Master? Perhaps the stage timber was stored there, though for this bit of speculation there is no real evidence whatever.

More entrances at the upper end?

The university orders of 1628–9 explicitly prohibit unauthorized entrance into the master's lodge, then proceed to limit passage 'through any dore of the said lodginge, or through the tyringe house into the hall, to the Comoedy'. The possibility that more than two upper-end doors led into the hall is reinforced by the orders of 1624–5, which warn unauthorized persons not to 'goe thorough the said lodgeinge into the Hall or thorough any of the doores that open at the vpper ende of the Hall'.

In 1920 the bay behind the upper-end wall of the hall was extensively reconstructed. Floors were stripped to their girders and joists, walls to their underlying masonry. Photographs taken during this reconstruction (figs. 26–7)[16] reveal four openings in the upper-end wall:

(1) The western doorway at the dais level, which remains functional.
(2) The eastern doorway at the dais level, now blocked.
(3) An eastern opening about eight feet above the dais, the top half of which now serves as a window on to the hall.
(4) An unexplained western doorway about eight feet above the dais level.

The four openings are roughly symmetrical. The two dais-level doorways are symmetrical of course, as they stand behind the symmetrical decorative doors in the panelling. The upper-level opening on the east is offset toward the centre of the hall by the whole width of a doorway, while that on the west is offset toward the centre by slightly less than this amount.

The history of the bay to the north of the hall is complex. As shown in a plan of about 1555 (fig. 24), the west range, inherited from Michaelhouse, was extended first north from the old *aula communis*, and then east. Much of this reconstructed west range and all of the eastward extension, however, were demolished under Nevile for the sake of the new hall and its kitchen to the south, and for the sake of a new master's

Fig. 26. Trinity College photo, 1920, east side and centre of upper-end wall of 1605 hall, from adjoining bay. Hand-written caption: 'Looking South'. Dais-level door at bottom left corner is now blocked; upper-level square opening above timber floor is now a waist-level look-through.

lodge which lay to the north so as not to intrude into what became the college's Great Court.[17]

Among the older masonry walls absorbed into the new construction of 1605 were those of the old *conclave magistri* at the former north-west angle, and some portion of the bay or bays to the south, including at least part of the bay which was to contain the tiring chamber. Could the upper-storey openings revealed in the 1920 photographs be ancient passages between adjoining bays of the 1550s construction? Willis and Clark indeed show the northern face of the upper-end wall of the 1605 hall as dating from 1553–5, the southern face from 1605 (fig. 25). The more recent drawings of the Royal Commission on Historical Monuments, in contrast, show the entire upper-end wall as

Fig. 27.   Trinity College photo, 1920, west side of upper-end wall of 1605 hall, from adjoining bay. Hand-written caption: 'Looking South; "doors" to Dais'. Dais-level door below is still in use; upper-level opening above left is now blocked.

belonging to 1605.[18] In fact, the 1555 plan does not show a cross-wall where the upper-end wall now stands, but even if some of the openings were traceable to the construction of the 1550s, the upper-level opening at the north-west corner of the hall clearly is not, as it lies entirely outside and to the west of the 1550s structures.

Even the dais-level openings present mysteries. Willis and Clark assign the north-west door to 1614–15, citing a payment for five days' work 'diging of a dore out of the lodging into the Hall & carring rubbish'.[19] Already in 1612–13, however, for the entertainment of Prince Charles and the Prince Palatine, the Trinity College stage platform served its subsequently standard function of separating dignitaries above the stage from humbler persons below. The earliest apparent reference to the tiring chamber, in this instance called the repeating chamber, is 1613–14, a year before the new door was dug from the lodging into the hall. Finally, in 1614–15 (as we have noted), locksmiths provided locks for *two* doors at the upper end: one door into the master's lodge, and another into the tiring chamber. If one of these two doorways was indeed cut in 1614–15, the other must have been available from the beginning.[20]

An alternative scenario to that proposed by Willis and Clark is that the door newly dug between the master's lodge and the hall in 1614–15 was the upper-level north-west door. Nor would such violence upon the fabric of a building have been unprecedented, for in 1564 (as we have seen) a door was made in King's College Chapel, and in 1566 a passageway was cut through a thick masonry wall at Christ Church, Oxford, for the convenience of Elizabeth, leading to a specially constructed bridge which allowed Elizabeth free passage to the college hall, bypassing the crowds below.[21]

The north-west upper-level opening must have been approached from the back by means of a gallery from the upper storey of the master's lodge. The opening would have led directly to the doctors' seats in the gallery above the stage, while the dais-level door would have provided separate access to the floor beneath.

The master's lodge was perhaps felt to comprise the rooms in the *upper* level of the northern part of the western range, as witness a payment of 1614–15:

> Item [for whiting] our Masters lower hall, *the stayres vpp to the lodging*, the long gallerie to our Masters kitchin, with the porche at the entrance to the lodging xxiiij s[22]

If the 'lodging' was essentially at the upper level, then a door leading from the lodge into the hall may also have been at the upper level.

On the occasion of three separate royal visits in the late seventeenth and early eighteenth centuries, a raised platform was installed at the upper end of Trinity College hall. For the reception of William III on 7 October 1689 the royal table was raised five steps above the floor, and tables were placed along each side of the hall. For the reception of Queen Anne on 16 April 1705 a throne was erected on a platform 5′ high. For the reception of George II on 25 April 1728 a scaffold was built with an ascent of six steps; scaffolds for women of the county were constructed along the sides of the hall; and an ascent for drummers and trumpeters was built at the screens end, facing the dais.[23] On any or all of these occasions, royal access to the raised dining platform at the upper end of the hall would have been easier from the eight-foot level than from the dais-level doorways.

The putative upper-level doorway on the west is not only speculative, but open to possible disproof since the panelling now in place at the upper end of the hall shows no sign of disturbance in this area. If the panelling was installed in 1605 and never subsequently altered or replaced,[24] then, except for the surviving look-through, upper-level openings could not have communicated with the hall. Eccentricities in the surrounds of the lower-level doorways – visible particularly behind the north-east (blank) door – suggest that the panelling has somewhat less integrity than has been assumed. The unanticipated openings revealed by the 1920 photographs, moreover, particularly the opening at the north-west, cry out for an explanation.

The comedy room

In the autumn of 1990 workmen excavating between Trinity College's back buildings and the river encountered a brick foundation. A century earlier, Willis and Clark (II, pp. 624–5) had proposed that a structure called the 'comedy room', with a floor-plan of approximately $25' \times 75'$, once stood some $85'$ behind the master's lodge in the direction of the river, at the end of a long gallery (fig. 25). Willis and Clark's proposal has been endorsed this century by the Cambridge theatre historian Moore Smith, by the historian G. M. Trevelyan (Master of Trinity 1940–51 and author of a small history of the college), and by the Royal Commission on Historical Monuments.[25] Is it then surprising that on 14 November 1990 the *Cambridge Evening News* could announce that a 'seven-strong archaeology team' had discovered 'a comedy wall – part of a 14th [!] century play-house which eventually disappeared under the newly-created college [of 1546]'?

I will argue that the comedy room was not a playhouse $85'$ to the west, but a room or set of rooms well within the traditional limits of the present master's lodge.

Cosimo de Medici, Duke of Tuscany, visited Cambridge in 1669. According to town Alderman Samuel Newton, the Master and seniors 'brought him to the Master's Lodge, and then they went to the Comedy House where they had a Comedy'.[26] Newton's 'Comedy House' does not necessarily imply a separate building: the university commencement stage, for example, was often called the 'Commencement House' from 1610–11 onward even though it was not an independent structure but merely an interior transformation of the nave of Great St Mary's.[27]

The official Italian account is more circumstantial: 'The evening coming on, his highness was introduced into the theatre, a room rather small than spacious, where was represented by the scholars a Latin comedy.'[28] College records of this year contain a unique archival allusion: 'for the hire of 4 haircloths for the windows in the Comedy-room 8 s'.[29]

Willis and Clark bring several additional pieces of information to bear on the matter of the comedy room. In 1710 fellows of the college submitted articles to the Bishop of Ely against Richard Bentley, Master of Trinity from 1700 to 1742:

Why did you, without any Authority, take into the said Lodge, or appropriate to your own Use, a great deal of room never before used with it, particularly one Room, which was formerly used for the acting of Comedies; which the lecturers of the College, are by the Statutes obliged to make against Christmas, besides other Rooms?[30]

The room is referred to again in a published reply to Bentley's published reply:

he, without any Authority, added more Room to his Lodge than ever was before; particularly a large Room formerly used for the acting of Comedies, which by the College Statutes the Lecturers are obliged to make every Christmas ...[31]

The second piece of supplementary evidence cited by Willis and Clark is a reminiscence by Dr Thomas Parne, whose college career extended from 1714 to 1749:

The Comedy room included both the long Room where the bow windows are and some of the present Master's Parlour, when they used to have leave to keep Christmas; the Senior Sophister and Bachelor were masters of the Revels and ordered all things in College. One came with drums, the other with trumpets before him; the fellows dined and supped promiscuously with the scholars.[32]

Willis and Clark add, whether with reference to this testimony or to college tradition more generally: 'It has been usual to identify the "Comedy-Room" with the large Drawing-Room [in the master's lodge].' Willis and Clark, however, resist the authority of college tradition: 'it is difficult to believe that a room in that position could ever have been regarded as not properly belonging to the Lodge, which was evidently the case with the room annexed by Dr. Bentley' (II, p. 624).

A number of considerations suggest that Willis and Clark's objections and counterproposal are finally untenable. The reply to Bentley characterized the 'Room formerly used for the acting of Comedies' as 'large', but the college theatre is described by the de Medici correspondent as 'a room rather small than spacious', an impression more appropriate to the surviving single-storey bow-window room with a floor-plan of approximately $28' \times 42'$ than to Willis and Clark's building with a putative floor-plan of approximately $25' \times 75'$ (which, after all, would have been considerably larger than Queens' College hall, though not so large as Trinity College hall).[33]

Three separate archival records identify a parlour as a venue for comedies. In 1611–12 the college paid 'for rushes and dressing the parlor at the Commides'. For a play performed on 16 March 1663, at the visit of the Duke of Monmouth, work was undertaken 'about the Stage in the Parlour'. In 1664–5 comedy expenses included repair 'to the Low parlour windows'.[34]

Thomas Parne's identification of the comedy room with 'the long Room where the bow windows are' seems clear, but this is not quite so helpful as it might seem, for both what Willis and Clark call the dining room, on the ground floor of the master's lodge (fig. 25), and also the drawing room, immediately above, are characterized by prominent bow windows. (In contrast, no significant evidence survives to suggest that the gallery or its extension had bow windows.)[35]

The tradition reported by Willis and Clark that the comedy room was 'the large

Drawing-Room' may require correction only with respect to level (it was apparently the 'Low parlour' at ground level). As for the intramural dispute over ownership, it could well be that the lower bow-window room was legally under the control of the fellows rather than of the master, which would certainly explain why the fellows were so exercised over the loss of 'a great deal of room'.

The acting chamber

Whereas a comedy room is named once only in the college accounts, an 'acting room' or 'acting chamber' is mentioned some twelve times between 1668–9 and 1695–6. About half the time the room is named in reference to play productions. It was almost certainly used for its nominal purpose at least for the four years 1668–9 to 1671–2 (the latter apparently the last year of play production in Trinity College); a final reference occurs in 1695–6, for repairs when the room had ceased to be used in connection with plays, though its former use was still remembered.

The only college account which definitively names the comedy room, from 1668–9, contains a separate payment of 3s 'To young Chapman for running of Errands, making fires, keeping the dore in the Acting chamber'. While the two different names in the same account may seem to imply two separate rooms, Willis and Clark are probably correct to equate them,[36] since on the occasion of a visit by Charles II on 4 October 1671 the king watched a play in the college (Appendix 6, 1671–2, headnote), and it would be logical to conclude that he watched it in the acting room which the college caused to be whitewashed that year.

The accounts of 1670–1 include a payment for 'two dores into the Acting-roome out of the Auditt Chamber': evidently the audit chamber, whose location is not independently known, was adjacent to the acting room/comedy room/low parlour. Although the audit chamber cannot be pinpointed exactly, the combination may recall Thomas Parne's asserted juxtaposition of 'the long Room where the bow windows are' with 'some of the present Master's Parlour'.[37]

The audit chamber evidently housed a press for playing costumes, installed in 1663–4:

> For a presse for the comedie cloaths, & carriage to the Audit Chamber 1 01 00
> Iron worke & a locke to the presse barre 00 03 06

Another college chamber had a similar press in 1668–9:

> Item for work done in the Common Chamber about the Presses to hang the Actors cloathes in for sliting the Boords 1s a lock 1s a row of pins 1s 2d ... 01 01 10

This second reference to a costume press, like many other Trinity College documents from this period, survives in duplicate manuscripts, one of which contains the highly abbreviated 'Com:' chamber, while the other expands to 'Common' chamber. Is it conceivable that the modern editor Moore Smith, who transcribed the former version, expanded correctly to 'Comedie' chamber, while the contemporary scribe of the latter version expanded incorrectly to 'Common' chamber?[38]

Archival evidence 1605–1642

Archival evidence for Trinity College plays from the completion of Nevile's new hall to the Civil War[39] is intensive rather than extensive. The enormously detailed depositions taken after a riot between the students of Trinity College and St John's College on 5–6 February 1611 illuminate many aspects of play production, but afford only the briefest glimpse into Trinity College hall itself. Crowd control was given over to college stagekeepers, including a dozen members of the college and at least one townsman. The stagekeepers were colourfully costumed in light defensive gear, and carried torches and links. The torches would have provided illumination for the crowd entering the hall about 5:00 p.m. (dusk in early February), and leaving in full darkness, but seem to have been even more useful as staves for directing crowd movement, and as weapons.

On the first night playgoers were admitted to college grounds as usual by the main college gate in Trinity Street. Admission to the hall itself was by the stairs leading up to the screens passage – stairs which were then rectangular in plan (fig. 22) rather than semi-circular as they are today. Thomas Layfield of St John's sought admission, but was thrown down the stairs by a stagekeeper. Robert Oxley of St John's sought entrance into the hall after the play was well underway:

> The said Robert Oxly the same night he came into the Hall all things being quiet between the 4th and 5th Act & ther within the skreen the same stagekeper before described came vnto him againe & lookt vpon went back & strock him ouer the shoulder with a club. & bad him be gon, who awnswering I am gone: & so went forth the stagekeeper following, & linking him [= striking him with a torch] to the hall dore.

John Webster, a townsman, claims to have been linked at the same time (p. 453).

For the second night's performance the main college gate was locked and admission instead was through Queen's Gate in Trinity Lane – also called Piss Pot Lane[40] – more remote from rival St John's College. Robert Mason of St John's managed to get to the hall door by the good offices of one stagekeeper, but was then chased back to the gate by two stagekeepers threatening him with their links (p. 440). Many St John's men did manage to get into the hall, but not without harassment at the hall door (p. 1034). Nicholas Auger was assaulted as he left the hall at the conclusion of the play (p. 430).[41]

Our one brief glimpse into the hall is afforded by the testimony of John Scarlett of Pembroke College (p. 465):

> he sayeth that he satt nere Mr Smyth with mr Perrin vppon a syde Scaffold at the fyrst Comedye & did see when as Mr Smyth styrred him selfe & rose vpp that the hyltes of a sworde scayne or rapier or such like weapon did before in his gowne playnly appeare to this examinates sight who looked full in mr Smyths face when the hyltes appeared.

Unfortunately for us, Scarlett was deposing about the riot and not about the theatre.

The following year, 1611–12, as we have seen, the college paid 'for russhes and dressing the parlor at the Commides', suggesting a play in the parlour rather than in the hall. The year after that, in 1612–13, Trinity College played host to Prince Charles and his new brother-in-law the Prince Palatine. Since the hall was to be set up for plays, the college distributed money for dining in the town.[42]

An extensive building account survives for the comedies of this year. Great quantities of timber and board were purchased, including fir timber, two loads of jeece, planks, and spars. Carters and sawyers were hired to transport and prepare the timber. Painters were active in the preparation of props including a 'pastorall clothe' and a 'centaure'; they were also paid for 'the howses 2 nights' and for painting candlesticks.

A smith provided candlesticks, and another candlestick was brought from Huntingdon. Durdon provided 172 pairs of white lights, and Samuel Smith provided torches. Coal was purchased, some of it from Chapple. More than three dozen mats were supplied, including mats for the Princes' seat, and an upholsterer was reimbursed for 'windows stopping with matts'. Haircloths were hired from Samuel Smith; holly, ivy, and sedge were provided, probably for the hall; and Kemp was paid for glass, probably for repairs. Smiths provided iron work, including six pulleys, and two men were paid for watching two nights.

The most elaborately recorded expenses are day-wages for carpenters: from these we can determine that construction on the stage started about 23 February in preparation for productions on 2 and 3 March: this left the carpenters about eight working days, but since many carpenters and labourers worked on the project simultaneously, the total number of man-days spent on putting up the stage and taking it down again was approximately 191. Peare seems to have been in charge, but Dowsing (= Dowsey) was also an active participant. Although the college theatre was by no means new this year (side scaffolds had already been constructed in 1610–11), the fresh expenditure of £180 may have provided the standard of elegance and finish that made the theatre so appealing in subsequent years to its royal visitors.

Also of interest are many references to carrying, not only of timber (both by cart and by water), but of trunks from Ware, another(?) trunk belonging to one Mistress Green, apparel from the home of the Earl of Southampton (in Great Shelford, near Cambridge),[43] wine from Royston, and musicians from London.

In 1614–15 several townsmen were paid 'for watching the College chambers the 4 Commedie nightes at the Kings first coming'. The London painter James Manutius[44] received the large sum of £5–7–6 'for paynting the stage', and he or another received further sums 'for paynting the Rayles on the stage', 'for paynting the Sayleirs' (celures, or stretched fabric), and 'for glew and nayles about the trees & stage'. Some 1800 of pit coal were purchased 'in the tyme of Commedies repeating', probably consumed in the fireplace mended this year 'in the Attyring chamber'.

Not only Trinity College, but St John's and Clare mounted plays on the Trinity College stage for the benefit of the royal entourage. Trinity itself had to spend £9–16–4 'for altering the stage and fitting it for our Commedies'. Beyond this, agents of the king devoted eight days to 'the Hall in Trinytie colledge for fower Comedies'.

This was the year in which the king returned to Cambridge for a repeat performance of the play which so caught his attention, George Ruggle's *Ignoramus* (REED, pp. 541–4, Appendixes 4–5).

Only one further scrap of useful information survives for subsequent years to 1642, from a Star Chamber case resulting from an incident which occurred in March 1632. Theodore Kelly, who issued a challenge to Sir Arthur Gorge, testified:

> That in Lent last there being a play to be acted att Trinity Colledge in Cambridge before the King, there was a great Preasse of people which thrust him this Examinate vpon Sir Arthur Gorge that he turned to this Eximanat & said he would Cudgell him this deponent or that he deserved to be cudgelled. The said Sir Arthur ledd a Lady or gentlewoman by the arme.

Not much information, true, but we do hear of the press of people seeking admission, and attendance by a couple. (Although women could not have made up a large proportion of the audience, they are known to have attended Cambridge plays on numerous occasions, even when plays were not in English, as this one was.)[45]

Archival evidence 1662–71

In 1661–2 the Master and Senior Fellows authorized the Senior Bursar to put £8 'toward the charges of a stage, & properties, & a Supper & for encouragement of the Actors of a Comoedy out of the Commencement moneys'. To this sum was added £20 from the Junior Bursar for 'the Stage & other Charges for the Latine Comedie' produced by Hill senior, and 16s 8d for 10 lb of wax candles 'for the use of two Commodyes'.[46]

The performance site for the 1661–2 plays is unknown. In 1662–3 a smith was paid for 'Worke about the Stage in the Parlour'; in 1664–5 work about the comedies was devoted to 'the Low parlour windows'. In 1668–9 haircloths were provided for the windows of 'the Comedy-room', called by Alderman Newton (as we have seen) 'the Comedy House'.[47] In this same year and in the two years following, provisions relevant to plays were made for 'the Acting room'. Evidently, then, from 1662–3 onward, and perhaps already in 1661–2, Trinity College plays were performed in the parlour, called the comedy room.

In 1661–2 the college purchased 10 lb of wax candles for the plays. The stage in the parlour in 1662–3 required 32 'standers' and 520 'quarters for bearers for the scaffold', along with 44′ of timber for the bearers, suggesting one or more extensive raised structures. A total of 31′ of rails (painted) with 28 turned ballasters may have been for the perimeter of the stage. Wax and tallow candles, links, and torches were provided, along with six hooks for hanging the candles. A haircloth was provided for unspecified purposes. Setting the stage up required nearly 60 man-days, taking it down again, 23; general assistance came to 16. The work of seven painters came to a total of 33 man-days. John Shuter was paid for hangings, a long cushion, and curtains, while Porter and Brewers were paid for keeping the gates.

For the next year, 1663–4, we have only a totalled carpenters' bill for £3–17–0, along with entries for candles, wax, and tallow, 'for a presse for the comedie cloaths', for carriage to the Audit Chamber, and for iron work and a lock 'to the presse barre'.

Comedy expenses including glass and related repairs in 1664–5 'to the Low parlour windows' again suggest a performance in the parlour. Great expenditure was made on light and heat, including 6 lb of tallow candles, eight tin candlesticks, links, wax candles, torches, earthen candlesticks, and a further 8 lb of candles, in addition to three sacks of sea coal, two bushels of sea coal, carriage, fires, and attendance. Painters were paid for 'a deaths-hed carved & painted', and for 'Inscription of the 2 Scenes'. Wax was supplied 'to make Ticketts', the first known reference to an apparent entry control. Itemized labour amounted to only 15 man-days this year, along with further payments for 'watching & defending the walls' and for doorkeepers. Deals, nails, and wages were supplied 'for the Scaffold work', along with new stuff, nails, tacks, mending 'the Entrance hangings' and 'the vpholsterers pains'.

No further payments are recorded until 1668–9, when items are listed under 'both the times of the play was acted' ('of publick acting'). This was the year of the visit of Cosimo de Medici. Once again payments for labour were relatively small, only 14 man-days being required for the stage. Four haircloths were provided 'for the windows in the Comedy-room', along with a dozen mats. John Shuter supplied sixteen yards of green baize 'to cover the stage'.[48] Seventeen deals and four slit deals were required in the way of materials. The painter Griffith was paid 'for painting NOLA upon the stage',[49] Chapman and James were paid for making fires and keeping 'the dore in the Acting chamber', while George Scarrow was paid 'for keeping the gate'.

Activities continued the next year, 1669–70, for a play 'before the Duke of Ormond & before the University'. A payment to William Caton the joiner 'for work done in the Acting Roome' is the only reference to the possible construction of a stage. 25′ of quarters were purchased for 'the Musick's Lattice', and work was undertaken 'in the Common Chamber about the Presses to hang the Actors cloathes in for sliting the Boords': a lock and a row of pins were also provided. Similarly, Timothy Caverly supplied a lock and two staples 'for the Acting roome'. 28 lb of wax candles were secured, and Gam provided two sacks of coal. Gam and Scarrow kept the doors 'at the Comedy', while Killingworth and Coolidge were paid 'for keeping the King's-gate & carrying charcoale'.

Further provisions included two mats and three haircloths, along with eighteen yards of cloth 'for the Oake Trees and the Well'; in addition, two hoops were provided for the well. The painter Wisdom was reimbursed 'for the Oake-trees Painting & writing 2 names'.

In 1670–1 a play was 'acted before the vniuersity' and also 'for the prince of Orange'. Timothy Caverly provided iron work, locks, and keys in the 'Acting-room', while an 18′ piece of timber was purchased for the stage, along with twenty-two deal-boards. Two new doors were installed between the acting room and the audit chamber. Carpentry work amounted to 15 man-days, not counting Coolidge's attendance over four days and the work of Caiton the joiner undertaken 'at the Lodge when the Duke of Yorke was here'. Porters were reimbursed for keeping the gates. Candles were provided, along with 24 lb of wax, four large tin candlesticks, eighteen additional candlesticks, and a lantern 'for the Hall Staires'.

John Shuter was closely involved with the plays this year, providing nails and tape 'for the Musick grate', setting on the green cloth, providing tenternails and leather, for 'taking up & laying the green cloth on the stage', for flocks and mats, for 'laying againe the stage cloth', for 'taking down and putting up Dr Cudworth's hangings', for three yards of green baize for enlarging the stage cloth, for twenty-two and a quarter yards of broad baize for hangings for the stage and adding to the floor one yard, and finally for thread, tape, and cord for hangings.

In contrast with this abundant documentation, little information survives concerning a performance on 4 October 1671 other than that the acting room was whitewashed for this last known occasion of play performance in Trinity College before modern times.

Coordinating the performance 1608–71

From 1608–9 to 1641–2 most Trinity College plays were performed in the new hall, although in 1611–12, and perhaps at other times, private performances were given in the master's parlour. Although the place of performance in 1661–2 is unknown, performances from 1662–3 to 1671–2 may all have been in the room denominated the comedy room or the acting room.

Preparations began with rehearsals in the tiring chamber (alias repeating chamber) through 1641–2, and in the comedy/acting room thereafter. Perhaps two weeks before any public performance in the hall, the tables and benches were cleared so completely that fellows were paid to dine in the town instead. Carpenters brought the stage timbers from their storage place, and set about transforming the hall into a theatre.

The college tiring chamber being located just behind the upper-end wall, props and costumes were close to hand. Night watchmen and stagekeepers were hired to guard against vandalism and to protect costumes and props of value.

The audience attending plays in the hall was in three parts. The master, doctors, visiting noblemen, and other social or academic dignitaries, including the king if he was in attendance, entered from the master's lodge through a door in the upper-end wall, possibly at the eight-foot level. Persons of higher dignity sat closer to the stage, the monarch reserving the right to sit on the stage platform; those of lower dignity sat in the upper-end galleries against the sides of the hall, or at floor level.

Regular members of the college, students from other colleges, and townsmen entered the hall through the screens. Masters of Arts had permission to go beyond the rail which cut across the lower end of the hall. Some at this end sat in the side galleries or perhaps over the screens; the rest stood or perhaps sat on benches on the ground.

It was not necessary for all actors to be in the hall for the duration of the play, since exits and entrances could be made and the play's progress could be monitored through the upper-level opening. For the most part actors entered on to the stage platform from the stagehouses, which provided house fronts, though direct access from the tiring chamber may also have been available. An actor might speak his lines from the platform, from within one of the side houses, or from the raised areas over the houses; if he had to move behind the scenes from the house on the east to the house on the west, he could move beneath the upper-end gallery.

Colourfully dressed stagekeepers carrying torches and wearing masks or visors controlled the behaviour of playgoers, and also controlled admission; a system of tickets was evidently in place by 1664–5. Normal admission to the college grounds seems to have been by the great gate on Trinity Street, although the college had other entrances, including the Queen's Gate in the south range of Great Court. General admission to the hall was by means of the stairway to the screens passage.

Once the play was finished, costumes and props were returned to their proper places, whether in the tiring chamber or (in later years) the audit chamber or common(/comedy?) chamber. The carpenters dismantled the stage and returned it to store. The hall or parlour was swept, tables and benches being returned to their normal position.

Performances in the parlour or comedy room were not directly accessible from the tiring chamber, but communication was still possible through rooms in the master's lodge. Performances here required less in the way of scaffolding, perhaps no more than a stage platform surrounded by chairs or benches appropriate to the dignity of the various spectators. Although painting had always been important in the preparation of Trinity College plays, in this more modest venue painting, lighting, and the use of fabrics were evidently more pronounced. Caution had still to be exercised against theft and vandalism.

4

Other colleges

March, 1579. The hall of St John's College. For more than a month, members of the college have been in rehearsal for perhaps the most ambitious dramatic performance ever attempted in England (before or since): *Richardus Tertius*, by Thomas Legge, Master of Gonville and Caius College, a play in three parts given on three successive nights, running to a total of some 10,000 lines, with the same actor taking the lead role on all three nights.[1]

The hall is filled with scaffolding; student actors in rehearsal attempt to capitalize on the traditional design of the stage and stagehouses as well as on the natural characteristics of the hall to realize Legge's elaborate stage directions:[2]

> ... let the singers singe. Or being placed on the toppe of some of the houses in the meane season lett such ceremonyes be used for the coronation as the chronicle declareth ...

> ... let gunnes go of[f] and trumpets sounde with all sturre of souldiers without the hall vntil such tyme as the Lord Stanley be on the Stage redy to speke ...

Over the course of the three nights *Richardus Tertius* makes a powerful impression on audience and actors alike: the text of the play is quickly transcribed in fair copy for publication at the university press and multiplied in manuscript; the performance takes a firm hold on the consciousness of educated readers throughout England; and the leading actor, John Palmer, later Bishop of Peterborough, is deemed by his enemies to have been spoiled for life by identifying too closely with the title role which he has played with such evident natural ability.[3]

Far more information can be recovered about the stages in Queens' College hall and in Nevile's hall at Trinity College than about the performance sites of any other colleges, or indeed about all of them put together. Nevertheless, the halls and the archives of other colleges, including Trinity College before 1605, are worth studying because of the considerable bulk of information recoverable, and as a check on consistency or variability of performance traditions from college to college.

The halls of no fewer than ten medieval and early sixteenth-century colleges survive more or less intact: Christ's College hall, rebuilt in the late nineteenth century; Corpus Christi, now the kitchen; Emmanuel, entirely refitted in the eighteenth century; Gonville and Caius, now a library reading room; Jesus; Magdalene; Peterhouse; Queens'; St John's, elongated in the nineteenth century; and Trinity Hall, refitted in the eighteenth century.[4] The halls of Magdalene and Trinity Hall will not concern us since no plays are known to have been performed in them; performances at Emmanuel are so conjectural that I will confine my comments on that college to a note.[5]

Several additional halls known or thought to have been used for plays have been demolished and thus can only be understood through documentary reconstruction: those of Clare College, King's College, King's Hall, and Michaelhouse (the latter used for performances by Trinity College from c. 1547 to c. 1605).

For the most part we are concerned only with play performance, which generally required the construction of a stage, but college halls were used for the performance of music as well. John Mere, in his diary entries for 1556–7, notes the presence or unusual absence of the town waits in the halls of Gonville, Peterhouse, Clare, Pembroke, and King's. At Trinity College in 1592–3 the town waits were paid for 'playing in the Hall'; from 1628–9 onward waits were paid for playing in King's College hall and Chapel. College shows were sometimes performed in halls, as at St John's in 1594–5, but on at least one occasion, at Trinity in 1556–7, and perhaps more frequently, the show was in the college court. Lords of Christmas, both collegiate and lay, seem often to have processed through the town, with drums and trumpets before them, and to have ended up in a college hall.[6]

In the discussions which follow, Queens' College hall will be taken as the standard against which others will be judged as large, standard, or small. As we have noted, the hall of Queens' is approximately 27′ wide by 44′ from the upper-end wall to the screens, giving a floor area approaching 1200 sq. ft.

References to upper and lower ends of college halls should be unambiguous in all circumstances, but references to the one side or the other will require additional clarification. Compass directions are of limited use in comparisons since halls might be oriented in any direction. As an expedient I will refer to the right and left sides on the understanding that the observer is standing at the lower end, looking toward the upper end. (For an impression of Trinity College hall seen from this perspective, please turn to the frontispiece.)

King's Hall

The history of King's Hall is well documented from 1337 to the demise of the college in 1546.[7] Plays were performed in the college perhaps by outsiders at first, but certainly by students from 1503–4, and possibly more than a century earlier. There can be little doubt that performances were in the college hall; evidence, however, is lacking.

The college's first hall, the house of Robert de Croyland, is known through an audit of 1337, and through building accounts of 1338 which reveal that it was then extended in length by 18′. The groundplan of Croyland's house has been reconstructed by Willis and Clark, who describe it as 'the usual arrangement of a large medieval house, in which the Hall has commonly the best apartments at one end, and the kitchen and the inferior rooms at the other'.[8]

King's Hall was rebuilt in a campaign lasting from 1375 until about 1390. The new hall was approximately 50′ in length to the screens by 30′ in width, larger in both dimensions than Queens' College hall. The primary entrance was via screens at the lower end; there may also have been a door at the upper end. This hall survived the dissolution of the college by less than a decade, and was not used for plays by Trinity College, which exploited instead the hall inherited from Michaelhouse.[9]

King's College

Play performances are clearly attested in the hall of King's College beginning in 1466–7, more than half a century earlier than for any other college. Most recorded hall performances were by visiting players, but an entry from 1469–70 refers to a play in the hall organized by a college scholar, and it seems certain enough that college disguisings, recorded from 1456–7 to 1489–90, and college plays, recorded from 1465–6 to 1614–15, were normally performed in the college hall.[10]

The original court of King's College was ceded to the university in 1829, the college subsequently building on lands south of its famous Chapel. The old hall stood on the south side of what is now the west court of the Old Schools (between King's College Chapel and Gonville and Caius College).[11]

The first hall on this site was evidently built to a plan presented by the college's founder, Henry VI. Willis and Clark give the following interpretation of the royal specifications:

> The Hall is placed on a vault 12 feet high, for the Cellar and Buttery (which is mentioned twice), and its breadth is 34 feet, with a bay-window on each side. It was to be entered at the north extremity, and there of course the usual screen would be placed, cutting off a passage within the walls of the Hall containing the usual doors of entrance. ... The Kitchen was not included in the range, but was placed on the west side of the Hall, and formed part of the north side of a small courtyard, 80 feet square. From its position ... it is clear that it could not have been reached by a central door and passage between those offices, as usual in the Halls of Cambridge, but probably by a door opposite to the entrance into the Hall, which is also usual when the kitchen has a lateral position. (I, p. 374)

Willis and Clark believe that the hall was rebuilt in 1562:

> The plan taken about 1635 ... shews that the Hall was then 50 feet long by 25 feet broad, with an oriel on the south side; and Storer's view ... shews two other windows on that side, plain oblong openings, subdivided by a mullion and transom, which may belong either to 1562 or 1634. (I, p. 537)

If the early King's College hall really was 34′ wide and proportionally long, it was substantially larger than Queens' College hall; the hall as putatively reconstructed in 1562, however, was shorter by 4′ and narrower by 2′.

The earliest payments clearly for a stage date from 1548–9, when Robert Bell purchased 200 boards 'pro le stagg' along with 400 nails. Payments for an 'apparatus' for a play in 1473–4 and 1489–90, however, with cords and nails in the former year and the large sum of 20s paid in the latter year, are consistent with the assumption that a stage was traditionally constructed for plays. Painters were hired to help prepare a disguising in 1484–5, and candles were provided for a play in 1498–9.

Payments in 1552–3 for a performance of *Hippolytus* testify to a remarkably developed theatrical event. Bell and two of his men put in a total of 12 man-days setting up the stage and half a day each (= 1.5 man-days) taking it down. One Stevennage was paid for supplying five planks. Ames the cooper supplied hoops and materials for a tent. Banks the blacksmith supplied nails of various kinds as well as locks(?) for the stage. John Burwell the apothecary supplied a dry vat for making the sound of thunder. Others supplied gunpowder, female wigs, lightning, paper boards, music, and hunting dogs. An inventory of this same year reveals that liturgical vestments 'transposyd into players garmentes' were kept 'in a chest on the sowthe syde of the Churche [= Chapel]'. (At least one chest of an appropriate style and age survives *in situ*.)[12]

Once again in 1555–6 Bell set up the stage, requiring a total of 8 man-days between himself and his man, while he and three men took half a day each (= 1.5 man-days) to take it down again. In 1561–2 the carpenters William Dowsey and John Grene spent three days each on the stage (= 6 man-days). In the year of the royal visit of Elizabeth, Rowland and his man spent one day each on the stage, and also supplied nails. In 1592–3 one Wharton, possibly a timber merchant, supplied 700′ of inch-board and ten pairs of studs for the comedy. In 1594–5 (John?) Cutchie, the carrier, was paid for the carriage of board, timber, and other things for the comedies, while (John?) Hames (= Ames?) was reimbursed 'for certen tymber for the said Commedies'. In 1595–6 one Peere, a carpenter, spent two days in the hall on the stages with one assistant; three other workers joined in, for an apparent total of 7 man-days.

Fifteen dozen candles were supplied in 1561–2, a locksmith was paid for four dozen candlesticks in 1563–4, while links were provided in 1578–9. A collier was reimbursed, presumably for coals, in 1606–7. In 1614–15, in preparation for a play before the king which in the event was not performed, King's College spent the vast sum of £114–6–7 for 'apparrell, Fees, stage, candles, torches, & other things necessary to the Comedy'.

In 1578–9 supports for the tables, possibly trestles, were broken at the plays and required repair. In 1595–6, in a year when stages were built in King's College hall and comedies performed there, its windows were the target of stones hurled by students of St John's, Clare, Queens', Caius, Christ's, and Corpus. Great damage ensued, the hall suffering most in spite of the fact that its windows were apparently hung with '9 haireclothes'. It is in connection with this event that we first learn of stagekeepers at King's.

A decade later, in 1606–7, a more serious riot occurred on the occasion of a comedy, despite the college's precaution in hiring one Elarye[13] for 'watching the commodie night about the porters lodge'. Several students and young men of the town threw stones at the hall windows, particularly on the Caius College side; the hall was 'full not only of the inferior sort, but also of diuers yonge noble men doctors Bacchelors in diuinity and masters of Arts', who suffered 'great offence and anoyaunce and disturbaunce'. When stagekeepers issued out the front gate they themselves became a target of the stonethrowers. The rioters pulled up a great post standing before the college gate and battered it open. Richard Cole, whose master was Peere, the carpenter who built the college stage in 1595–6 and doubtless in other years, was required, with his master's help, to 'mend vp the gate or else sitt 2 howers in the stockes at the bullring'.

Christ's College

The hall of Christ's College is named in connection with plays in 1537–8, 1551–2, and 1562–3, and it seems probable that the connection was invariable.[14] The hall, built soon after the refoundation of the college under the direction of John Fisher in 1505, survives, although it was taken down and rebuilt in 1876–9 with 6′ added to the height of its walls. As far as possible, original materials, including the beams of the roof, were preserved and returned to their original place.[15]

Christ's College hall measures 26′ in width by 46′ in length to the screens, somewhat longer but marginally narrower than Queens'. Historically it had a single oriel on the west (left) side (that on the east being modern), and a louvre (apparently first provided in 1544–5). At some time a fireplace was provided in the upper-end wall, with a tall chimney-stack. The original screens survive, having been covered up in the eighteenth century but restored in 1876–9. The modern wainscoting is a close replica of the original. Two interior windows overlook the upper end of the hall from the master's lodge.[16]

The college stage at Christ's is the earliest specifically recorded in Cambridge, for in 1529–30 we learn that a carpenter received 16d 'for settyng up the stages ij tymes'. Payments for the stage are recorded in 1532–3 and also in 1534–5, when the carpenter is named as (Roger) Pereson. In 1551–2, among expenses for Sir Stevenson's play, is listed 12d 'to the carpenter for removing the tables in the haull & setting them vp ageine with the houses & other thinges'. (This Sir Stevenson was doubtless William Stevenson, and the play may have been *Gammer Gurton's Needle*: REED, pp. 749, 897–8.) In 1559–60 carpenters worked at two plays, while in 1561–2 'a carpenter & his boye' spent three days 'at Mr Chathertons playe'; in 1567–8, for the last known performance, carpenters were paid for 'settinge vpp the scaffold at the plaie'.

Nails were purchased for the stage in 1532–3 and again in 1551–2, this time along with candles. A 'sugar cheyst' was purchased in 1534–5 'for the players ornamentes', while in 1550–1 a lock and key were provided 'for the cheste where the plaiers gere lieth'. Sedge was provided in 1552–3 when Christmas lords came at Candlemas 'with shewes'. In 1539–40 coals and faggots were provided 'in Chrystynmas abowte settyng furthe of playes'; in 1552–3 the college purchased 11s worth of coals 'at sondrie rehersinges of the tragedie betwen christenmas and fastingham: and in the plaie time': evidently the rehearsals went on for some six weeks. Coal fires were provided not only for rehearsals, but for the performance proper. Coal was purchased again in 1553–4. In 1563–4 the college purchased 'xij socketes for the candlesticke for plaies'.

In 1537–8 Christ's paid Roger the glazier 'for the reparyng of the Hall Wyndowes brokyng in dyuerse places at the tragedy'. This is the earliest reference to the damaging of windows in the course of a play. In 1563–4 (William?) Barnes was paid 'for paving in the haule after the plaies'.

St John's College

The performance tradition at St John's College began in 1521–2 or perhaps earlier, and continued until 1619–20. This was the venue of Legge's *Richardus Tertius* of 1578–9, and Legge may have had the same college in mind for his *Solymitana Clades* or *Destruction of Jerusalem*, a play never in fact performed.[17] That the hall was the primary site of plays in the college is sufficiently evident from the statutes of 1529–30, to a direct declaration by Simonds D'Ewes in 1617–18. A colourful description of the hall is provided by Roger Ascham, who wrote from Antwerp in 1550:

> Good God, (it is) the wealthiest mart not only of Brabant but of the whole world. By its shining and magnificent construction it achieves such pre-eminence that it surpasses in that respect all the other cities which I have seen, just as the hall of St John's (College) (when it is) decorated theatrically after Christmas, surpasses that (city) itself ...[18]

Construction on St John's College hall started about 1511 and was finished by the end of 1513. The screens at the lower end were originally doorless; the walls were hung in 1518–19 with green say (a fabric); wainscoting was installed between 1528 and 1539.[19]

The hall survives essentially intact, though in a building campaign launched in 1862 three bays were added to the upper end, with the panelling from the original upper-end wall moved to the new terminating wall. To visualize the earlier hall it is necessary to imagine the present upper-end wall with its panelling moved forward to cut off the hall at the end of the fifth bay from the screens end. The original hall was 29′ 6″ in width by approximately 60′ in length to the screens, substantially larger than Queens' College hall.

In 1534–5 the college spent 2s 3d for 'settynge vp, removynge & takynge downe the stage', an expense which continued with regularity thereafter. In 1540–1 two carpenters received a total of 4s for 'settyng vp the stage and taken yt dovne'. In 1544–5 three carpenters were paid for two days each (= 6 man-days) 'making tressils and setting vp the stage'; in addition, a carpenter and his man were paid for one and a half days for work on the stage and on a repair to the entry to the kitchen; and a labourer received payment for helping the carpenters take down the stage. The carpenter John King and his man were paid in 1548–9 'for settyng vppe the stage and takyng yt downe', and similar payments are recorded for 1556–7 (Bell the carpenter) and 1559–60. Payments in earlier years were a matter of shillings, so the payment in the latter year of £7–4–6 'for the hole stadge' must mean either that an entirely new stage was built this year, or that the payment is for the full costs of the play. In 1579–80 four men were hired for a total of 33 man-days in the weeks of Christmas and Twelfth Night at a total cost of £1–11–2: perhaps this was for the construction of the stage.

The trestles newly made in 1544–5 are mentioned again in 1548–9 and 1575–6: evidently the college stage platform consisted of trestles with boards over them. Boards were purchased or borrowed in 1544–5: boarding was taken in from diverse places in the town, and some was returned by boat to Michaelhouse (up the river a short distance, shortly to be made part of the new Trinity College). Other boards and trestles were placed in a storehouse. Damage to the stage was repaired in 1538–9 and again in 1575–6 (trestles and forms). Cords were purchased in 1538–9 and (along with packthread) in 1540–1. Unidentified 'eles' (= nails?) were purchased in 1538–9 and a pole in 1540–1. Links, candles, or torches were provided on numerous play occasions between 1538–9 and 1579–80: an inventory of 1541–2 lists 'xxvj Candlestikes in the cofer in the buttre [= buttery] & vj taied [= ?] in the candlestick'. One 'Henry the paynter' was hired in 1564–5. In 1579–80 the hall was whitewashed, evidently in preparation for a play.

Elaborate costume inventories allow costume chests to be traced from 1540–1 to 1565–6:[20] one chest was kept in the Master's 'inward chamber', the other in the 'outwarde chamber' (1540–1); these are also called the 'great Chamber', housing 'a great Chest'; and the 'Middle Chamber', housing 'a great Cofer of wainscot' (1546–7). In 1548–9 the chest in the Great Chamber is more narrowly described as 'an owld great chest of firr tree (= wood)', and now a third chest is also recorded, 'a Long great Chest lined with linen & barred with Iron'. At least one of the chests was fitted with a lock and key. In 1556–7 the three chests are described as 'Twoe greate cofers' and 'a great Long Cofer'.

In 1556–7 and 1561–2 equipment stored with the chests in the master's lodge included a portal (of wainscot). In 1541–2 a 'Phanum' (presumably a temple) and a thunder-barrel were stored in the buttery.

Glass was mended after plays at St John's in 1568–9, 1575–6 (connection with plays uncertain), 1578–9, 1594–5, 1597–8, and 1601–2; stagekeepers are mentioned in the latter year. In 1578–9 and 1594–5 nets were hung over the hall windows, perhaps in a failed attempt to forestall breakage.

Trinity College to 1605

When Trinity College was established in 1546, it inherited a hall from each of three antecedent institutions: King's Hall, Michaelhouse, and Physwick Hostel.[21] The college statutes of 1559–60 require that nine of the fellows – those with the title of domestic reader – 'shall be responsible for putting on ... comedies or tragedies in the hall privately or publicly', and college accounts from 1547–8 (perhaps the year of the first Trinity College play) to 1598–9 reveal that the hall was the normal place of performance.[22]

Willis and Clark demonstrate that the common hall (*Aula communis*) shown in the architect's plan of 1555 (see fig. 24, p. 46) was the hall inherited from Michaelhouse (II, pp. 465–7). It had screens at the lower end, a single door in the upper-end wall leading to a bay which apparently had no other exit, an oriel on the east (left), and a central louvre, presumably serving a firepit directly below. The hall measured approximately 42′ in length to the screens by 25′ in width, slightly smaller than Queens' College hall (II, p. 468).

In 1547–8 Trinity College's stage materials included 'xij staging trystles ix long & thre short' together with 'feete for the same tristles' and 'A little ladder for the stage'. Nine long trestles might have been arranged in three rows of three each, while the three short trestles might have constituted a fourth row. Whether long and short in this context meant wide and narrow or high and low is uncertain, but perhaps the latter is more likely: a low platform for the seating of dignitaries next to a higher stage platform conforms to what we may infer of the stage erected in King's College Chapel in 1564 (see fig. 5, p. 11).

In 1556–7 the carpenter William Hardwyke and his man were paid for one day's work 'mending formes & makynge Howses for the players'. Two years earlier, in 1554–5, William Carpenter – probably William Hardwyke – constructed 'a payre of lytle gallowes for the shew'. In 1557–8 Lame the painter was hired, evidently for a play or show.

In 1548–9 unnamed carpenters received 24s $8\frac{1}{2}$d 'when the playes were in hand', while another unnamed carpenter, his man, and two other men spent a total of 12 man-days 'occupied about the stage'. In 1559–60 William Hardwick and his man spent six days setting up the stage and taking it down again (= 12 man-days). In 1562–3 Richard Bell, Edward Dorrell, and Matthew Brewer logged a total of 7 man-days 'setting vpp the stage & Raile at christus Triumphans': a payment in the same year to William Hardwick and his man for 12.5 man-days setting up and pulling down 'the Raile' (together with an apparent 4 man-days from Rowland Richardson) must have been for the same kind of effort. In 1567–8 a carpenter and an unknown number of labourers were reimbursed 'for removinge of staig'.

In the week including 10 February 1571 William Hardwick was again paid 'for framing the stage' along with John Thaxted, Nicholas Odam, John Forrest, William Butcher, and 'Botes': assuming that Hardwick put in six days like the others, the total was 25 man-days. On 22 February Thomas Watson, William Parkin, D. Butcher, William Dowsey, and George Sterne spent a total of 30 man-days 'about the stage'. In 1572–3 Thomas Watson alone was paid 'for viij dayes work abowte the stage, and other necessaries in the Colleadge'. In 1586–7 the college made an otherwise unspecified payment, doubtless to carpenters, 'for making the stage at the playes' and for 200 planks and other boards.

Finally, in 1598–9 some board and timber was hired and more was purchased 'for the setting vpp of the Stage and Galleries'; an unknown number of carpenters received £4–8–0 'for setting vp & taking downe the same'; and the porter was paid 'for his helpe & ouersight therof'. A carter was hired 'for the carring & recarring of Tymber & other stuffe for the stage', while others 'fetched formes and tymber from St Maries[23] & helped to carie the stage stuffe after it was taken downe'.

Purchases in connection with the stage in 1554–5 included pins; in 1559–60, cord, whipcord, and packthread, along with tenterhooks and 'trashe nayl'.[24] Tenterhooks were purchased again in 1560–1. Cord was purchased in 1570–1, in 1598–9 'nayles of all sortes'. In 1570–1 were purchased 'certeyne hoopes occupied about the stage'.

The accounts of 1552–3 note that two shows were performed at night. Since shows, unlike plays, were sometimes mounted out of doors, we can draw no conclusions from this evidence about the time of day plays may have been performed.

In 1547–8 the college purchased 'A great Rownd Candlesticke for the stage In the hall'; in 1559–60, 'A knot of Corde to hange vp the great candlesticke'; in 1560–1, 'a greate nosell for the stage lantehorne'. In 1547–8 the college had in its possession 'A staple to sett candlestyckes in'; in 1559–60 a smith provided 60 candlesticks; in 1560–1 the college purchased 30 iron candlesticks. Candles were purchased in 1549–50, 1550–1, 1553–4, and 1557–8. The purchase of torches or links is recorded every year from 1548–9 to 1554–5 (except 1551–2). Presumably candles were suitable exclusively for indoor performances, while torches and links were used for either indoor or outdoor performances. In 1548–9 the college purchased 49 lb of pitch along with twenty-one 'frales for the cressetes': cressets were iron frames for holding burning material like coal, useful for giving off both light and heat; 'frales' were apparently the baskets which held the burning matter. In 1598–9 torches were used by night watchmen, and 'Charcole and wood' were purchased, apparently for heat.

The inventory of 1547–8 reveals that the trestles and other materials used for the stage were kept in 'the storehowse in phisike hostle hall', implying perhaps that the hall inherited from Physwick Hostel was itself used as a storehouse. In 1562–3 the college paid 'for a New Kei of the seller dore where the stage tymbre Lyethe', possibly a reference to the cellar beneath Physwick Hostel hall.

In 1547–8 the college maintained a stock of liturgical vestments, including some which had been made into playing gear, in the revestry of its chapel; apparently this was in the 'nether chapell', which contained 'foure grete chistes two wherein the plaing gere lieth'. In 1550–1 the same chests are described as 'the gret cheste in the chappell' and 'the lesse cheste'. In 1562–3 keys were provided for the two chests 'where the plaieres gere lieth'. Records of the storage of costumes in the college tower survive from 1580–1 and 1585–6.

In 1598–9 Trinity College paid substantial sums to men who watched the glass windows on comedy nights; a small payment in 1570–1 to carpenters 'for ther paines taking in the night aboue ther wages' might have been for watching windows, or perhaps it was a gratuity for overtime work. Stagekeepers are not named as such in college records before 1605, and only in 1578–9 (recorded 1579–80) is Trinity known from external sources to have been the subject of a deliberate attack. Nevertheless, the college was not immune from damage during its plays. Evidence of damage to glass, usually in the hall, survives from 1560–1, 1565–6, 1567–8, 1572–3, 1578–9, 1582–3, 1584–5(?), and 1590–1. In 1568–9 glass in the hall was taken down and repaired 'before the plaies', while in 1586–7 glass was taken down and set up 'at the plays'. In 1565–6 not only the glass but the hall itself required mending after the plays, while in 1598–9 a mason and his man spent a day and a half each 'mending the hall walls after the commodies'. In 1571–2 William Button was paid 'for newe dressing the clothes in the hale', apparently after plays. Finally, in 1588–9 the college spent 20d 'mending the Locke of the wickett thrise at the playes'.

Archival records from Trinity College are supplemented by the vivid personal testimony of John Dee, probably in reference to the academic year 1547–8:

> I did sett forth (& it was seene of the Vniuersity) a Greeke Comedie of Aristophanes, named in Greek Eirene, in Latin Pax. with the performance of the Scarabeus his flying vp to Iupiters Pallace, with a Man & his Basket of victualls on her Back: whereat was great wondering, & many vaine reportes spread abroad, of the meanes how that was effected.

Presumably 'Scarabeus his flying' was managed with ropes and pulleys, but Dee makes a virtue of his ability to disguise this fact.

The college commitment to plays seems to have continued unabated up to the construction of the new hall beginning c. 1605. A prime example of this commitment occurred in 1594–5, when Trinity College was visited by 'dyuers nobell men knyghtes and gentell men of worship, namly the Earles of Shrosberry, Rutland, & Essex, Barrons, my Lords Burros, Compton, MountIoy, Sheffeeld, Crumwell, Rich': these dignitaries saw two comedies and a tragedy at the college, 'the wich wear the causses of ther comeing downe …'

Not enough evidence survives to reconstruct the pre-1605 Trinity College stage in any detail; nevertheless, it would not be amiss to suppose that it followed the pattern of Queens' College stage and was a modest version of the post-1605 Trinity College stage. Support for this supposition comes from an observation made and a question posed by Moore Smith. 'The dramatis personae of Walter Hawkesworth's *Labyrinthus* acted at Trinity College 1602/3 are grouped by houses in various MSS.' These are *Domus dec. sup.*; *Domus Bac in med.*, and *Domus dec. inferioris* (houses of the Senior Dean, Bachelors in Medicine, and Junior Dean); other characters are listed as *Semper a foro* (from the marketplace). Smith continues: 'Does this imply that for the performance[,] structures or partitions already existing in the hall were adapted to stage purposes and obviated the need of building stagehouses *ad hoc*?'[25]

Since the assignment of seats by academic rank was *de rigueur* for virtually all college and university events, the identification of houses by academic rank probably indicates not the appropriation of pre-existing non-theatrical structures, but adjacency of theatrical houses to seats reserved to particular ranks of academic spectators.

John Mere reports for New Year's Day 1557: 'a shew in trinite college in ther courte of the wynninge of an holde [= castle] & takinge of prisoners, with waytes trumpettes gonnes & squybbes'. The college plan of 1555 (fig. 24) reveals the shape and dimensions of the court, which though substantial was considerably smaller than the new court later laid out by Nevile.

Corpus Christi College

Corpus Christi, commonly known as Bene't College until well into the eighteenth century, was apparently active in play production from at least as early as 1550–1 to the early 1620s, but precious little detailed evidence of this activity survives.[26] In 1557–8 two comedies were played publicly in the hall; in 1550–1 torch links were supplied for the plays; in 1579–80 it was noted that an attack on a stagekeeper had occurred the previous year. In 1581–2 carpenters named Lamb and Porter were paid for making houses at the comedy; the following year the scholar Thomas Evans of Pembroke College was committed to prison for three days because, among other things, he 'laid about with a club and threw stones when the stage plays were being shown at Corpus Christi College'.

The college's medieval hall, originally built at or soon after the foundation of the college in 1352, was converted to kitchens about 1825; fortunately, its external walls and roof survive mostly intact. The hall was just over 27′ wide by 35′ in length to the screens, exactly the same width as Queens' but considerably shorter. By 1515 a side chimney replaced an earlier square brazier in the middle of the hall beneath a lantern. The wall at the upper end was plastered before 1553, while between this year and 1574 the old lantern was removed, the entire hall wainscoted, and a triple screen (creating two doorways?) installed at the lower end. The window sills were raised to 9′ and the windows glazed. The hall was adorned once again about 1597, the windows being enlarged and new screens envisioned if not actually installed.[27] Edmund Carter described the hall in 1753 as 'a large Room, having two beautiful Bow-Windows'.[28]

Jesus College

Records of college play performance in Jesus College span the long period 1561–2 to 1622–3.[29] Extremely sparse, the records include a unique instance of the English word 'theatre' applied to a Cambridge college stage (1563–4). The college chapel is the only sixteenth-century Cambridge performance site still regularly used for plays.

On 5 January 1578 Thomas Wilshaw, a fellow, was given 23s 2d 'towardes the Stage & other charges of the Comoedie pleyed publiklie in the Hawlle, in Christmas'. A decade earlier, in 1568–9, two fellows of the college received £4–6–0 'spent at the playes in the chappell', a payment which recalls another from 1567–8 for 'glasse for the chappell after the playe'. Like King's, then, but without the pressure of a royal visit, Jesus College performed plays in both its hall and its chapel.

The hall of Jesus College was inherited from the nunnery of St Radegund at the foundation of the college under John Alcock in 1496.[30] Willis and Clark describe the hall as

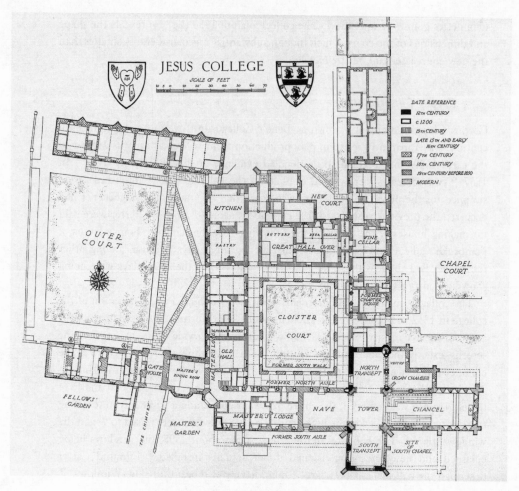

Fig. 28.   Jesus College, plan showing Chapel and Great Hall (RCHM, England).

a very handsome and well-proportioned Refectory, still retaining an open roof and
ancient stone corbels, but ... marred in effect by later panelling and screen. The oriel on
the north side is an exceedingly elegant specimen of the architecture of Alcock's period,
and the rich panelling of the soffit of the arch which separates it from the hall is especially
beautiful. Opposite to it, on the south side of the high table, is a large window of three
lights, divided by a transom. The rest of the windows were originally small, of two lights
each, like those we have found employed at Pembroke and elsewhere. They are shewn in
this condition as late as Loggan's time ...; but have since been made longer, by lowering
the cills about three feet. (II, p. 160)

Overall Jesus College hall is 64′ long by 25′ wide. In its original configuration an
internal stair coming from below at the lower end robbed the hall of 21′ 6″ of usable
length, resulting in a main floor area 25′ in width by 42′ 6″ to the screens, close to the
dimensions of Queens' College hall. In 1875 the hall was altered by the reconfiguration
of the staircase, by the removal of the screens 13′ 6″ in the direction of the lower end,

and by the installation of a new floor a foot higher than the original; panels in the wainscoting were altered to fit the new level. The modern screens, originally constructed about 1703, replaced older screens of 1610–11, which in turn replaced screens repaired in 1567 and constructed earlier. In 1569–70 the hall was hung with a tapestry at the upper end and on part of the side walls; this tapestry survived until at least 1614–15.

Jesus College chapel was also inherited from the nunnery of St Radegund, and again certain alterations were undertaken to suit collegiate use (fig. 28).[31] The nave beyond the third bay from the crossing and the nave aisles were blocked off: together with other alterations this yielded a cruciform groundplan of the following parts and dimensions:

nave (33′ 9″ × 24′)
south transept (23′ 6″ × 25′ 9″)
north transept (23′ × 26′)
chancel (64′ × 23′ 3″)
crossing (32′ 6″ square)

Assuming that the chancel was reserved for sacred use, the area available for theatrical use was approximately 3060 sq. ft. Presumably the stage platform was set up within the crossing.

Only snippets of further information useful to an understanding of play performances at Jesus survive: in 1562–3 the servant of an unidentified 'Suttell' was paid for a day and a half 'at the playing of Curculio'. In 1613–14 12s was devoted 'toward the stage'. In 1564–5 the college purchased two torches 'for the diologge and shewe in Christmas', while in 1595–6 candles weighing a total of 2 lb were purchased for a show. In 1567–8, as we have seen, chapel glass was repaired after a play; a window in the room of William Jenks, a fellow, was mended in 1622–3 after it had been 'brouken at the commodie'. The college clock was repaired in 1568–9, having been 'broke once at the playes and one other tyme'.[32]

Peterhouse

The hall of Peterhouse was fitted out with a stage or theatre (*theatrum*) for plays in 1562–3, 1571–2, and 1572–3.[33] The oldest of all Cambridge colleges, Peterhouse also has the oldest hall, constructed about 1290.[34] Restoration and partial reconstruction in 1870 disguised or eliminated some features while adding an oriel and exterior buttresses. By the middle of the fifteenth century the hall (including its windows) was heightened, and a fireplace was installed on the right side in the early sixteenth century. For all the changes over the years, the floor area has been unchanged at a width of approximately 25′ and a length of 48′ to the screens, slightly narrower and slightly longer than Queens' College hall. Entrance to the hall is by two screens doors in the lower end and by a door in the right-hand upper-end corner.

In 1572–3 nails and benches were supplied for the college stage. James Silcock was responsible for the construction in 1571–2 and 1572–3; a painter was hired in the latter year. The theatre was lit by candles and candelabra, and evidently both lit and warmed by cressets (1571–2, 1572–3). Repairs were made to the hall glass after the plays of 1562–3, and to tripods and hall wainscoting after the plays of 1575–6 (by Naze, a joiner).

Clare College

Very little is known about Clare College plays from college records, only that mayhem in 1611–12 resulted in damage to the college windows and injury to its stagekeepers. More informative but of less certain relevance is a long list of expenses from 1614–15 for the preparation of *Ignoramus* for performance before King James on 8 March 1615: that performance was in Trinity College hall.[35]

Since Clare College was wholly rebuilt during and after the reign of Charles I, nothing now remains of the hall built in 1524 to replace another destroyed by fire in 1521. A plan, however, is preserved in a plan of the entire college evidently drawn up in anticipation of the Caroline reconstruction. The hall was 27′ in width by 33′ in length to the screens, the same width as Queens' College hall, but some 11′ shorter.[36]

The seventeenth-century Cambridge historian Thomas Fuller reports that *Club Law* was performed (in 1599–1600) before town dignitaries who were themselves the target of the play's satire. The townspeople were assigned to a 'convenient place' while students who impersonated them 'acted on the Stage'.[37] It is reasonable to assume that this event occurred in the college hall.

In anticipation of the royal performance of 1614–15, a carpenter was paid 'for hire of Timber for a stage to repeate vpon in our Colledge'. Carpenters were paid again for their 'work about both stages', presumably the rehearsal stage and the stage at Trinity College used for the actual performance. The making of fires over seven weeks suggests that rehearsals began in the middle of January for the performance on 8 March. More than a hundred bushels of sea coal and three tons of pit coal were purchased as 'fireing for the acting chamber', doubtless during the same seven weeks. This acting chamber was probably the room reserved for play rehearsals, but conceivably the reference is to the tiring chamber at Trinity. Rehearsals were evidently lit with candles purchased by Mr Bargar, a college fellow who was closely involved with the production and who acted in the play.

Although it is not possible to distinguish absolutely between expenses incurred for rehearsals at Clare and those for the hall at Trinity College, it seems that in addition to carpenters' work on the Trinity College stage Clare paid for torches and wax candles, and also paid a carpenter named Burton for a 'darte' and 'for setting up & remouing the painters frame'. Painters were given dining subsidies amounting to more than £16 in addition to a direct payment of more than £23. Of a total of £242–07–08, therefore, the painters received more than £39, nearly one-sixth of the whole cost of *Ignoramus*. Musicians from London received £44–15–6, nearly one-fifth of the whole cost.

Gonville and Caius College

Records of dramatic performances at the college of Gonville and Caius are extremely sparse.[38] The statutes of 1573–4 approve private performances only, and then only in the daytime. The proscribed public performances would have meant 'a great influx of scholars or others'; private performances, by implication, were limited to members of the college and to specially invited guests. The college statutes also insist on daytime performances 'because of the danger of crowds'. Perhaps it was for these reasons that Thomas Legge's three-day public extravaganza *Richardus Tertius* was performed at St John's in 1578–9 rather than in the college where he was master.

Despite statutory precautions, in 1579–80 a scholar of St John's named Punter (given name unknown) 'vncased (as they call it) one of the stagekepers of Caius colledge pluckinge of[f] his visor'. In 1615–16 the windows of the college hall were damaged in the course of a play performance, as was a door near the chamber of one of the fellows.

The college hall, originally built in 1441, had an interior plan 23' 6" in width by 46' 6" in length to the screens, 4' narrower but somewhat longer than Queens'. Although the hall survives, it has been altered almost beyond recognition. Its floor was raised in 1589, the hall was remodelled in 1792, then an intermediate floor installed in 1853–4 divided the hall into chambers below and a larger room above, the latter made into a reading room for the college library in 1910.[39] Willis recorded his impressions at the time of the nineteenth-century alterations:

> This Hall was remarkable for the strict proportion of its dimensions. During the changes in 1854 I had the opportunity of accurately measuring and delineating it. Its length was double its breadth. The height of the corbel above the floor was half the breadth. The height of the wooden cornice above the floor is the diagonal of the square formed by half the breadth. (I, p. 196)

Willis and Clark inform us:

> The old Hall on the first floor [= upper reading room] retains much of the original roof although reconditioned and incorporating much modern material; it is of five bays...
>
> The oblong windows of the Hall were shortened in 1589 by taking away the lower part that was not glazed, but were made to admit more light than before, and were new glazed at the expense of various persons whose arms were placed therein. The lower part of these windows was evidently closed only by shutters beneath a transom, a very common arrangement. The wooden floor was raised about five feet above the level of the court, so as to admit of a space beneath about seven feet high. This was employed as butteries and cellars, for, owing to the small dimensions of the site, the kitchen was obliged to be built at the west side, and there was no room at the end of the Hall for the usual position of the butteries. (I, pp. 196–7)

A payment of 1625 reveals that the hall had screens and was wainscoted, with side posts supporting the roof. Prior to 1565 the hall had no provision for a fire:

> Hereupon a new brazier, of large size, capable of being moved upon wheels, cleverly fashioned of new iron, was placed in the Hall in October, 1565. It weighed 353 pounds,

so that at the rate of sixpence per pound, it cost in all eight pounds, seventeen shillings; less the value of one pound of metal. A fire was first lighted in it on All Saints Day in the same year. Before this no fire had ever been lighted in the Hall ... (I, p. 198)

Pembroke College

Only two records survive of play performance in Pembroke College: a university judicial record of 1582–3 to the effect that Miles Moses, a Pembroke fellow, broke the head and shed the blood of Robert Thexton of Corpus 'while the stage production was being put on in Pembroke Hall' (*aula Pembrokia*); and an account entry of 1585–6 for coals purchased at the plays.[40] Although *aula Pembrokia* is name of the college and does not itself refer to the hall used for dining, we may assume that stage production did indeed occur in the college hall.

A building campaign begun in 1862 swept away the medieval hall, which however was described by Willis before its destruction and is well documented in various pictures and plans. The old hall measured approximately 27′ in width by 40′ to the screens, the same width as Queens' but slightly shorter. It was approached at the lower end through wooden screens with two doors (earlier screens rebuilt in 1634). At the upper end a door communicated with the combination room or parlour. Unusually for Cambridge, the hall had a second storey and thus a flat ceiling. (The new college hall, though somewhat larger, retains many characteristics of the old hall.)[41]

The university

On very rare occasions the university rather than a particular college sponsored plays. For the visit of Queen Elizabeth in 1564, King's College produced several plays, but the university produced Plautus' *Aulularia*. In addition to a lump payment of £9–13–9 to John Lane, M.A., the university audit book records payments to Rowland and his man for one day each (= 2 man-days) and for nails, to a locksmith for four dozen candlesticks, for wax, and to 'a paynter for payntinge Buckeram & mockado for the Plaies'. Fabric purchases came to four yards of mockado and two of buckram. Finally, a total of 5s 4d was expended in an unspecified manner 'in Rehersinge of the Playes' – perhaps for food. The purchase of candlesticks and wax sorts oddly with Stokys's insistence that only torches held by the guards were used to light the plays. Perhaps these lighting materials were purchased for the stage in King's College hall which was dismantled in favour of the stage in King's College Chapel.

In 1577–8 an unknown comedy was presented to Elizabeth at Audley End: musicians were paid 'at the rehersyng of the commodye' but little else can be discerned from the records. George Ruggle's *Ignoramus* of 1615 may perhaps be considered a university play, since roles were taken by students of several colleges, but it is so closely identified with Clare College that I have assigned it to the college rather than to the university.[42]

5

The university commencement stage, 1464–1720

2 December 1673. Cambridge. The university Senate votes a resolution (called a 'grace') for the construction of an academic theatre (*Theatrum Academicum*). A similar grace is passed on 27 March 1674, and an empowering resolution by the Syndics is taken on 6 April 1675 (though the appellation 'Theatre' is cancelled in favour of 'Musaeum').[1] During the academic year 1675–6 the university pays the local mason and architect Robert Grumbold for 'surveying ground, for the Theator'.[2] Christopher Wren submits architectural plans for a hall with perimeter galleries reminiscent of college theatres.[3] A dream expressed by Anthony Sparrow, President of Queens' College, in a letter to William Sancroft, then Dean of St Paul's, seems close to fulfilment: 'we have, I hope, made sure of the ground on the side of the Regent walke, next Caius College, for to build a Theatre … to rescue God's House from Commencement prophanation (*Faxit Deus!*)'.[4]

Of all the roles played by the two English universities (as distinguished from their associated colleges), the most important was the granting of degrees. In early modern Cambridge, B.A. degrees were conferred during Lent, while M.A. and higher degrees were conferred at the 'Great Commencement' early in July, generally on the first Tuesday. ('Commencement' was an expression peculiar to Cambridge: candidates were regarded as 'commencing' in their new status as M.A. or as Doctor; the equivalent ceremony at Oxford was generally called the 'Act'.) B.A. degree ceremonies were held in the Schools; until the opening of the Senate House in 1730, the great commencement was held in one of several churches, preeminently Great St Mary's, the University Church.[5]

After the Restoration, both universities constructed buildings specifically for the granting of degrees: Oxford its Sheldonian Theatre (1664–9), Cambridge its Senate House (1722–30). The Sheldonian, designed by Christopher Wren, is modelled on an idea of the classical theatre; the Senate House, designed by James Gibbs, on the Banqueting House in Whitehall, designed by Inigo Jones for banqueting and masques.[6]

The idea that a structure used for the granting of degrees should be called a theatre did not occur in Cambridge merely as a reflex of Oxford nomenclature. Matthew Stokys, in his description of the 'great and ample stage' in Great St Mary's Church in August 1564, observed that the royal secretary William Cecil was responsible for explaining to the queen the 'placyng of every parson within that theatre' (Appendix 1). James Tabor, Registrary from 1600 to 1645, observed in 1620–1 or thereabouts, as he was puzzling out the history of the university's relationship to Great St Mary's: 'That the vniuersity had a Theatre, I find in the Auditt booke, about the yeere 1545 ...' (Appendix 7). In 1636 William Laud received a formal complaint in anticipation of his official visitation:[7]

> St Mary's Church at every great Commencement, is made a Theater, & the Prevaricatours stage, wherein he acts, & setts forth his prophane and scurrilous jests besides diverse other abuses & disorders then offered in that place.

The interpretation of the Cambridge commencement stage as a theatre was in fact much older than even James Tabor realized. The term *theatrum* was first invoked for this purpose in 1498–9, while the English equivalent, 'stage' or 'stages', goes back a decade further to 1489.[8] Among alternative Latin terms used up to 1543–4 for either the whole stage or its constituent parts are *fabrica* (1501–2), *machina* (1533–4), *locus* (1536–7), and *scaena* (1539–40); among alternative English terms are 'frame' (1523–4) and 'place' (1524–5). (Many of these terms, particularly *locus*, *scaena*, and 'place', are familiar to historians of medieval theatre.) The interpretation of the commencement stage as a theatre persisted, for during the years of its construction the Senate House was often called a theatre (in English) by its builders and caretakers.[9]

Records of the construction of the commencement stage from 1464 to 1720 are of interest because they reveal, with even greater clarity than records of college plays, carpenters and co-workers engaged in the specialized craft of creating, assembling, disassembling, and storing the demountable stage platforms, seating galleries, and similar structures which made up the theatres of early modern Cambridge.

Historical overview

For nearly a quarter of a millennium – from the latter half of the fifteenth century until the early years of the eighteenth – Cambridge M.A. and higher degree ceremonies were held in one of several churches routinely transformed into theatres. First recorded in 1464–5, the Cambridge commencement stage was variously set up or stored as a heap of timber in the church of the Austin Friars, in Bene't Street; in Great St Mary's; and in the church of the Franciscans or Minorites (Grey Friars), later incorporated into Sidney Sussex College. From 1539–40 onward, following the disestablishment of the religious houses, Great St Mary's became the regular venue until the construction of the Senate House in 1730.[10]

Expenditure on stages and linen cloth (for skirting) beginning in 1489 implies the use of raised platforms for the commencement stage. In 1507–8 the university paid 4d to Robert the carpenter 'for the marking of the parts of the stage (to show) the way they are put together' (*pro signatione partium stagiorum quomodo coniungerentur*). In 1527–8 the stage was amplified and renewed, measured timber being purchased for this purpose. In 1560–1 the university spent over £12 on the stage, perhaps for wholesale enlargement and reconstruction: by contrast, the royal visit of August 1564 cost the university only £3–10–6 for setting up the existing stage plus £6–16–10 for extras including a separate 'Stage for the Queenes maiestie' (fig. 6, p. 12).

The commencement stage was enlarged in 1572–3, the back of the physicians' stage in 1577–8. The 'backstage' broke in 1579–80, requiring repair. Work in 1589–90 resulted in a distinction between the 'ould commencement stage' and the 'newe inlarginge of the seates within the said stage': the next year occurs a reference to 'a new staire'. In 1591–2 the church was provided with a 'new Musicke stage' for commencement, and work was also undertaken on 'the inwarde seates & two paire of staires & foure particions about the stage': these 'inwarde seates' may have survived as 'ascends' used for fellow commoners at the royal visit of Prince Charles and the Prince Palatine in 1612–13.[11] The year 1596–7 witnessed 'a new stage next to the steple which hath not vsually bene set vp heretofore'.

Permanent side galleries, installed in Great St Mary's in 1610 but removed in 1617,[12] were evidently used during the royal visits of 1612–13 and 1614–15. In 1632–3 the university paid for 'the new gallerie in the Chansell setting vpp and takinge downe'; a similar reference to 'the gallery in the Chansel' occurs the following year (1633–4) along with a payment for 'oxford mens gallery'.

In 1651–2 provision was made for a music act in King's College Chapel, while in 1657–8 'a new Scaffold, at the west end, next the steeple' was constructed. Galleries are mentioned again in 1659–60. A new pair of stairs was provided in 1677–8; two new pairs are mentioned in 1678–9. In 1680–1 'new Timber for the Musik room' was provided along with 'timber for the musicke Scaffalls', deal-boards, nails, and workmanship; the 'musek scaffoll' was erected again in 1683–4. From this time forward the commencement stage was set up infrequently: although the timbers survived until 1720, the last time the university had the stage set up in Great St Mary's was in 1713–14, an occasion celebrated by Laurence Eusden in *Verses at the Last Publick Commencement at Cambridge*.[13]

Organization of space

The stage as set up for Elizabeth in August 1564 has already been described.[14] For the royal visit of 2–3 March 1613 by Prince Charles and the Prince Palatine, 'The wholle stage was set vp as at the Great Commencment' except that the 'Ascends vpon both sides within the Church' were 'left out' (REED, p. 508). These ascends were raked scaffolds (probably rising from ground level), normally used by the regent and non-regent masters. Far from being omitted altogether, the ascends were moved to the west end in order that 'fellow commoners might sit there' (fig. 29). The eastern half of the permanent galleries on the north side was reserved for doctors in divinity, the same half of those on the south for doctors of law and physic; the western halves of both

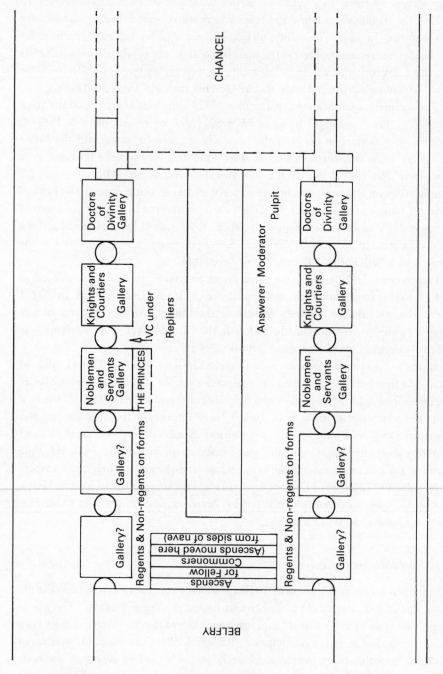

CHANCEL

Doctors of Divinity Gallery

Doctors of Divinity Gallery

Knights and Courtiers Gallery

Knights and Courtiers Gallery

Answerer   Moderator

Pulpit

VC under

Repliers

Noblemen and Servants Gallery

Noblemen and Servants Gallery

THE PRINCES

Gallery?

Gallery?

Regents & Non-regents on forms

Regents & Non-regents on forms

Gallery?

Gallery?

(Ascends moved here from sides of nave)

Commoners

Ascends for Fellow

BELFRY

Fig. 29.   Commencement stage in Great St Mary's church arranged for royal visit of 1613, schematic plan.

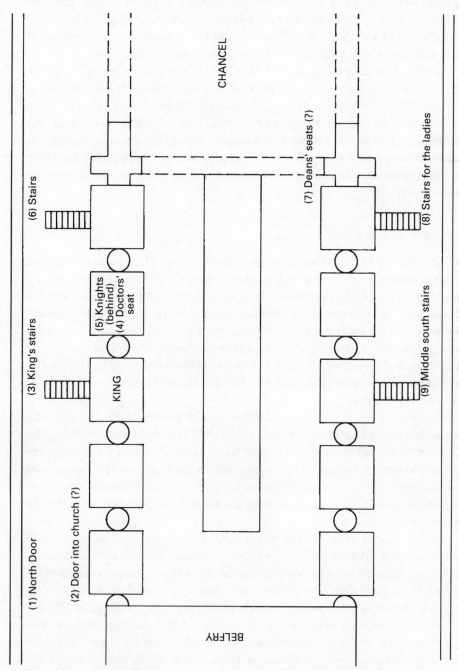

(1) North Door

(2) Door into church (?)

(3) King's stairs

(4) Doctors' seat

(5) Knights (behind)

(6) Stairs

(7) Deans' seats (?)

(8) Stairs for the ladies

(9) Middle south stairs

KING

CHANCEL

BELFRY

Fig. 30. Commencement stage in Great St Mary's church arranged for royal visit of 1615, schematic plan (see Appendix 5).

galleries were reserved for non-university guests, called 'strangers'. Also on the north side of the church, jutting out from the noblemen's gallery and two steps lower, was a platform, with two chairs, specially constructed for the two princes; the entire north side was hung with rich tapestries, its stairs covered with matting.

James I visited Cambridge on 7–11 March 1615. The security plan drawn up for this occasion (Appendix 5) covered the commencement in Great St Mary's as well as Trinity College. At least five stairs may be discerned in the plan (fig. 30): the 'king's stairs', stairs near the north door, stairs 'for the Ladyes', middle south stairs, and belfry stairs: thus on each side were central stairs and east stairs; in addition, west-end stairs led to the belfry gallery. Some of these stairs may have been part of the church galleries which survived until 1617, while others may have been installed specially for the occasion.

Stage construction

By now we may begin to visualize some of the structures which made up the usual commencement stage: a long – and probably narrow – stage running the full 75′ length of Great St Mary's Church like a runway; seating on either side, whether benches on the floor or raked ascends; raised galleries (during some periods), temporary or permanent, nestled between the pillars, with stairs and doors at the back; seats for the Vice-Chancellor, Proctors, and visitors from Oxford, at or near ground level (provided during some periods with doors like theatrical boxes); partitions with doors separating structure from structure, and also creating a perimeter wall, probably within the side aisles.

Construction bills reveal the scantlings of some of the constituent timbers, and – more often – their lengths (Appendix 9). In the 1560–1 timber inventory, the apparent verticals[15] are listed as $2 \times 4s$, $3 \times 6s$, and $4 \times 4s$. Girders were all $4 \times 6s$ positioned with the longer side vertical. Of the two sorts of rails, the longer were $4 \times 5s$ positioned with the longer side vertical, while the shorter were $4 \times 4s$. Scantlings are given for two sets of jeece in 1662–3, one pair 14′ long, another pair 15′: both were $4 \times 6s$ like the girders of 1560–1.

Timber lengths must be interpreted with some caution: it is necessary to distinguish measures of length from measures of volume (in board-feet); lengths may refer to a total in running-feet rather than to individual pieces; and longer pieces might have been cut into two or more shorter pieces. Measures of length are not impossible, however, to distinguish from measures of volume; prices may allow us to tell piece measure from running-feet; and it must be assumed that carpenters did not often purchase longer pieces for cutting when they could get shorter pieces: despite an apparently constant price per volume of board, longer pieces without defects will always be more highly valued by timber dealer and carpenter alike.

From the lengths of the timbers, it may occasionally be possible to guess at the dimensions of a finished platform, and here we will start with heights. The presumably vertical timbers purchased in 1560–1 were in lengths of 4′ 6″, 7′, 9′, 10′, and 12′. In

1582–3 three 7′ studs were provided, in 1591–2 five pairs of 9′ studs, evidently for the new music stage. An elaborate bill of 1662–3 records three studs apparently 7′ each. Stud lengths in 1667–8 ran from 4′ to 8′ in even feet. Presumably a 4′ 6″ stud implies a stage platform of 5′ allowing for horizontal beams and flooring. Longer verticals may have served for higher platforms, for multi-storied structures, or for carrying a rail above platform level. Verticals of evenly graded lengths may have been used for ascends.

Most horizontally disposed timbers recorded up to 1651–2 are multiples of 3′ in length: a single timber purchased in 1527–8, possibly for a horizontal, was 9′; horizontals recorded in 1560–1 include girts of 6′ and 9′, and rails of 6′, 9′, and 12′; the stage for the music act in 1651–2 required 14 joists of 6′ each. These numbers suggest platforms of a standard 6′, 9′, or 12′ width or depth. The stage for the music act of 1651–2 – held not in Great St Mary's but in King's College Chapel – required fourteen joists each 6′: assuming deployment of the joists at 12″ on centre, this would result in a platform 13′ wide and 6′ deep. Timber purchased in 1667–8 included two girts of 11′ each; twelve jeece of 5′ each; and rails of 9′, 10′, and 14′. The 12 jeece at 5′ each might make a platform 11′ wide by 5′ deep: the two 11′ girts purchased at the same time may have been for the same structure.

Boards were thinnish pieces of oak, elm, fir, or spruce, perhaps 4″ to 6″ wide, and approximately an inch thick, cut to length by the carpenter but not otherwise worked, nailed rather than pegged, and commonly used for flooring (*OED*, s.v. board). Boards were apparently distributed over the structure as suited the fancy of the carpenters of the year. They were consumed at a much higher rate than timber, and sometimes were hired or borrowed rather than purchased.

Board purchases are first recorded as early as 1488 (*asseres*), and thereafter are so common that they scarcely warrant individual mention. Occasionally, however, an acquisition may be suggestive, as in the 1527–8 purchase of 21 boards each 18′. At a width of 6″, these would cover a platform 18′ in length by 10′ 6″ in depth; at 4″ the platform would be 7′ deep.

The stage platforms mentioned in connection with these timber purchases were far from the only structures erected by Cambridge carpenters for the commencement stage. Galleries were provided for the 1564 commencement before Elizabeth, but are not recorded again over the next several decades. The new stairs of 1590–1 seem to imply a temporary gallery, and even when the church had a permanent gallery, from 1610 to 1617, an additional gallery was installed for Prince Charles and the Prince Palatine in 1612–13 ('for nailes for the gallery making'). In 1614–15 reference is made to a belfry gallery, but whether this was part of the church or part of the commencement stage (for example, the 'new stage next to the steple which hath not vsually bene set vp heretofore' in 1596–7) is unclear.

Elizabeth was placed in an elevated room at the east end of Great St Mary's in 1564, but no evidence survives to suggest how she got up there, nor how the doctors got up into their temporary galleries. The ladder (or steps: *scala*) provided by William Dowsey in 1561–2 may or may not have been used by participants in the academic ceremony, but certainly the queen would have ascended to her platform by stairs and not by a ladder.

In 1590–1 the university purchased 'stufe for a new staire on the North side of the Churche', along with 'a paire of dore hingells and nailes on the northe side where the staire was new made'; the following year work was undertaken about 'two paire of staires & some particions aboute the stage'. These stairs may have been used to approach the new elevated seating platform erected about the same time. In 1594–5 the duties of watchmen included 'kepinge of staires at the comensement'. Stairs were in use in 1612–13 and 1614–15,[16] though these may have belonged to the galleries which remained permanently in the church from 1610 to 1617.

In 1523–4 the university spent 12d 'for kepyng the dorres off the stage'. This payment may have been for men who guarded an entrance door in the fabric of Great St Mary's, but it is clear that the commencement stage in due course had doors of its own. Associated with the construction described in 1590–1, for example, 'on the northe side where the staire was new made', was a door provided with a pair of hinges. A new door was also provided in 1594–5, while in 1596–7 6d was spent 'for settinge vp of a dore vpon the stage next to the place where Mr Vicechauncellor sat'. The security plan for 1614–15 includes the guarding of an internal door leading to deans' seats[17] (exact location unknown), and perhaps a door at the head or foot of each of five stairs.

Some doors may have been for the commencement equivalent of theatrical boxes or church pews: thus, for example, 1s 2d was spent in 1619–20 'for mending the anserrers seate doore and for a pair of Ioyntes for it', and 8d was spent in 1651–2 'ffor a paire of Ioynts for the seat doore'. Others seem to have been full-size, practicable doors with locks to them. The clearest and for us the most intriguing example is from 1610–11: 'for mending the lockes and making a new key for the comencement dores, after they were altred at Trinitie Colledge'.

Because the commencement stage was provided with doors to control its perimeter, it was logical that the stagekeepers should sometimes be called doorkeepers, and so they frequently were from 1623–4 to 1696–7.

Carpenters' tasks and charges

An impression of the increasing complexity of the commencement stage over the years may be gained by an analysis of carpenters' man-hours recorded for setting up and taking down. In 1479–80 two carpenters required five days each (= 10 man-days). This figure remained relatively constant through 1501–2, but with the construction of a stage in the church of the Franciscan Friars in 1507–8 the total rose to 19.5 man-days. In 1523–4 the carpenters required 20 man-days for setting up; in 1534–5, 31 for setting up and also taking down.

New construction in 1560–1 required 83 man-days, not counting four days each put in by two sawyers. In 1582–3, a time of no significant new construction, William Dowsey counted 50 man-days to set up, charging a shilling a day for skilled work and slightly less for unskilled work. He then charged 14s for taking the structure down again, implying 14 man-days on the assumption that Dowsey used skilled labour, for an estimated total of 65 man-days. Charged at a shilling a day, the cost would have come to 65s or £3–5–0, just short of the subsequently standard £3–6–8. Dowsey charged for a total of nine days each for himself and his man in preparing new work for the stage, from which we may infer that work began at least nine working days in advance of commencement, or perhaps a fortnight counting holidays.[18]

No further detailed lists are available until 1650–1, when 51 man-days were required to set up, and 20 to take down. The numbers dropped in 1651–2 to 28.5 and 21 respectively, in 1652–3 to 26 and 15, and in 1653–4 to 24 and 12. Roughly the same figures are recorded in 1654–5, 1657–8 and 1658–9. In 1662–3, however, the figures rose sharply to 67 man-days for setting up and 18 for taking down, a total (= 85 man-days) reached again exactly in 1697–8. Finally, in 1713–14, when the stage was built one final time, the total reached a record of 116 man-days for setting up and 44 for taking down, 160 man-days in all.

Even when inflation is taken into consideration, the increase in financial costs over the years is impressive. The carpenters' overall charges for building the stage increased from 5s in 1479–80, to approximately 10s at the turn of the century, to 20s in 1511–12, where it remained (with variations) through the 1550s. After the new construction of 1560–1 costs rose to approximately £3–8–6; after new work in the early 1590s, to £4–0–0. By 1632–3 the standard charge was £4–6–0, though back in 1627–8 the cost of old work and new work together was £7–12–9, and in 1628–9, £7–15–0.

In many years the carpenters received a flat fee for the usual work and submitted an itemized bill only for the additional work. This is very evident in 1589–90, when Dowsey received exactly £4–0–0 for work described in general terms, and an additional £4–11–4 for work and materials described in detail and clearly specified as 'for the inlarginge of the seates within the Stage at the Commencement', and work 'more then heretofore hath bene done over and besyde the usuall charge'.

Decoration

From very early days the commencement stage was provided with an ornamental skirting to give it an appearance of solidity. In 1489 the university spent 9d *pro panno lynnio pro ly staghys tempore inceptionum* (for linen cloth for the stages at the time of commencement). Linsey-woolsey, a relatively inexpensive and coarse textile made of mixed flax and wool, often green for stages, is first specifically named in the accounts for 1560–1, and it is named again in 1574–5, 1582–3, and 1619–20; other fabrics, usually green, are mentioned from 1612–13 to 1667–8.

In 1560–1 skirting-cloth purchased for the stage ran to $57\frac{7}{8}$ yards, or nearly 174′, perhaps an indication of the combined perimeters of the various stages. An enlargement of the stage in 1574–5 required 9 yards or 27′ of linsey-woolsey: assuming the new platform was square and skirted on all sides, it measured approximately 5′ 3″ on a side; if skirted on three sides only, the sides were 9′ each.

The width of the cloth may have been related to the height of the platforms. The linsey-woolsey purchased in 1619–20 was 'the broadest'; similarly, 'broad' cotton was purchased in 1652–3. The standard width of broadcloth was two yards or 6′: assuming that the long side of the cloth was attached to the edge of the stage platforms, and that the skirts reached to the floor, this would yield a normal stage height of 6′, a figure which tallies with the length of the 24 studs purchased in 1667–8.

The commencement stage was decorated with flowers and strewing material. In 1540–1 the entire theatre was washed down and provided with herbs. Rushes (*sirpis*) were purchased in 1559–60, and again in 1560–1, along with strewing. From this time onward such decoration was commonplace. The provision of rushes, and later flowers, was generally in the hands of the schoolkeeper, who also (rather than the carpenter) often supplied specialized nails called 'trashes'[19] for the stage fabrics.

Storage

In 1500–1 and 1501–2 the commencement stage was apparently stored at the Austin Friars' and erected at Great St Mary's, but beginning in 1507–8 it was apparently stored in the Schools and erected at the Franciscan Friars'. In 1523–4 the Friars agreed to store the stage for an annual payment of 10s, an arrangement which lasted until 1536–7 and put a temporary end to the annual carrying of materials with the exception of certain forms borrowed from Great St Mary's. By 1539–40, however, the stage, though still stored at the Franciscan Friars', was erected in Great St Mary's.

The place of storage immediately after the Franciscan Friars' property went into other ownership about 1540–1 is unknown. The university had a storehouse, mentioned in 1582–3, 1587, and 1634–5,[20] though in none of these years is it certain that the stage timbers were preserved there. From 1597–8 to 1609–10 the carpenter John Wade paid the churchwardens of Great St Mary's to allow him to store commencement timber in the church; the continuation of this practice seems to be confirmed by the Churchwardens' Accounts of 1617–18.[21] Almost two decades later an informant of Archbishop Laud declared that 'All the year after a parte of it [= Great St Mary's] is made a Lumber House for the Materials of the scaffolds, for Bookbinders dry Fats, for Aumeric Cupboards, & such like implements, which they know not where else to put.'[22]

Beginning in 1661–2 the university hired a stable belonging to the New Inn, on the site of what was to become Senate House yard, as a place to store the stage timber.[23] The rent of £2 per annum can be traced over the next sixty years. (For much of the first half of the seventeenth century, the university similarly rented a house to store the timber for the proctor's booth: see Appendix 10.)

Stagekeepers

As early as 1523–4, when the university spent 12d 'for kepyng the dorres off the stage', men were hired to guard the stage as night-watchmen, ushers, or both. In 1548–9

Bissell and other workers were paid *pro avectione theatri et custodia eiusdem* ('for transporting the stage, and for keeping it safe'), while in 1552–3 watchmen were paid for the nights of 11 and 14 July, possibly commencement days that year. In 1589–90 numbers are given for the first time when seven men were paid 'which kept the passages vpon the stage': these seem to have been ushers. The account book for 1593–4 contains a payment 'to 14 men keepinge the scaffolde at the commensment'. In 1594–5 the carpenter John Wade received a payment 'for kepinge of staires at the comensement two dayes for himselfe & his man'; the university made a separate payment to 'the Stagekeepers'.

In the accounts for 1602–3 Benjamin Prime the Yeoman Bedell is first named as head stagekeeper; he usually had assistants, numbering six in 1603–4, eight in 1605–6, seven in 1606–7, and four in 1608–9. Prime is last called by name in 1611–12. From 1623–4 to 1696–7 the stagekeepers are frequently called 'dorekepers'. Complete lists, with respectively eight and nine full names, survive from 1650–1 and 1652–3.

Breakage

Despite precautions taken by stagekeepers and others, both the commencement stage and the building in which it was erected were subject to damage, probably both from normal wear and tear and from occasional abuse by ill-disciplined students. Among the casualties were seats and forms (from 1488), window glass (from 1507–8), stage platforms (1566–7 and 1579–80), cloth and cushions (1581–2), church-yard gates (1632–3), and church pillars (from 1639–40).

Glass windows were broken with extraordinary frequency. Payments for glass, for a glazier, or for a plumber (to repair leading) occur in 1507–8 (Franciscan Friars') and 1515–16, sporadically until about 1566–7, and almost annually thereafter. Payments for taking down the glass, or for taking it down and putting it up again, may suggest that glass was removed from all the windows as a precaution against damage, but the sums paid are so irregular that evidently only those panels actually broken were taken down, mended, and set up again.

The earliest records of putative commencement activity, from 1464–5 and 1479–80, include payments for new benches, but beginning in 1488 payments are made for the repair of benches, and other instances occur so frequently thereafter that they are scarcely worth noting individually. Payments continue almost without a break through the penultimate commencement in Great St Mary's in 1697–8, and doubtless some damage occurred again in the final commencement of 1713–14.

The university made some attempt to limit such damage. Beginning in 1584 undergraduates were under specific instruction not to stand on forms, while under the vice-chancellorship of Benjamin Lany (1632–3) they were additionally ordered not to stand in the church windows.[24]

6

Secular playing sites

The Guildhall

25 July 1606. Cambridge. John Duke and Thomas Green, leaders of Queen Anne's Company of professional actors, have come to Cambridge in expectation of putting on a play.[1] Duke and Green secure an audience with the mayor, John Edmunds, an ancient foe of the university[2] who grants them permission to act in the Guildhall on the market. Mayor Edmunds orders town carpenters to build a stage in the hall, and for a precaution commands that the glass be taken down from the windows. He entrusts the key of the hall to Duke and Green, who anticipate that they will be able to come and go at will as they get ready for their performance.

The company of professional players does not escape the vigilance of university officials. Richard Clayton, Master of St John's College and Vice-Chancellor of the university, for all his vehement anti-Puritanism[3] is quick to dispatch the Esquire Bedells, who summon the players before the Vice-Chancellor's court. Duke and Green take refuge in their transactions with the mayor, but are informed in no uncertain terms that the mayor has no right to infringe on the prerogatives of the university, one of which is the right to exclude all players from five miles' compass of the town centre. Under threat of arrest Duke and Green sign and seal an obligation:

> The Condicion of this obligation is such that if at all tymes hereafter the above bounden Thomas Greene & Iohn Duke & either of them doe wholely & altogether give over & leave of[f] to act or playe any maner of playes or enterlewdes what soever within the vniversity & Towne of Cambridge or within the Compasse of five myles of the sayd vniversity & Towne of Cambridge both by them selves & theire whole Company then this presente obligacion to be voyd & of none effect or else to be & abyde in full fourse & vertue/.

Green and Duke know that if they attempt to play now or in the near future they will be in acute danger of forfeiting the crippling sum of £20. Shaking the dust of Cambridge from their feet, they head immediately for Ipswich, the next town on their itinerary.[4]

Various sources confirm that the Guildhall was a traditional place of performance. On 23 May 1557, for example, John Mere noted in his Diary (REED, p. 199):

> On sonday very warme & fayre & no sermon throwghe the towne. Item my lord of Norfolkes players played in the hall & at the folken.

We know from other sources that actors coming to a town often played first before the mayor and aldermen, and only then moved to such venues as inns (here, the Falcon) for performances before the public.[5] Perhaps Thomas Duke and John Greene were preparing such a mayoral performance when they were forestalled by university officials on 25 July 1606.

The nineteenth-century Cambridge architect T. D. Atkinson studied the Guildhall, also known as the Town Hall, which incorporated the town prison called the Tolbooth:[6]

> The Guildhall or Tolbooth was rebuilt in 1386, and though it appears to have been diminutive in size and unpretending in its architecture, the building then erected continued in use for just four hundred years. Like almost all medieval Town Halls, it consisted of an upper storey supported on arches, the space below being open to the Market Place.

> ... the building of 1386 consisted of a hall used for leets and general meetings; a parlour in which the aldermen sat, at the east end of the hall; a pantry used by the Four-and-Twenty, on the south; and a kitchen to the west. These rooms were all on the upper floor and appear to have been reached by an outside staircase.

> 'After the sermon', says Alderman Newton, 'the whole company went to the Towne Hall everyone in order two and two, and first the Threasurers, that new came in, then every one according to his place and seniority. When the Treasurers came to the Hall staire foot doore, there they stood untill the Attorneyes first and then the Mayor &c followeinge went upp into the Hall; after the Commonday was done, dinner being prepared wee went to it.'

(The 'Commonday' was the 'common-day' meeting of the council; it is not an idiosyncratic spelling of 'comedy'.)

The Guildhall was sometimes let out to private persons for marriage feasts, as revealed in the Town Treasurers' accounts:[7]

> 1552: For ij brydalls kept in the Guyld halle, ij s
> 1562: Item, of Thomas Clarke for a brydale kept in the hall, xx d

The Treasurers' accounts also contain information more germane to our interest in performance venues (REED):

> 1488–9 (Latin original): Likewise as rewards given various persons playing in the common hall 8d
> 2s as rewards given to the same earl's [= Oxford's] entertainers ... in the guild-hall

> 1530–1: Item payd for v players at the gyldehalle by the commaundement of Master Mayer iij s iiij d

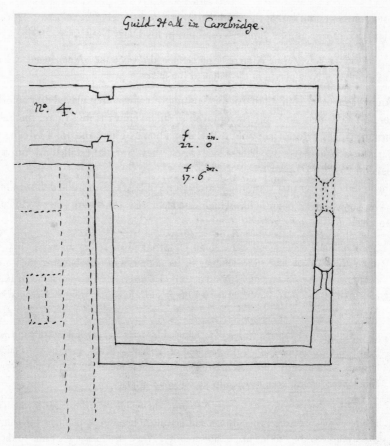

Fig. 31.   Cambridge Guildhall, upper level, by James Essex, 1781 (copy by William Cole, British Library Add. 5183, f. 130v; original not traced). Drawing is apparently oriented with lower end of hall at top. Accompanying drawings of the ground-level walls and arches are reproduced in Atkinson, *Cambridge Described*, p. 83; and REED, p. 724.

1547–8: Item to players at the hall by the comaundement of Master Mayer Mr Chapman & Mr Rust ij s

1567–8: Item paid masen [= Mason] for plaienge at the guilde hall at the comaundement of master maier & the counsell xiij s iiij d

1569–70: Item to Gibbons for playeinge at the hall vpon Hocktuisdaie xvj d

1611–12: Item to the town waytes ... for musicke at the hall xvj d

Of these seven payments (1488–9 counted as two), the first and second are probably, the fifth to seventh certainly for musicians, while the third and fourth may be for acting companies. Musicians, including William Gibbons, may have performed for meetings of town officials, but acting companies must have mounted plays which constituted the principal reason for the assembly. The Queen's Men, who visited Cambridge with some regularity from 1561–2 to 1596–7 (REED, p. 1283), must have played often in the Guildhall.

The Cambridge Guildhall was pulled down in 1782, but not before James Essex, designer of the new town hall, had made drawings for posterity (fig. 31).[8] Although some aspects of his drawings are elusive, it appears that the principal room was an oblong chamber measuring 22′ by 17′ 6″ raised on arches which defined the open ground level beneath. Access was by an outside stairway leading to an entry-way in the south-west corner. Opposite were two windows overlooking the market, probably the windows from which glass was to have been removed in 1605–6.

The squarish floor-plan of the hall needs to be reconciled with a highly elongated rectangular groundplan discernible in the 1592 Hamond map and the 1688 Loggan map of Cambridge.[9] Apparently the 'hall' in its totality consisted of a central hall supported on a masonry arch, flanked by lighter structures carrying the additional rooms mentioned by Atkinson, that is, a parlour to the east and a kitchen to the west. Even the largest room of the Guildhall was fairly small by modern standards: a relatively minuscule interior space, at 385 sq. ft. roughly a third the floor area of Queens' College hall, could suffice for the performance of a professional play.

The testimony of John Duke and Thomas Green gives an unusually clear picture of their proceeding in July 1606: 'both saye that mr Maior did give them absolute authoritye to playe in the Towne Hall & did give order to some to buyld theire Stage & take downe the glasse windowes there & did also give theym the Key of the Towne Hall'. Apparently the town stood the expense of constructing the stage and of taking down the windows; like many other towns of the period, including Norwich,[10] Cambridge may have owned a demountable stage which could be set up in the hall at command.

Inns

Sunday, 3 January 1557. The Falcon Inn, Petty Cury, Cambridge. Despite the plague, which is ravaging Cambridge yet again, crowds cannot resist a play. Last Friday, a clear but chilly New Year's Day, Trinity College provided an outdoor show in its court. Today, warmer though still overcast, a troupe of professional players has come to Cambridge – indeed possibly two troupes, for one play is to be performed at the Falcon, close to the Guildhall, another about a half mile distant, near the main bridge, at the Saracen's Head (REED, p. 199).

John Mere was Esquire Bedell of the university from 1530 to 1543, then Registrary to 1558. The year 1556–7 had been filled with tension: official visitors appointed or at least approved by Queen Mary were scrutinizing the university, both as an institution and as a corporation of sometimes fractious and sometimes heretical members.[11] As Registrary, Mere was keeper of university documents, any one of which might be subject to inspection; as a highly visible though not personally powerful official, both duty and private interest made him keen to keep track of what was going on. Mere also had a personal devotion to play performances: an inventory taken at his death in 1558 lists several players' costumes kept in his garden house along with more ordinary household possessions (REED, p. 204).

In his diary for 1557 (REED, pp. 199–200), Mere twice notes the activities of professional players in Cambridge (we have previously noted the second instance, p. 89):

> (3 January) On sonday fayre & close wether & no sermon throuwghe the towne … Item a play at the fawkon & a nother at the saresins hed …

> (23 May) On sonday very warme & fayre & no sermon throwghe the towne. Item my lord of Norfolkes players played in the hall & at the folken.

On 3 January plays were performed at the Falcon and at the Saracen's Head (possibly by two different companies). On 23 May the players of Lord Norfolk[12] performed twice, first at the Guildhall, presumably for the mayor and aldermen, and then at the Falcon before the general public.

Although a romantic history of plays at the Falcon as frequently promulgated by Cambridge antiquarians includes a performance before Queen Mary in 1557, or performances before Elizabeth at unspecified dates ('probably watching Shakespeare or Marlowe acting in the yard'),[13] no performances apart from the two of 1557 and certainly no performances before royalty are capable of being documented for the Falcon, and no performances at all before modern times for the only surviving Cambridge galleried inn, the Eagle.[14] The two performances at the Falcon are nevertheless twice as many as can be documented for three other Cambridge inns: the Saracen's Head (3 January 1557), an ancient but obscure inn;[15] the Elephant (27 February 1596); and the Bear (28 May 1600). We know, however, that professional players visited Cambridge with some regularity into the 1590s, though their place of performance is scarcely ever recorded (REED, pp. 723, 725).

The generic inn

The generic Cambridge inn is well described by Atkinson:

> Cambridge seems to have been well supplied with good inns, in some measure, probably, owing to the fairs and especially to that at Stourbridge. These inns presented a comparatively narrow front towards the street. This front contained a large gateway which gave access to a long and narrow court yard; round the yard ran open galleries from which the principal rooms were entered, the ground floor being devoted to menial offices. At the further end of the court another archway led through into a second yard containing the stables. The yard straggled irregularly back for some distance to join a street in the rear. An exit was thus provided for waggons which could not possibly have turned in the confined yard. In this way some inn yards have gradually become public thoroughfares and others may be seen at various stages of transition, while some have been closed and kept private. (pp. 71–2)

The 1798 Custance map of Cambridge (fig. 32) shows at least six inns of the kind Atkinson describes. Clockwise from bottom left, these are the Black Bull, now

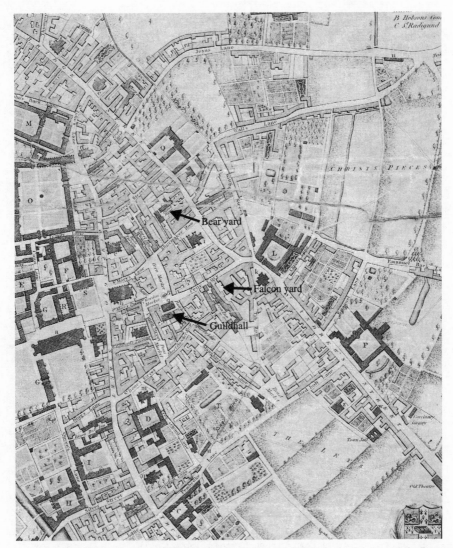

Fig. 32. Custance map of Cambridge, 1798, with sites of Guildhall, the Falcon, and the Bear indicated.

incorporated into St Catharine's College; the Rose, now Rose Crescent; the Bear, whose courtyard-thoroughfare survives as Market Passage; the Red Lion, whose passageway is reflected (though not very accurately) in the modern Lion Yard development; and the Falcon, in the first courtyard east of the Red Lion.

The Falcon

Had it not been for the temerity, not to say brutality, of Cambridge officials in the 1960s, the Falcon, which was established by 1513–14,[16] would not have had to be

1883 – 1896 TDA

Fig. 33.   Falcon Inn yard, 1883 (after a sketch by T. D. Atkinson), looking north, showing galleries on west side of yard. From Atkinson, *Cambridge Described*, p. 75.

reconstructed in the imagination at all, for it was only razed in 1972. The Lion Yard development, which entirely obliterated the site of the Falcon, houses – ironically – the Cambridgeshire Collection, a research library for local history.[17]

Atkinson, who knew the Falcon as it was toward the end of the nineteenth century, describes it as follows:

The Falcon has now ceased to be used as an inn, but it is a very good example of the old arrangement. Till quite recently the court was entirely surrounded by the timber buildings of the fifteenth or sixteenth centuries, and the west and south sides still stand almost unaltered. The buildings are in three floors, the two upper of which have open galleries, projecting slightly over the ground storey. The galleries probably ran all round

Fig. 34.   Falcon Inn yard, photo by Arthur Nicholls, c. 1860, looking south, showing galleries on west side of yard. Cambridgeshire Collection, Cambridgeshire Libraries, O.Fal.J6.267.

the court originally. ... The galleries on the east side appear to have been destroyed in the last century to form a large reception room, the three round-headed windows of which appear in our illustration. (pp. 73–4)

Atkinson's illustration (fig. 33) is taken from a sketch made by himself in 1883; a photograph survives from an even earlier date (fig. 34).[18] An early nineteenth-century drawing shows the timber construction of the galleries in fine detail (fig. 35).[19] Atkinson's sketch looks north: through the gateway can be seen a glimpse of Petty Cury, the narrow but important thoroughfare from which carriages entered the yard. The photograph looks south: through the gateway can be seen the second court which presumably held the stables. An estate agent's published plan from about 1880 gives the exact dimensions of the yard, probably little changed since the sixteenth century: it was 66′ 4″ long, narrowing irregularly in width from 17′ at the south end to over 18′ at the north end leading to Petty Cury.[20] At approximately 1160 sq. ft., it was slightly smaller than the area enclosed by Queens' College hall. Presumably the stage was set up in the centre of the yard, while spectators watched from the galleries or from the ground.[21]

Fig. 35.   Falcon Inn gallery, detail, from Buckler Drawings, c. 1820. British Library MS Add. 36435, f. 177.

The Elephant

In August 1596 John Crowfoot, M.A., was disallowed as a compurgator or witness in an adultery trial: as evidence of his unsavoury character the defence alleged that he had been 'drawen by the heeles from a common playe' (REED, p. 365). Contemporary university depositions ascribe what is probably the same event to the Elephant. The innkeeper at this time was Thomas Knights, the inn located in the parish of St Sepulchre, the 'Round Church'. This parish also contained the Hoop, whose site is known;[22] but we can only guess where the Elephant may have been located.

Richard Ridding, Esquire Bedell, tried to arrest Crowfoot at the Elephant, calling on the assistance of Edward Smith and Benjamin Prime:

> [Crowfoot] resisted and layed hould on a post from whence this deponent and otheres dyd pull him and going down the stayrs he sawe Crofoot drawe his dagger and offer to smite at Mr Riddinge ... and before he came to the stayrs and vpon the stayres and in the entry of the house and soe allong the streats going to the toulbooth dyd often repeat these wordes viz Riddinge I wilbe revenged on you base Rascall ...

Prime deposed much the same, adding that Crowfoot cried aloud 'in the courte yard' of the Elephant after he had been dragged down the stairs (REED, pp. 1229–30).

The depositions are not sufficiently detailed to reveal whether the play occurred indoors or in the yard, but nothing is inconsistent with the assumption that it occurred in the yard: the stairs may have led to galleries; the 'courte yard' in which Crowfoot yelled may have contained both actors and audience.

Earlier the same year, on 14 June, the innkeeper Knights himself had been hauled before the Vice-Chancellor on the complaint that 'there was kept and suffered within the said Knightes his house a bearebaightinge and by that occasion a great disordred multitude of schollers and townsmen and other persons vnlawfully assembled': this bearbaiting must necessarily have taken place out of doors, doubtless in the yard of the Elephant.

The Bear

The keeper of the Bear in 1600 was Mary Gibbons, widow of William, who was head of the Cambridge waits from 1567 to 1576, and again from 1590 to his death in 1595. Mary seems to have retained legal control of the waits until her death in 1603. (She was the mother of Orlando Gibbons, who may well have grown up at the Bear, and probably lived there during his student days if he did not live within the walls of King's College; he would have been about seventeen in 1600.)[23]

The following extract records an incident of 28 May 1600:

> for that yt was aparant to the sight and knowledge of mr vicechancellor that the sayed Pepper was this present day in a tumultuous and disordered meeting beholdinge certayne playes and interludes at the signe of the beare without the habite of his degree and

haveinge deformed longe lockes of hayre and vnseemely syde [= long] and great breaches vndecent for a graduate or scholler of orderly carriage. Therefore the sayed Pepper returninge to the consistorye was there suspended ...

Unfortunately, this extract conceals what most concerns us: exactly how and where the plays and interludes were performed.

Chesterton

2:00 p.m., Sunday, 22 April 1581. Chesterton, near Cambridge. Though it is Sunday sermon time in Cambridge, the yard of Jackson's inn has been teeming with activity for over an hour. In the centre of the yard a bear is chained to a stake. Huge dogs lunge at the bear: those which escape unhurt, or wounded but alive, are either brave and lucky, or graced with cowardice. Excited spectators standing in a circle whose radius is the length of the chain include the bearward himself; Jackson the innkeeper; Thomas Parris the high constable; and Richard Parris, his brother.

The crowd's attention turns to a knot of university officials who have appeared suddenly, clearly intent on putting a stop to this unlawful game: they are Thomas Nevile, M.A., Senior Proctor; Henry Farr, M.A., Taxor; Martin Wylliams, B.A., vicar of the Chesterton church; John Hutchinson and Samuell Farr, both M.A.; John Standish, Esquire Bedell; and William Dant, Christopher Gryme, and Anthony Bende, servants of the university. Nevile as Proctor asks the bearward on what authority he is baiting his bear in this place. On the authority of my patron Lord Vaux (replies the bearward) and by warrant of the Justices. Nevile responds that the bearbaiting violates the university's jurisdiction within five miles' compass of Cambridge, a prerogative superior to that of Lord Vaux and the Justices. Informed that he is under arrest, the bearward agrees to place himself and his bear in the custody of Standish.

Nothing the university officials could have said or done is so certain to irk this crowd, which has had its bellyfull of university restrictions on its harmless pleasures. Richard Parris shouts a challenge to the bearward: 'Do not go with him, for if thou do, thou art a fool!' John Daniel, a lanky bystander familiarly known as Long John, cries: 'Thou shalt not go!' and places himself between the bearward and Standish.

The crowd, encouraged by this show of resistance, surges forward, cutting off Standish's escape and crowding him to the bear so that he can scarcely keep from harm. Fearing for his life, he cries for assistance. Long John Daniel, experienced enough to know that an actual injury to Standish will have the most dire consequences for him and the crowd, relents, telling Standish he might well go, for he has no legitimate concern with the bearbaiting.

Regrouping and confident of their authority, the university officials complete their mission in spite of threats and arguments from the Parris brothers: the bearward and the bear are marched off to Cambridge; within days Thomas and Richard Parris are cooling their heels in a Westminster jail; the intervention of Lord North himself barely suffices to free them nearly a month later (REED, pp. 295–305).

Chesterton bore approximately the same relation to Cambridge that Southwark bore to London: it was a site of often dubious activity which the university tried, with only limited success, to regulate.[24] Two Chesterton incidents similar to the bearbaiting of 1581 – but less charged with violence – involved plays whose performance sites can only be guessed. Both incidents involved the Queen's Men, the first in 1589–90, when a warrant was sent to the constables:

> ymmediatelye vpon the receipte hereof you do in her Maiesties name will and requiere the partie within the said towne in whose house or grownde within that sayed towne the sayed Players have alreadye presumed to playe, or anie other at whose hands they may herafter happen there to requeare or desire the lyke lybertie – not hereafter to suffer them or any of them so to do within anie of theire houses or grounds within that sayed towne.

The broad legal language prohibits performances which might occur within houses or grounds, probably signifying in this instance the yard of an inn. A warrant issued for the second incident, on 1 September 1592, conceives of even more possibilities: 'as namely from the sufferinge of them, or of any of them to take the vse, of any theire roomes, houses or yardes in that towne to that end and intent'. On 18 September Vice-Chancellor Robert Some and the heads of colleges complained to Lord Burghley:

> How slightly that warrant was regarded aswell by the Constables and thinhabitauntes of Chesterton as by the Players them selues (whereof one Dutton is a principale) apeared by theire bills sett vp vpon our college gates, and by theire playeinge in Chesterton, notwithstanding our said warrant to the contrary.

(Here we observe the method by which professional plays were advertised, that is, by bills posted on college gates.) The Vice-Chancellor and the heads wrote to the Privy Council the same day:

> Wherefore wee are most humblie to craue of your good Lordships, that you would be pleased to cause to be called before your Honores aswell the said Plaiers and the Constable, as also the partie in whose house the Enterludes were plaied...

Although both indoor and outdoor performances are prohibited, it again seems likely that the place of performance was the yard of an inn, perhaps the very yard where the bear was baited in 1581.

Open-air sites

Saturday, 15 July 1620. The Iron Age Wandlebury Round in the Gog Magog Hills south-east of Cambridge. Robert Scott, Master of Clare College and this year's Vice-Chancellor, has caught word of impending sports and games at the Gogs. Approaching in the company of James Tabor, Registrary, Scott is astonished to meet young Simonds D'Ewes, whose curiosity has clearly got the best of his notorious piety, already returning from the site of the games.

Surmounting the ancient earthworks, Scott descries numerous booths and widescale preparations for 'horseraces, bull bayting, beare bayting, Loggattes, ninehoales, ryflinge [= gambling], dicinge', as well as for bowling, running, jumping, shooting, and wrestling. (D'Ewes was later to report that all this activity went 'under the designation of the Olympic games'.)

Vice-Chancellor Scott quickly learns that John Adamson of Ware, the entrepreneur, expects activities to continue for at least three weeks, and perhaps as many as five. Scott and Tabor, both confident of knowing who's who and what's what, bind over a crowd of suspicious Cambridge characters: the widow Juda Hudson, a suspected bawd and whore commonly known as Jumping Judy; George Cook and George Clark, victuallers; John Fardell, carpenter, whose wife is a known and noted whore; Thomas Whaley, innkeeper; and John Cochey, carrier.

Under threat of arrest, Adamson signs the bond prepared for him by the Vice-Chancellor, agreeing to 'cause all his booths which he hath buylded at Hoggmagogg Hills to be removed & taken awaye, & dischardge all his Companie that he hath drawne together thither, & cause them to departe presentlye without any delaye, or returne agayne ...' (REED, pp. 570–3).

Most performances in Cambridge and vicinity occurred either fully indoors, as in college halls, chapels, and the Guildhall; or within bounded areas, as in college courts, innyards, or the bullring on the market.[25] Some performances, however, occurred in the open air. An apparently minor open-air venue was the Howes, about a mile north-west of the town centre on the Madingley Road, now recalled by such names as Howes Place and the White House. In September 1580 one Robinson, a neighbour of Sir Francis Hinde of Madingley, obtained a licence 'to showe, & exercise certaine games at or nigh vnto the howse next Cambridge'; in 1611–12 the university acted to stop a bearbaiting there; and in 1618 D'Ewes reported that he had played bowls at 'a green about a mile from Cambridge called Howse', and received refreshment at 'the cottage that standeth there' (REED, p. 727).

Of much greater consequence is Wandlebury Round some three miles south-east of Cambridge town centre (fig. 36).[26] With an outer circle nearly 1000′ in diameter, enclosing an area of 13.5 acres, and with a smooth inner bowl, this seems to have been a perfect place for open-air playing. The university accounts of 1572–3 reveal that John Baxter, Esquire Bedell, went 'to gogmagog hils at the tyme of playes'. From letters written by Vice-Chancellor John Whitgift in May 1574 we learn of impending 'onlawfull gamyng of dyuers kyndes', 'lewed games', and 'playes or games'; we also learn that the entrepreneur, the same Robinson (doubtless) who was active at the Howes in 1580, was already notorious as a promoter of games.

Clearly the (man-made) geographical features of the Gog Magog Hills, including the inner and outer earth rings of the hill-fort, were useful for crowd control, for guaranteeing the payment of gate receipts, as raked seating for the spectators, and perhaps as boundary markers for races, whether horse or foot. We are also reminded of performances in the round suggested by such East Anglian plays from the late middle ages as *The Castle of Perseverance*, *Mary Magdalene*, and the N-Town cycle,

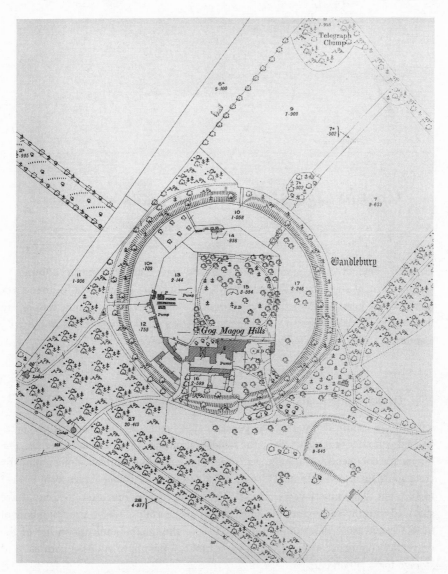

Fig. 36. Wandlebury Round, Gog Magog Hills. Detail reproduced from the 1927 Ordnance Survey map.

and we may find here grounds for speculation about the characteristic use of circular constructions and of demountable wooden booths or scaffolds for outdoor games and plays.[27]

7

Cambridge staging practices

Granted some diversity among college stages, and granted that the university's commencement stage erected annually in Great St Mary's was not a theatre in the service of the genuine dramatic enterprises of Cambridge, various general lessons can nevertheless be learned from the history and details of all known stages in the early Cambridge tradition, including the commencement stage.[1]

Demountable stages

Virtually all Cambridge stages were permanent structures in the sense that they were erected year after year, generally in the same location and with the same materials. The university commencement stage was assembled and disassembled almost annually from approximately 1464 to 1714, some 250 years, Queens' College stage from 1546–7 to 1639–40, some ninety years. The Trinity College stage from after 1605 may have survived into the early years of the Restoration. Doubtless few if any fragments of timber lasted from the beginning to the end of the quarter-millennium life of the university commencement stage, but most timbers must have endured both use and storage for years on end.

Many colleges had demountable stages, while the town of Cambridge may have had a demountable stage for its Guildhall. In addition to theatrical and commencement stages, the university maintained a booth which it erected annually at Sturbridge Fair (Appendix 10), as did the Mayor and Aldermen.[2] Merchants kept booths for use at the fair,[3] just as traders in the Cambridge market keep booths to this day. Visiting showmen set up booths at the Gog Magog Hills in 1620–1, carting them away on the order of the Vice-Chancellor.

Timber joints may have had to be cut somewhat looser for demountable wood-built structures than for permanent structures, but that temporary and permanent structures were both built with similar techniques by the very same carpenters is abundantly clear.[4]

Storage

It is just conceivable that the fifteenth-century commencement stages were broken up and their materials dispersed after each use, but from at least as early as 1500–1 a demountable stage was annually set up, used, taken down, and then stored for the rest of the year. Benches and desks may have been temporarily appropriated from the Schools or from churches including St Mary's itself, and other elements may have doubled for use in the B.A. ceremonies in the Schools. Most of the timber scaffolding, however, must have been appropriate for no other use, and thus required storage for perhaps fifty weeks of each year.

The early commencement stage was stored variously at the Austin Friars', the Schools(?), and the Franciscan Friars'. After 1540–1 it may have been kept in a storehouse in the Schools, though by 1597–8 much of the timber was kept at Great St Mary's itself. From 1661–2 to 1719–20 the timber was kept in a rented stable. (During the early seventeenth century the university also rented a house for storing the proctor's booth.)

All colleges with demountable stages must also have had appropriate storage places. Queens' College had a *lignarium* or lumber-house for storage in 1540–1, St John's a 'store howse' for the 'bordes and tressils of the stage' in 1544–5, while Trinity College appropriated the old Physwick Hostel hall in 1547–8 as a 'storehowse' and used a cellar (of the same hall?) in 1562–3. The storage place used by Trinity College in 1614–15 is a mystery except for the fact that it was protected by lock and key; I have suggested (p. 48) that it might have been the ground-floor room behind the upper-end wall of the hall. A storehouse used by Queens' College in 1633–4 was replaced by a purpose-built structure whose construction dates from 1637–8. Both this extra-mural storehouse and the university's stable at the New Inn were known at times as 'stagehouses'.

Transportation

Timber which was stored had to be transported. The timbers of the university commencement stage, along with benches and other furniture, were carried and re-carried almost annually, from as early as 1488, when the charge was 4d, and 1500–1, when the carrier was Robert Pryce who took three cartloads for 2s, to 1713–14, when the charge was a more substantial £1–4–0. Notable records of carriage occur in 1529–30 (12 loads), 1534–5 (4 loads of forms), 1538–9 (2 carts), 1560–1 (4 carts), and 1578–9 (forms from the Regent House and St Michael's Church).

In 1544–5 St John's College hired a boat to bring boards for its stage to Michaelhouse; in 1546–7 Queens' paid Martin Avesse, John Gayttes, and Margaret Vetule for the carriage back and forth of boards from Corpus and St John's; in 1548–9 the same college paid John Frost for a trip to Steeple Bumpstead to fetch planks for the tragedy: his charges included labour, horse hire, and the use of three waggons. In

1594–5 Cutchey transported board and timber for the comedies of King's College. In 1598–9 Trinity College paid 'for the carring & recarring of Tymber & other stuffe for the stage by Carte' along with another similar payment. The highly detailed 1612–13 accounts for Trinity College comedies are a mine of information about the carrying of stage timber.

The relative proximity of college storehouses to their respective halls meant that timber might be hand-carried by labourers rather than moved in carts by professional carriers: thus in 1633–4 Queens' paid 'for layinge the stage in the storehouse', perhaps to labourers rather than carriers.

Materials other than timber and boards also required transportation. In 1547–8 John Frost and John Graves carried a large chest for Queens' College stage costumes. The celebrated Cambridge carrier Thomas Hobson carried 'certaine stuffe at our playes' for Queens' in 1579–80, and 'Targettes & other thinges at the Tragedy' for St John's in 1582–3. Again, 1612–13 Trinity College comedy accounts contain numerous references to the carrying of costumes and props.

Timber

All Cambridge stages were framed with oak of square or squarish scantlings (= cross-section), cut to length, and fastened with mortise-and-tenon joints. Scantlings for the commencement stage, as recorded in 1560–1 and 1667–8, run from 2×4s at the smallest to 4×6s at the largest. The shortest recorded studs are 4′ (1667–8), while more representative may be the 20 timbers at 4′ 6″ purchased in 1560–1 or the 24 at 6′ purchased in 1667–8. Although we have noted a propensity for purchasing verticals in multiples of 3′ from 6′ to 12′, perhaps non-uniformity is a more significant overall characteristic, suggesting platforms of non-uniform height. Of the horizontally disposed timbers, girts and rails run from 6′ (1560–1) to at least 14′ (1667–8) and perhaps 17′ (1662–3), jeece from 5′ (1667–8) to 14′ (1662–3).

Our knowledge of timber purchased for college stages is vague by comparison, since colleges did not often preserve the original bills. In 1592–3 King's College purchased ten pairs of studs, in 1594–5 'certain timber'. Trinity College purchased timber for framing the stage in 1570–1, and board and timber in 1598–9 including forms and timber from St Mary's. In 1614–15 Clare College hired timber for a rehearsal stage: its play was scheduled for performance in Trinity College hall.

Fastening the joints

Timbers were normally fastened with mortise-and-tenon joints secured by wooden pegs. In 1500–1 the university purchased *C pynnys de meremio* and *ly pynne de ferro* (100 pins of wood and one pin of iron) for the commencement stage; in 1502–3 the payment was for *ducentis clauis meremij* (200 wood pins). Many annual accounts from 1593–4 to 1607–8 include purchases of ash poles: some (1589–90, 1602–3) are specified as being for the seats, but in 1596–7 John Wade was reimbursed 'for a peice of ashe which was bought to make pinnes on [= of] for the new stage'. 'Pinwood' is mentioned on numerous occasions from 1651–2 to 1677–8. The purchases of 'pynnes to owr masteres shew' by Trinity College in 1554–5 may also refer to wooden pegs for timber joints.

Probably most pegs could be saved and reused, but many must have been broken each year, either from the violence of being driven in and out, or perhaps because they became frozen in place and had to be bored out with an auger.

Marking

In 1507–8 the university paid 4d to Robert the carpenter 'for the marking of the parts of the stage [to show] the way they are put together': clearly Robert marked the individual timbers which made up the stage to show how they were to be joined again. This procedure demonstrates the care and foresight that went into the maintenance of the stages over time, and how clearly the stages were intended for disassembly and reassembly.

The Queens' College inventory of 1640 reveals how actual carpenters' marks were used, along with paint, to identify matching mortises and tenons: marks placed on the two timbers making a joint include letters of the alphabet, numbers, astrological symbols, and geometrical arrays such as rows of one to six dots. Carpenters' marks are known from other contexts,[5] but rarely in such detail, or for the reassembly of structures which spent most of their lives in storage.

Boards

Boards are thin planks, 4″ to 6″ wide, as opposed to the squarish timbers used for framing. Beginning in 1573–4 the thickness of boards purchased for the commencement stage is suggested with some frequency by the designation 'ynche bourde'. The 'hoching boord' of 1582–3 is probably also inch-board. The Cambridge use of this term is nearly seventy years in advance of the earliest instance cited by the *OED* (1646). Both university and college records suggest a free commerce in boards, which by their very nature might be used interchangeably for virtually any stage in Cambridge.

The earliest references to boards for Cambridge stages come from the commencement records of 1488 and 1493 (*asseres*, 'burdys'). During the sixteenth century the purchase of boards, often in lots of 200′ to 500′, is commonplace. Boards were secured from lumber dealers, donated by friends of the university (1560–1), or purchased at Midsummer Fair, which was more logical given its proximity to the July commencement than a single recorded purchase at Sturbridge Fair (1594–5), which concluded at Michaelmas.

In 1544–5 St John's College paid a carpenter 'for takinge bording in diuerse place of the towne for the stage'; some of the boards were brought by boat to Michaelhouse, and others carried 'in to the store howse'. Queens' acquired boards in 1546–7 from Corpus Christi and St John's, reimbursed St Catharine's College in 1547–8 for 59′ of boards ruined by cutting, and acquired planks in 1548–9 from college lands in Steeple Bumpstead. Other purchases of boards in lots of 200 are commonplace, though the 700′ of inch-board bought by King's College in 1592–3 is impressive even by the standard of the commencement stage.

Platform heights

Since the minimum stud length for the university commencement stage was 4′ 6″, we may guess at a minimum platform height in Great St Mary's of 5′, but the more common stud length of 6′ may imply a greater average height. The use of broadcloth for skirting may also imply a height of 6′ for the main central stage. A range of lengths for vertical timbers seems to suggest a variety of platform levels.

Galleries are recorded in 1564, 1612–13, 1632–3, 1634–5, 1659–60, and 1661–2; Thomas Buck's 1665 'ceremonial' shows that at the Restoration, if not before, the stage at the belfry end of the nave had a lower and upper platform.[6] References to stairs from 1590–1 onward suggest complex vertical elaboration.

The only Cambridge stage heights directly reported by an observer were those for Elizabeth in 1564: the stage in King's College Chapel was 5′ high; the raised throne platform in Great St Mary's, 8′. The minimum height of structures beneath which people might stand or move (all evidence taken from non-Cambridge stages) was apparently 7′. I have adopted the 5′ stage height and the 7′ minimum headroom for my reconstructions of stages at Queens' and Trinity.

Trestles

The system for supporting the stage platform at Queens', as revealed by the 1640 inventory, seems somewhat less than ideal, since the platform apparently stood firm only by virtue of being pinched between flanking houses. St John's College stage platform apparently rested on trestles (with four feet), newly made in 1544–5 and recorded subsequently in 1548–9 and 1575–6 (those in the latter year were not necessarily for the stage). The nine long and three short 'staging trystles' at Trinity College in 1547–8 suggest a stage of two levels, or (more doubtfully) two widths. The music scaffold for commencement in 1583–4 required '5 girts for the tresses thare', but this is the only mention of trestles in that context. Other devices such as tripods and *sustentacula mensarum* may or may not have been used for stage platforms.[7]

Stairs

Stairs, a feature of the developed commencement stage, must have been provided for Elizabeth in 1564, and are recorded from 1590–1 onward, sometimes – as for the royal visit of 1614–15 – in abundance. Colleges also used stairs in conjunction with their platforms, as at Queens' College in 1540–1, when five spikes were provided for fastening the steps to the stage; and at Trinity College, where in 1547–8 the storehouse in Physwick Hostel contained 'A litle ladder for the stage'. In 1564 Elizabeth approached the stage in King's College Chapel by means of a 'bridge'; the 1640 inventory of Queens' College lists or implies slope boards and slope rails, presumably for access to the stage.

Stairs and ladders must have been a more prominent part of college stage platforms, houses, and galleries than surviving documentation reveals: by what other means are we to imagine that college visitors, scholars, and actors negotiated their way around the raised scaffolds which made up the college stage?

Stairs were also a feature of inns, important for giving access to upper levels, as the image of John Crowfoot clinging to a post to avoid being dragged down the stairs vividly reminds us.

Doors

The commencement stage had doors within Great St Mary's to control access to particular areas of seating. In its final year, 1713–14, iron work largely devoted to hinges, locks, and keys for these doors totalled nearly £8.

Access to college halls was controlled at the outer hall doors and screens (and, at Trinity College in 1614–15, at the trap-door and one additional upper-end door). The 1640 Queens' College stage inventory reveals the existence of a door at the back of the stage platform as part of the recent additions – though this may have been hung with a curtain rather than provided with a wooden door on hinges, if indeed it was not merely an archway. Inventories of St John's in 1556–7 and 1562–3 record a 'portall of wainscotte', though its connection with college plays is not established.

College stagehouses had openings which stood for doors, though they may have been hung with curtains rather than being provided with hinged wooden doors. The side chapels at King's College Chapel which served for houses in 1564 did have wooden doors, which may have been put to use for plays.

Rails

Rails figure prominently in the 1640 Queens' College stage inventory (see fig. 19, p. 31), and were a virtually inevitable part of raised spectator galleries, including both theatrical stages and the commencement stage in Great St Mary's. A different kind of rail, intended as a barrier to separate spectators of lower dignity from those of higher dignity, was part of the Trinity College theatre in the first half of the seventeenth century (figs. 20–1, pp. 41–2), and perhaps in the latter half of the sixteenth.[8] Yet another kind of rail is implied by a Trinity College payment in 1614–15 to James Manutius 'for paynting the Rayles on the stage': these may well have been low rails at the front (and rear?) edge of the stage, of the kind depicted in the famous *Roxana* frontispiece.[9]

Houses

Stagehouses, perhaps an invariable part of Cambridge college stages, are recorded at Queens' College in 1522–3, and again in 1545–6. Christ's had stagehouses in 1551–2, while for Trinity College in 1556–7 William Hardwick the carpenter and his man made 'Howses for the players'. Plays produced by both King's College and the university made use of side chapels in King's College Chapel as stagehouses in 1563–4. In 1581–2 the carpenters Lamb and Porter made 'houses at the Comoedie' for Corpus. Houses were constructed, painted, and guarded overnight at Trinity College in 1612–13, while in 1615–16 the same college's plays at Royston were provided with 'a stage with particions on the sides... in the Chamber of presence'. The houses described in detail in the 1640 Queens' College inventory clearly did double duty as stagehouses and as tiring houses. Stagehouses are by rule named in the plural, and on at least three occasions – 1563–4, 1615–16, and 1640 – were clearly facing pairs.

Moore Smith notes most of the houses which I have just cited, and in addition cites references to houses from stage directions and from Cambridge play texts (*CP*, pp. 26–9), including the houses named after the Senior Dean, the Bachelors in Medicine, and the Junior Dean in the *dramatis personae* of *Labyrinthus*, performed at Trinity College, 1602–3.

Other structures were house-like if not in fact houses. A shrine at Queens' College in 1540–1 was constructed by a carpenter, covered with fabric, and painted; a similar structure was built in 1548–9 of lath, pasteboard, and coarse cloth or canvas. In 1554–5 a Queens' College inventory included a shrine of Venus (*phanum veneris*). Earlier, in 1541–2, St John's also inventoried a 'Phanum', stored, along with a 'Thunder Barell', in the college buttery. Again, Moore Smith adds items to this list drawn from play texts, including temples and a sepulchre with functional doors (*CP*, pp. 26–9).

The 'spacious and hie Rome for the quenes maiestie which was by her owne servauntes Richelye hanged with arras and clothe' at Great St Mary's in 1564 must have had the general shape and appearance of a stagehouse, though of course it was single and much more magnificent. The upper and lower platforms at the west end of Great St Mary's implied in Buck's ceremonial of 1665 suggest a structure much like a college stagehouse.

Trap-doors

Although trap-doors are generally assumed as standard theatrical equipment, no stage traps are mentioned in any Cambridge records which have yet come to light. On the other hand, trap-doors were apparently features of the halls of both Queens' and Trinity colleges, and were exploited for stage construction and audience control respectively.

Seating

A throne was provided for Elizabeth in 1564 at the plays in King's College Chapel, and at commencement in Great St Mary's. Prince Charles and the Prince Palatine were provided in 1612–13 with seats covered with matting, doubtless comfortable as well as splendid in appearance, and we may be confident that James I, Charles I, and other royals were provided with something very like thrones whenever they witnessed a Cambridge academic play. Matting, generally used for the seating of dignitaries, is named in the university commencement records of 1599–1600, 1620–1, 1650–1, 1676–7, and 1697–8. Matting similarly distinguished the more comfortable seats for the doctors in the Queens' College stage complex from the bare racks provided for those of lesser dignity.

Placement was of course also determined by rank. The royal visitor always constituted a focal point: the presence of Elizabeth within the chancel of Great St Mary's in 1564 shifted the focal point further to the east than normal; the two princes in 1612–13 seated in a centrally located gallery jutting out beyond other galleries must have created a similar sense of significant presence.

At plays, the stage platform divided the hall (or chapel) into an upper part for those of higher dignity, and a lower part for those of lower dignity; at Trinity College in the seventeenth century a bar or rail further subdivided the lower end of the hall. The *dramatis personae* list of *Labyrinthus* suggests that this organization pre-dated the new stage erected after 1605: note also a rail at Trinity College in 1562–3. At Queens' the small lower platform immediately above the stage was reserved for doctors. Elizabeth sat on the stage itself in 1564; perhaps James did so in 1614–15, for the Vice-Chancellor Samuel Harsnett was ridiculed for being seated on the stage (REED, pp. 872–3), and it is impossible to imagine that he would have sat on the stage while James himself remained in the gallery.

Fabrics

The commencement stage was provided with skirting from 1489 onward, but skirting is virtually unknown for college stage platforms, perhaps because the press of the crowd inevitably made the understage area inaccessible to view in any case. Fabrics were also used for the infill of stage structures, as for the stagehouses at Queens' College in 1522–3, or the shrine at the same college in 1540–1. A payment in 1612–13 at Trinity College for the painting of a 'pastorall clothe' raises the possibility that hangings were used in some form as scenic backdrops (REED, p. 500).

Trash nails

Purchases of 'trash' or 'trasshes' occur frequently throughout the documentation for the commencement stage, first in 1502–3 ('trash nayle'), and subsequently in 1523–4 ('traces'), 1527–8 ('trashes'), 1537–8 ('thrasse'), 1559–60 ('trasshes'), and indeed routinely until at least 1669–70 ('Trashes'). Trinity College purchased 1½d worth of 'trashe nayle' for its theatrical production of 1559–60.

The 'trasshes' in the sense indicated here have hitherto eluded exact understanding and definition. True, it has been understood that these somewhat peculiar nails were used for attaching fabric to wood, but neither the *Oxford English Dictionary* (s.v. trash-nail) nor any other standard historical or dialect dictionary has succeeded in producing an exact definition.[10] The *OED*, moreover, knows of no use of this word before 1556–7: trash nails, however, were purchased as early as 1485 for the coronation ceremonies of Henry VII.[11]

John Bowtell, the Cambridge antiquarian who lived in the late seventeenth and early eighteenth century, gives the following virtually unnoticed explanation:

> Trashes: These are horse-nail-stumps driven into small pieces of s[t]iff leather which form proper heads to them in order to fasten hair-cloths upon the roofs of booths.[12]

A single entry among many occurring in the Cambridge University archives happily confirms Bowtell's definition: where parallel accounts from other years simply use the term 'trashes', the accounts for 1571–2 add the uniquely helpful detail: 'for iiij^or hundret tresshes *with leathers*'. Another confirming entry comes from 1650–1, when the purpose of the devices is specifically named: 'ffor Trashes for the cloath'.

The trash nail was an essentially expendable device consisting of a broad-headed nail driven through a bit of leather to attach fabric to a wood frame. In the case of the commencement stage, the fabric so attached was skirting for stage platforms.

In 1533–4 and 1534–5 trash nails were priced at 50 per penny: keeping inflation in mind, we can safely assert that Trinity College probably purchased no fewer than 50 trash nails in 1559–60 and no more than 75.

Rushes

Both the university commencement stage and college stages were decorated with flora, but the impression was different in each case. Rushes were provided for the commencement stage in 1559–60 (*pro sirpis*), in the same way as for some college stages (REED, pp. 177, 224, 228, 233, 490, 498, 530), but the commencement stage was also consciously decorated, with herbs (from 1540–1), frankincense (in 1561–2), and flowers (from 1574–5).

Painters and painting

Painters were hired only to repair damage to Great St Mary's after commencement, but they were employed directly in the preparation of many college plays. In 1484–5, for disguisings at King's College, painters were given food and accommodation for two weeks and more. In 1540–1 Thomas, a painter, received a reward from Queens' for 'painting the shrine and for the colours which the actors of the comedies used'. In 1557–8 Lame the painter was employed by Trinity College 'on Childermase day at my Lorde our emperoures instance': the 'Emperor' was the college Christmas Lord, who may well have been in charge of plays or shows on this occasion. A painter was similarly paid at Peterhouse in 1572–3. Trinity paid painters in 1612–13 for various work, rather mundanely in painting candlesticks, and more interestingly for a pastoral cloth, houses, and a centaur. One painter evidently was the enigmatically named 'papaly stag'; in 1614–15 Trinity College hired the more identifiable James Manutius 'for paynting the stage', and paid Manutius or another 'for paynting the Rayles on the stage' and 'for paynting the Sayleirs' – apparently canvas hangings. Clare College in the same year gave extravagant recompense to painters who, as we have seen, received something like a fifth of the total cost of the play, and who employed a 'painters frame' in their work. In 1637–8 Queens' gave the large sum of £2–2–0 'to the Painter for the Stage'. In 1662–3 at Trinity College painters invested 33 man-days in the play in the parlour; in 1664–5 they painted a death's head and 'Inscription of the 2 Scenes'; in 1668–9 Griffith painted 'NOLA' upon the stage. In 1669–70 John Wisdom painted oak trees and wrote two names.

Costume storage

Costumes, purchased and maintained in great quantities, were often stored in chests. Christ's College purchased a 'sugar chest' in 1534–5, evidently still in use in 1550–1. The costume chests of St John's College are traceable from 1540–1 to 1565–6, those of Trinity from 1546–7 to 1562–3. Costume chests are also recorded at King's College in 1552–3 and at Queens' in 1561–2. A 'press for the Acting cloaths' was installed in Queens' College in 1639–40, and another is reported at Trinity College in 1663–4 (in the audit chamber) and 1688–9 (in the common chamber).

Lights and lighting

The commencement stage was illuminated by natural light streaming through the clerestory windows of Great St Mary's church in daylight hours of early July. Plays, on the other hand, were regularly provided with artificial light. Many performances were at night.[13] Afternoon performances are recorded in 1594–5, 1622–3, 1627–8, 1628–9, 1631–2 (?), and 1641–2: in 1594–5 the plays were staged, 'the day being turned into nyght'; in 1622–3 the hall was 'darkened'.[14]

Candles, appropriate to indoor but probably not to outdoor performances, were purchased with such regularity from 1498–9 (King's College) to 1670–1 (Trinity College) that their mere mention in the records in any particular year is not of great significance. When their number or the weight of wax is specified, however, more interesting conclusions can be drawn. Candles necessarily imply candlesticks, which again become interesting when their construction or number is specified. The same may be said about other means of lighting, including unspecified lights, lamps, oil-lamps, lanterns, torches, and links, along with pitch: except that torches and links were by nature suitable to both indoor and outdoor performances. Cressets and frales, along with coal and wood, may have been used more for heat than for light, but would have provided both.

Torches are mentioned for Queens' College as early as 1522–3; in 1633–4 their number is specified as 48. Torches and/or links are mentioned in the accounts of St John's College from 1538–9 to 1568–9 (two torches), six and three torches respectively at two distinct entertainments at Queens' College in 1548–9, torches and links and 49 lb of pitch at Trinity College in 1548–9, and torch-links in the accounts of Corpus Christi in 1550–1. Torches are recorded at King's College in 1614–15, and 24 links were used by Queens' College in 1627–8. Torches were used by the night watch at Trinity College in 1598–9. The most vivid picture of the use of torches comes from the visit of Elizabeth in 1564, when the great stage in King's College Chapel was surrounded by her guard serving as torch-holders. That torches and links could also serve for crowd control is abundantly evident from their use as weapons by the Trinity College stagekeepers during the riot of February 1611.

Candles were used in large numbers, as at King's in 1561–2 (a total of 180), Peterhouse in 1571–2 (12 lb), Jesus in 1594–5 (2 lb), and Trinity in 1670–1 (24 lb). In 1540–1 Queens' paid for nails for the making of a candlestick and, in addition, purchased 38 candlesticks of iron and (silver-)plate. St John's kept 26 candlesticks for the plays in a coffer in the buttery. The university acquired 48 candlesticks for the plays of 1563–4, and in the same year Christ's purchased 'xij socketes for the candlesticke for plaies'. The candlesticks purchased by Peterhouse in 1572–3 were perhaps earthenware. In 1545–6 and 1548–9 *lucernae* are mentioned in the accounts of Queens': these may have been oil-lamps, though the fact that in the former year their weight is given as 9 lb, and their cost as 2d per lb, which is about the same as for candlewax, suggests that they might have been candles.

By far the most interesting apparatus for illumination (as the records have survived) was at Trinity College in the middle of the sixteenth century: 'A great Rownd Candlesticke for the stage In the hall' was purchased in 1547–8; an inventory of the same year lists 'A staple to sett candlestyckes in'; in 1559–60 the college purchased 'A knot of Corde to hange vp the great candlesticke'. In 1559–60 the same college acquired 60 candlesticks from the smith; in 1560–1 30 from the locksmith, this time specified as Leonard Tysetone. In this last year the college also purchased 'a greate nosell for the stage lantehorne', apparently a socket to hold a candle. The great candlestick may have held one large candle, but as a single candle, no matter how large, gives off a small amount of light, it seems likely that the great candlestick was in fact a large circular candelabrum, with sockets for candles, suspended by a heavy cord from a staple driven into the roofbeams.

Cressets, or metal baskets holding burning material, are recorded at Trinity College in 1560–1 (along with 'frales') and at Peterhouse in 1571–2 and 1572–3. Coal for heating was purchased at Christ's in 1539–40, 1552–3, and 1553–4; at Pembroke in 1585–6; and at Clare in 1614–15.

Haircloths and nets

Haircloths were commonly used to make roofs and walls for booths, as may be seen from Bowtell's definition of trash nails[15] and from records of the proctor's booth at Sturbridge Fair (Appendix 10). Nine haircloths were provided for a comedy at King's College in 1595–6, at which a riot occurred with much breaking of glass. In 1612–13 Trinity College hired haircloths from Samuel Smith on the occasion of two comedies presented to Prince Charles and the Prince Palatine; in the same year the university paid 'for nayling vp an hair cloth, to Cover the window at the Bachelers Commencement'.[16] In 1668–9 four haircloths were acquired for windows in the comedy room. Other records refer to nets hung over hall windows, as at St John's College in 1578–9 and 1594–5.

The principal function of haircloths in the context of indoor public assemblies may have been to protect the windows from flying stones (however effectively), but the haircloths would have had the additional effect of darkening the interior. A darkened hall seems to have been desirable for plays, but was probably less ideal for the B.A. commencement.

Carpenters and other workmen

Some carpenters worked on both college stages and the commencement stage. John Keyle, hired for Queens' College play in 1522–3, constructed the commencement stage from 1520–1 to 1529–30. A number of carpenters involved in the enlargement of the commencement stage in 1560–1 also built college stages: Father King was probably the man active in building the Queens' College stage in 1548–9, while King's servant assisted John Pople in the construction of the 'heaven' at Queens' College in 1551–2; Richard Bell built a stage for Trinity in 1562–3; and James Silcock built the Peterhouse stage in 1572–3 and 1573–4.

The Dowseys, a numerous family of carpenters including the patriarch John, his sons John, William, and Nicholas, and later a Thomas, variously active on the commencement stage from 1560–1 to 1588–9, were so much part of the construction and continuation of Queens' College stage from 1540–1 to 1553–4 that they may be characterized as the chief carpenters of the project. William was also active on King's College stage in 1561–2 and Trinity College stage in 1570–1. Some member of the Dowsey family worked on the commencement stage of 1610–11 and the Trinity College stage of 1612–13.

William Hardwick, whose name does not occur in university commencement records, assisted William Dowsey in the construction of Queens' College stage in 1546–7. His subsequent work was for Trinity College: he is probably to be identified as the 'Wylliam Carpenter' who made a club for the Christmas Lord in 1554–5; he made houses for the players in 1556–7; he was in charge of setting up the stage and taking it down in 1559–60, 1562–3,[17] and 1570–1.

A carpenter surnamed Peare (Peere, Peear) worked on the King's College stage in 1595–6, and in 1606–7 was required to repair the college gate following a riot because of the misbehaviour of his man, Richard Cole. Peare and his man were prominent among those who worked on the Trinity College comedy stage of 1612–13. The same surname occurs in a commencement document of 1651–2 and among Trinity College payments of 1662–3. The name John Piers occurs in 1662–3, and Peirce in 1663–4.

In exclusively post-Restoration years, a Goodman Newlin is recorded among those who helped erect the commencement stage in 1650–1; he is then listed as Goodman Newling in 1652–3 and 1654–5, as Edward Newlin in 1657–8, and simply as Newling in 1658–9. Edward Newling – perhaps the father – and William Neuling – evidently the son – were hired by Trinity College in 1662–3; a John Newland was hired in 1668–9, a William in 1670–1. The names of Alderman William Newling and John Newling occur among carpenters active in the construction of the commencement stage of 1713–14; William also had charge of storing the stage timbers at the New Inn from 1713–14 until 1719–20. Similarly, Thomas Silk, who fitted the scaffold for the music act in King's College Chapel in 1651–2, assisted with Trinity College stage in 1662–3, 1663–4, and 1670–1; evidently he was the father of the Abraham Silk who was in charge of building the commencement stage from 1695–6 to 1697–8, and who repaired the New Inn where the stage was stored in 1702–3.

Among non-carpenters, John Shuter, who seems to have sold or hired out fabrics in one guise and to have been a small property holder in another, appears in commencement-stage documents from 1662–3 to 1675–6; he also provided fabrics for Trinity College stage in 1662–3, 1668–9, and 1670–1. Similarly, the Simson who occurs in a Trinity College document of 1662–3 may bear some relation to a Rowland Simpson who provided fabric for the commencement stage in 1663–4, and/or to the Samuel Simson who laid up the commencement stage from 1694–5 to 1702–3.

The overlap in supervising carpenters should not be exaggerated: three successive carpenters engaged by the university for its commencement stage – John Wade (1589–90 to 1610–11), Nathaniel Bridges (1617–18 to 1640–1), and John Adams (1649–50 to 1683–4) – are not known to have been active in the construction of college stages.

Time, money, materials

The new commencement construction of 1560–1 required 83 man-days; of 1582–3, 75 man-days; while the total for Trinity College in 1570–1 was 55 man-days. Construction of the commencement stage in 1661–2 consumed 45 man-days; the larger effort of 1662–3, 85 man-days; while the total for Trinity College in 1662–3 was 83 man-days plus general assistance of 16 man-days. The record for the commencement stage was set in 1713–14, with 160 man-days. The record for any college stage was Trinity College in 1612–13, with approximately 191 man-days. Carpenters probably put in a greater effort on the commencement stage than on any given college stage, with the exception of Trinity College stage from c. 1605 to 1642.

In 1553–4 the university paid William Dowsey 20s 6d for the commencement stage, while Queens' College paid him 11s 3d for its stage, a ratio of nearly 2 to 1. In 1570–1 Trinity College paid £1–19–8, the university somewhat less at £1–5–4. In 1661–2 carpenters received a total of £6–7–10 for Trinity College stage along with properties and other expenses; in the same year the carpenters' bill for the commencement stage '& for new Timber then vsed' was £10–11–0. Except for major new construction or repairs, costs for college stages and for the university commencement stage were generally of the same order of magnitude.

Judging from the few cases which allow comparison, materials and labour seem to have contributed in approximately equal amounts to the cost of a stage. For the commencement stage of 1527–8 materials came to £1–0–8½, labour to £1–4–4. For the reconstruction of the commencement stage in 1560–1, Laurence the carpenter and his various assistants received a total of £4–1–2 for their labour, while Hillary (Cluxton) and Prime were paid 8s 11d *ob* for 'labor aboute the frame' for a total of £4–9–11½. The cost of supplying timber, even when one 'tymber tree' was donated (by Mr Hynde), was £5–1–9, while fabric came to £2–5–6, for a total materials cost of £7–7–2. In 1667–8 the cost of materials was £7–8–6, the cost of labour £7–1–4.

In most years, of course, the charges listed are for labour alone, or perhaps for labour and new boards, since the timber purchased and installed in previous years had been kept in storage. Timber was a valuable commodity, made even more valuable by the workmanship invested in the cutting of mortises and tenons: it was worth the storage, and even – in the case of Queens' College in 1638 – worth the cost of a new storage facility.

Stagekeepers

Whereas the colleges recruited stagekeepers principally from among their own members (occasionally recruiting a townsman as in the case of Trinity College in 1610–11), the university recruited stagekeepers from among townsmen exclusively, often under the supervision of the carpenters who built the stages, as in 1594–5 when John Wade and his man kept the stairs at commencement for two days. From 1602–3 to 1611–12 the stagekeepers were under the supervision of Benjamin Prime, a Yeoman Bedell of the university. Seven of the eight or nine names in the full lists of 1650–1 and 1652–3 occur in both lists, and in both cases the master carpenter John Adams seems to have been in charge.

Stagekeepers at commencement seem to have kept the doors and the stairs as well as the stage proper. No mention is made in the records of a costume or livery. College stagekeepers, on the other hand, were dressed in light defensive garb, carried torches as weapons, and sometimes if not always wore visors. It seems that stagekeepers at commencement dealt with a crowd which was inclined to be orderly, whereas stagekeepers at college plays were appointed to control potentially violent rivalries between various colleges; only they might, and often did, provoke the very violence they were meant to forestall.

'Stage keeper' is recorded by the *Oxford English Dictionary* as first occurring in 1586. The term is already fully fledged in Cambridge by 1579–80, however, in the description of the abusive student named Punter, who 'had vncased (as they call it) one of the stagekepers of Caius colledge pluckinge of[f] his visor'; similarly, Punter 'had priuely crept into Benet colledge, ... takinge vpon him the habite of a stage keper'. The thing, if not the exact name, occurs as early as 1548–9 in an inventory from St John's College: 'A blak nightcap to kepe the stage'.

Public and private

The St John's College statutes of 1544–5 and the Queens' College statutes of 1546–7 require public play performances. Queens' College accounts from 1552–3 twice specify public performances; at Corpus Christi College in 1558 a play was performed *publice in aula*; a comedy at Jesus College in 1577–8 was 'pleyed publiklie in the Hawlle'. In Restoration times, the Trinity College accounts of 1668–9 refer to 'publick acting'. According to their title pages, *Parnassus III* (St John's, c. 1601–3) was 'Publiquely Acted'; *Adelphe* (Trinity College, March 1613) was *bis publice acta* ('twice publicly acted'); and *Senile Odium* (Queens' College, 1630–1?) was *publice academicis recitata* (REED, pp. 913, 888–9, 922).

Explicit references to private playing are few. The 1573–4 statutes of Gonville and Caius College authorize private plays only, on account of the crowds they would otherwise bring (*quas priuatas esse volumus, ei quae fuerint, propter turbas*). *Aristippus* (Trinity College, 1625–6?) is described on its title page as having been 'Presented in a Private Show' (REED, pp. 890–1).

Occasionally private and public performances are contrasted. Trinity College statutes of 1559–60 permit public or private playing. In 1622–3 the Queens' College play *Fucus* (*Histriomastix*) was first given in Cambridge 'in a private Hall' (clearly the hall of Queens'), and then was taken to Newmarket, where it was 'acted before the King' 'in so publike a place' (REED, pp. 878–9). The July university commencement was always public until 1730, but private thereafter: until 1730 the university seems to have taken pains to exclude younger students but not the general public; since 1731 admission has been either by membership in the university or by specific invitation.[18]

Attendance at private college performances seems generally to have been restricted to members of the college and explicitly invited guests. Public performances, by contrast, could be attended by members of other colleges at their own volition, and perhaps even by the general public. Royal performances were apparently public in the sense that the makeup of the audience was not under the control of the college or university, and included many non-academics.

John Dee, recalling a play which he supervised apparently in 1547–8 at Trinity College, reports that it was 'seen of the university'. In 1614–15 *Æmelia* was 'acted before the King in Trinity College hall', while *Sicelides* was 'acted before the Vniuersity, in Kinges college' (REED, pp. 538–9). In 1669–70 and 1670–1 Trinity College plays were performed once before noble guests and a second time 'before the

University'. Apparently, performances before the king and performances before the university were both considered public: *Adelphe, bis publice acta*, was acted on one of the two occasions before Prince Charles; similarly, the two occasions of 'publick acting' at Trinity College in 1668–9 included one when Prince Cosimo de Medici was present, and one when he was not.

Large halls were doubtless more appropriate for public performances, smaller venues for private performances. The Queens' College plays of 1548–9 and 1560–1 which were evidently performed in the president's lodge may well have been private, as were perhaps the Trinity College comedies performed in the college parlour in 1611–12. This distinction, however, does not seem to apply to the Trinity College plays of 1662–3 and of 1668–9 up to 1671–2, which seem to have been given in the parlour only, both for visiting nobility, and for the university at large.

The Trinity College comedies of the 1610–11 riot were certainly public: members of St John's College had an implied right to attend, though many were first warned away and then driven away. *Club Law*, performed at Clare College c. 1600, looks at first as if it must have been public, since (if the narrator of the tale is to be trusted) the mayor 'with his Brethren, and their Wives, were invited to behold it, or rather themselves abused therein' (REED, p. 377); but if the invitations were formal, then perhaps it was private.

Tickets are mentioned for the first time in the Trinity College accounts of 1664–5: the implication that these were issued to the public, or at least to members of the university, seems beyond serious doubt.

8

Postscript: Cambridge to London

Friday to Sunday, 16–18 February 1990. One hundred and fifty archaeologists, architects, scholars, and Shakespeare buffs from Britain, Canada, and the United States gather at the University of Georgia, in Athens, to discuss 'New Issues in the Reconstruction of Shakespeare's Theatre'. Of the more strictly historical presentations, Simon Blatherwick delivers an archaeological report compiled by himself and Julian M. C. Bowsher on 'The Structure of the Rose'; C. Walter Hodges speaks on 'Reconstructing the Rose'; John Orrell discusses the Rose itself and implications for playhouses, particularly the Globe, 'Beyond the Rose'; John J. Allen draws comparisons between the London playhouses and 'The Spanish *corrales de comedias*'. In less formal presentations, Sam Wanamaker of the Shakespeare Globe Trust makes an impassioned plea for cooperation among scholars to promote the International Shakespeare Globe Centre whose construction has already begun on the South Bank; Theo Cosby presents his architectural drawings of the developing project, including the reconstructed First Globe.[1]

Scarcely ever has an academic conference exhibited such a retreat from previously held certainties and such a willingness to undertake fresh assessments of evidence. Confessions of error, patience, forbearance, and humility in the face of new data characterize most speeches and most speakers. From excavations in the mud by the Thames has come a breath of fresh air!

Comparative arguments derived from a study of theatres in Spain, or even as close as Cambridge, can scarcely hope to compete with evidence from excavations of the Rose or the Globe in the reconstruction of these or other London playhouses. Nevertheless, Cambridge is not absolutely disconnected from London, and some comparative observations may be in order.

Nomenclature: 'theatre'

A broad issue in English theatre history is whether the London playhouses from 1576 onward represent a further development of established traditions, or reveal a fresh infusion of architectural concepts from Greek and Roman theatres as interpreted by the classical architect Vitruvius and more immediately by his sixteenth-century epigone, Sebastiano Serlio. Orrell has argued that conscious tribute to this classical tradition is signalled by the very name assigned to the Theatre at its inauguration in 1576 (*HS*, pp. 44–5, 48–9, 60, 201–2).

The *Oxford English Dictionary* commits a pardonable error in implying that the word 'theatre' in its modern architectural signification was invented for the English language by James Burbage in 1576.[2] Cambridge scholars writing in Latin as early as 1522–3 (Queens' College accounts) and in English by 1564 (Jesus College accounts) used *theatrum* and 'theatre' comfortably in their modern sense as signifying a place for the performance of plays. The same term in either language could characterize the commencement stage in Great St Mary's in 1564: Matthew Stokys called it a 'theatre', while Nicholas Robinson called it a 'circus ... magnus' and a 'Theatrum magnificum', despite the fact that a structure less classical in its wooden angularity can scarcely be imagined.[3]

Architects or carpenters?

Even as Robinson would certainly have been mistaken if he imagined that the carpenters who built the commencement stage in Great St Mary's had seriously intended an imitation of a Roman theatre or *circus magnus*, so the tendency of foreign sightseers and moralizing preachers to compare London's polygonal playhouses to Roman theatres provides no warrant for imputing classical architectural intentions to joiner James Burbage and grocer John Brayne (*HS*, esp. pp. 45, 59–60, 150–63). In citing the professional identities of the projectors of the Theatre I do not mean to deny their intelligence or possible acquaintance with treatises on architecture; I do mean to suggest that they were men of practical bent, and that to impute to their commercial project architectural ambitions otherwise reserved to projects funded by royalty or nobility is to strain credulity.

The question of funding is important because royals and nobles, while not alone in being able to understand and appreciate classical concepts in architecture, were virtually alone in being able to afford them. The banqueting houses which have been claimed as precedents for London's polygonal playhouses were enormously expensive structures funded by the royal treasury (*HS*, pp. 30–48). The double-cube which characterizes Inigo Jones's Banqueting House in Whitehall is mightily impressive in its proportions, but patently extravagant in its exceedingly high and obviously costly ratio of enclosed volume to usable floor area.

The Theatre, built by Burbage and Brayne, was a commercial enterprise. An obvious strategy would have been to achieve a maximum area to accommodate prospective audiences at minimum construction cost. Just as half the cost of books in Renaissance England was the cost of the paper they were printed on, so perhaps half the cost of the playhouse fabric was the cost of the timber. (The land on which the playhouse was built was another consideration, and cosmetic finish yet another.) A polygonal structure approaching the circular requires less timber than a square structure to enclose the same area; all that is required is carpenters with sufficient experience, and we know from the prior existence of animal baiting rings that London had carpenters with the necessary skills.[4]

Joseph Moxon, writing more than a century after 1576, paid lip-service to architecture, but his practical building plan (figs. 2–3) reveals no hint of classical design, even in the age of Christopher Wren. The observations of a modern architectural historian seem perfectly apt:

> In England, before about 1620, the chief effect of the renaissance of Roman architecture was the addition of Italian ornamental features to buildings of predominantly Gothic design and construction. ... Between 1617 and 1635, however, Inigo Jones (1573–1652) erected several buildings in which the whole doctrine of Renaissance architecture was proclaimed. ... In the time of Inigo Jones, and even later in remote districts of England, old traditions of building lingered on.[5]

In short, 1576 may be nearly half a century too early to look for any substantial embodiment of the doctrine of Renaissance architecture in England. The Theatre and subsequent London playhouses, like the theatrical and commencement stages in Cambridge, were built by carpenters, not by architects. Ornamental features like the columns of the Swan or the satyrs of the Fortune and Globe (*HS*, pp. 46, 59, 153, 275 note 10) were probably sufficient to persuade contemporaries that they were bathing in the light of ancient Greece and Rome.

Architecture and mathematics

Moxon contrasts 'Mechanick Exercises' (blacksmithing, joinery, carpentry) with architecture, which he defines as a 'Mathematical Science'.[6] Cambridge documents testify to a 'Mechanick' rather than a 'Mathematical' approach to theatre design. Stages were adapted to existing structures, while principles of regularity and symmetry could be abandoned as readily as they were honoured.[7]

Nothing could better illustrate the mathematical approach to building design than the application of the *ad quadratum* principle of geometry. A circle is drawn which represents the outer circumference of a polygonal or circular building; within this circle is inscribed a square; within this square is inscribed another circle. Take away the square, and the result is two concentric circles with a particular mathematical relation of radii and enclosed areas. Applied to playhouse design, the inner circle defines the open space or yard, while the ring between the circles defines the space occupied by the galleries and back stage. The corner points of the removed square can be enlisted to inscribe a polygon whose sides are of a given number, ideally a multiple of four. Given certain requirements for the stage platform – for example, that its back corners intersect certain angles or mid-points of certain galleries, or that its fore-edge reach to the centre of the yard – it too can be laid out on geometrical principles.[8]

Much has been claimed for the *ad quadratum* method, most notably that it was well known to sixteenth-century builders, and that it or a variant (for example the *ad triangulum* method) was the *only* means available to medieval and Renaissance carpenters for setting out a building which was either round or regularly polygonal.[9]

The *ad quadratum* principle for the design of London playhouses, if valid, is a gift from the gods, not only for the original designers, but for twentieth-century theatre historians. It means in practice that if virtually any single horizontal dimension of a particular playhouse can be established, then (given an opinon as to the number of sides and the shape and placement of the stage) virtually all other horizontal dimensions can be extrapolated by the turn of a mathematical crank. Add to the *ad quadratum* hypothesis the argument that the Second Globe was built on the foundations of the First, and that the First Globe was a timber-for-timber reconstruction of the Theatre of 1576, then a single horizontal dimension from any one playhouse permits an accurate reconstruction of the groundplans of all three.

The *ad quadratum* hypothesis has at least one very odd consequence: the depth of the gallery (from back wall to front rail) necessarily becomes a function of the outer circumference of the playhouse rather than of the internal logic of gallery depth. Following *ad quadratum* logic, a playhouse 70′ in diameter must necessarily house shallower galleries than a 100′ playhouse, and the galleries of a 101′ playhouse must necessarily be yet deeper by a tiny amount.[10] A more logical assumption is that builders determined gallery depth by the number of rows of seats and the kind of aisles the gallery was planned to contain. Following this assumption there should be no necessary difference in gallery depth between playhouses of 100′ or 101′ diameter, and perhaps none between playhouses of 100′ and 70′ diameter.

Archaeologists discovered that the first Rose was a rough and ready polygon, apparently fourteen-sided and by no means perfect, for its angles and sides were only approximately uniform and the polygon was flattened at one end. The second Rose abandoned all pretence of regularity.[11]

Whereas the Rose excavation placed the *ad quadratum* theory under severe strain, the Globe excavation ruled it out of court as essential to the design of polygonal playhouses in Renaissance London: the galleries were apparently much shallower than they should have been, given the apparent overall diameter of the polygon.[12] If the equation Second Globe = First Globe = Theatre is maintained, then the Theatre of 1576 itself was not constructed using *ad quadratum* geometry.

In his *Mechanick Exercises* Moxon presents considerations which seriously undermine arguments for *ad quadratum* design and mathematical exactitude. In assessing these considerations it should be kept in mind that Moxon, royal map-maker and publisher of technical treatises including a book on architecture, was a master of Euclidean geometry; by contrast, we have no certain knowledge that Burbage, Brayne, and other builders of the early London playhouses commanded any of the mathematical techniques which have been attributed to them.

Moxon instructs his reader to set out a regular polygon of eight sides by drawing a circle 'of any bigness, but the larger the bet[t]er: Devide this Circle into eight equal parts, and from every point draw a line to the Center: Draw also straight lines from every point to its next point'. Moxon then explains that a polygon may be made 'of either five, six, seven, eight sides &c.'; 'for any number of sides you devide the Circle into the same equal parts'.[13]

The division of a circle into seven equal parts, and thus the construction of a regular heptagon, is a classic conundrum in the same league as squaring a circle; both are in fact literally impossible. (Equally impossible is constructing a regular polygon of fourteen sides!) Moxon must certainly have been familiar with the problem, but since he makes nothing of it we may conclude that he meant his reader to divide the circle into equal parts by enlisting the perfectly practical system of trial and error, that is, by successive approximations.[14] Burbage and Brayne would similarly have discovered – had they had the knowledge to make the comparison – that trial and error would give them their polygon at least as quickly and with as much practical accuracy as strictly Euclidean methods.

Moxon also explains that buildings were initially laid out on a sheet of paper – called a 'Draft' – at a reduced scale (for example, $\frac{1}{8}'' = 4''$, or, as we would say, 1:32), rather than with stakes and surveyor's chains directly on the ground. We know that a draft, called a 'platt', accompanied the original Fortune contract, and was a material part of its technical description.[15] Measurements and angles may be taken from the draft, and need not be entirely re-calculated on the ground.

Finally, Moxon explains that structural timbers as initially prepared could be only approximately correct: the master carpenter is instructed not to tighten up individual timber joints and lock them with pegs too early in the process of final assembly of the carcass, lest it be 'out of square'. Instead, the timbers were to be set in place loosely, held together temporarily with 'hook pins', and then gradually closed up (p. 136).

English Renaissance carpenters were perfectly capable of producing buildings with proportions pleasing to the eye, but geometrically based architecture which could supersede building traditions representing centuries of practical experience came to England only with the advent of Inigo Jones – and even then the new rules could be bent in the interest of local contingencies (*HS*, pp. 126–7).

Antecedents

Although animal baiting rings can be detected in London by 1546, a full thirty years earlier than the first polygonal playhouse, recent scholarship has challenged the precedent on the grounds that baiting rings were insubstantial by comparison with playhouses (*HS*, pp. 14–20). An Italian visitor, however, describes the Paris Garden baiting ring in 1562 in much the same terms as would apply to the Theatre. In a publication of 1576 William Lambarde alludes to a 'gate', 'Scaffolde', and 'quiet standing' at Paris Garden, with no implication that these amenities were of recent date. In 1583 the 'old and vnderpropped scaffolds, round about the Bear-garden, commonly called Paris Garden' collapsed (*HS*, pp. 8, 17–20). Surely these 'old ... scaffolds' had stood for more than the seven years since 1576?

Yet another apparent precedent for the design of London playhouses in 1576 and after is the innyard, claims for which have been disputed in recent decades (*HS*, pp. 7–12). Inns (if not innyards) were traditional sites for play performances, and in London at least six are known before 1600: in alphabetical order they are the Bel Sauvage, the Bell, the Boar's Head, the Bull, the Cross-Keys, and the Red Lion. For two of these – the Red Lion of 1567 and the Boar's Head of 1598 – enough documentation survives to make hypothetical reconstruction of the playhouse in the yard possible.[16]

The objection to the innyard hypothesis is based on two main arguments: first, while it cannot be denied that inns were used for performances prior to 1576, it is not certain that plays were performed in their yards rather than indoors; second, the Red Lion was not an inn.

To take these topics in reverse order, if the Red Lion was an inn then the innyard hypothesis is undeniably viable. Since one of the two projectors of the Red Lion playhouse was John Brayne, moreover, if the Red Lion was an inn, then the Theatre was in part built by a man with personal experience of an innyard playhouse. I believe in fact that it is a mere quibble to insist that the Red Lion was not an inn. It is true that the property is described as a 'messuage or farme [= rental] house called and knowen by the name of the Sygne of the Redd Lyon ... sometyme called Starke House', but this designation does not prove that it was not an inn:[17] more important, the innyard hypothesis assumes performances not so much in yards of legally licensed inns as in outdoor yards of any kind, given the definition of a yard as surrounded by buildings or walls and not merely an open field. The objection to the Red Lion as an inn must boil down to the correct observation that its buildings or walls cannot be shown to have contributed materially to the form of the playhouse.

The argument that plays performed at inns are not known to have been performed in the yards of those inns is admitted not to apply after 1576, on the evidence of the Boar's Head of 1598 and a performance in Norwich in 1583. William Lambarde, writing in 1576, applies his references to a 'gate', 'Scaffolde', and 'quiet standing' for 'Beare Bayting, Enterludes, or Fence playe [= fencing]' not only to Paris Garden, but to the Bel Sauvage 'or some other suche common [= public] place'.[18] Conceding that this is the earliest known certain reference to the performance of an interlude in an innyard, it must also be noted that the date of publication by no means precludes a tradition of long standing.

The conclusion that 'before 1576 innyard theatres were rare' (*HS*, p. 10) is probably unwarranted, for inns are known to have been used for plays since the 1540s, and what small evidence there is points to a tradition of outdoor rather than indoor performances. The Bel Sauvage was the site of a fencing competition in 1568, and George Gascoigne wrote of 'Bellsauage fayre' in 1575 without implying novelty – on the contrary, he treats the (presumably outdoor) fair as common knowledge.[19]

Cambridge records are of significance to this debate in two respects: first, they contribute clear evidence – earlier by some months than the first indisputable evidence from London[20] – that inns if not innyards were venues for plays; second, in the Falcon they provide the very pre-1576 details missing from the Red Lion documentation: an enclosed yard, controllable entrances, and multi-storey galleries. Granted the absence of final proof that on 3 January 1557 plays were performed in the yards of the Falcon and the Saracen's Head at Cambridge rather than indoors, it would be wrong to insist positively that they could not have been performed in the yards.

Sources and analogues

Cambridge college stages may also shed light on London playhouses. I have elsewhere urged one important negative argument: Tudor hall screens are not an architectural source for the *frons scenae* of professional playhouses such as the Swan or the Globe.[21] Until recently, proposed reconstructions of the Globe were designed on the assumption that indoor plays had routinely been performed using hall screens as backdrops, hall doors as stage entrances, and minstrels' galleries as balconies. Evidence from Cambridge and elsewhere, however, shows that the usual place for performance was the upper rather than the lower end of the hall.

The disposition of the 'typical' Cambridge college stage does bear some similarities to the disposition of London playhouses. Much of the audience, especially those of lower dignity, occupied both the ground in front of the stage platform and raised galleries surrounding that open space. More prominent members of the audience watched from above the stage – from the upper-end galleries at Cambridge and from the 'Lords' Room' in London playhouses.[22] Still others, including those who insisted on being seen as well as seeing, sat on the stage itself.[23] Entrance for the majority of the audience was through access doors below the stage, while persons of higher dignity used more exclusive entrances above the stage. The disposition of the audience may have meant bi-directional focus for the actors in both cases, and action meant to be seen in silhouette, though presumably the drama was chiefly projected over the front edge of the stage.[24]

Stagehouses provided curtained entrances and exits as well as recessed spaces and raised areas above. Professional London tiring rooms were probably more similar to the behind-stage tiring chamber of Trinity College than to the shallow, dual-purpose tiring houses which flanked the stage at Queens'.

Clearly, a major difference between the open-air playhouses and the Cambridge hall theatres concerns the area at the back of the stage at stage-platform level: in London this was available to actors for their entrances and exits, whereas at Cambridge actors entered almost exclusively from the sides of the stage. Some exceptions seem to have been in force in both communities, however: Queens' College provided an addition which may have enabled entrance by actors from the Doctors' Gallery immediately above the stage; and the Rose excavations suggest that entrances may have been through angled flanking doors defined by sides of the polygon as much as through an entrance at the middle back of the stage.[25]

A final matter concerning London's open-air playhouses is whether their stages and tiring houses were integral with the square or polygonal gallery structures, or independent units. Documents from Cambridge, including the Queens' College inventory, the descriptions of the stage in Trinity College, and the records of the commencement stage in Great St Mary's, all suggest that non-integral construction was the rule. One obvious exception – the lower-end galleries in Queens' College sharing a post – is of little consequence, since like was joined to like. The additions set between the tiring houses and the second face of the great gallery in Queens' College show that originally separate structures could be made to interrelate through subsequently inserted connecting timbers.

Of course, the Cambridge hall theatres are likely to have borne more similarities to London private indoor theatres than to open-air playhouses. Detailed reconstructions of the Blackfriars theatre in particular have been undertaken in spite of the fact that practically no real evidence survives: in effect, the presumed structure of open-air playhouses has been squeezed into the confined rectangular space known to have been contained within the walls of the Blackfriars hall.[26]

Although I do not propose a reconstruction in fine detail, it would be a useful exercise to imagine the timbers of Queens' College stage (fig. 19, p. 31) transferred to Blackfriars hall, but with the tiring house and costume store behind the upper-end wall, on the model of Trinity College hall. This proposed reconstruction has the advantage of offering an explanation of an event of 1636 described in a document discovered by Herbert Berry.

Sir Charles Essex, attending a play at Blackfriars with Lady Essex, had his view blocked by Lord Thurles who was standing on the stage as Sir Charles and Lady Essex sat in a box; Thurles and Essex had words leading to an attempted swordthrust. Berry concludes that the box was level with the stage, either at the side or at the back; he then provides arguments in favour of the latter, conceding that he has no absolute warrant from contemporary evidence.[27] Cambridge documents now constitute a warrant for at least imagining boxes at the back of the stage.

Temporal priority

Much has been claimed for the priority and innovation of London playhouses, and it may be that most innovations did originate in London, but it must also be said that many firsts are capable of being documented elsewhere, particularly in Cambridge. There, as we have seen, the Latin word *theatrum* was applied to scaffolding for a place of assembly by 1488 and for a place of play production by 1522–3, while English 'theatre' was used in its modern sense by 1564. Stagehouses – possibly doubling as tiring houses – can be traced to Queens' College in 1522–3.[28] A fully fledged dramatic stage tradition can be documented in Cambridge from the 1530s, while a well-developed if not finally developed theatrical stage which survived until 1640 can be detected at Queens' College beginning in 1546–9. Permanent (though demountable) stages were built indoors in Cambridge college halls long before any stage was built at

Blackfriars in London. Full costume and prop inventories were plentiful in Cambridge from the 1540s to the 1560s. Evidence of highly elaborated stage action as complex as anything known in London before *A Looking Glass for London* (1590)[29] is available from the King's College accounts of 1551–2. Machinery for making descents was installed at Trinity College probably in 1547–8, and at Queens' - where it was called a *coelum* or 'heaven' – in 1551–2, anticipating recorded London practices by forty years.[30] Costuming considered archaeologically accurate for its time was imagined if not implemented in Cambridge as early as the 1580s.[31]

Looking outside the college halls, Cambridge performances are recorded at the Falcon and Saracen's Head inns on 3 January 1557, some months earlier than in London: the Falcon is a text-book instance of a galleried Tudor inn. Credit for the first demonstrably self-conscious perspective set – probably the earliest certain embodiment of the Renaissance theory of theatre design – goes to Oxford, with Simon Basil and Inigo Jones's Christ Church theatre of 1605 (*HS*, pp. 119–29). Outdoor entertainments and games recorded at the Gog Magog Hills outside Cambridge in the 1570s and again in 1620 anticipated a projected London amphitheatre of 1620 – only the project for London never came to fruition (REED, pp. 1243–4).

I conclude with a negative curiosity: while trap-doors are mentioned in connection with stage records at both Queens' College and Trinity College, in neither case was the trap-door situated in the stage platform or part of the stage action; in both cases the trap-door was instead a feature of the hall.

No doubt some or perhaps all of my claims for the relevance of Cambridge records to the London theatre tradition are rooted in an exaggerated passion for a beloved subject. Nevertheless, I believe I have shown that provincial traditions such as those documented for Cambridge ought to be given lip-service at least, and serious consideration at best, by future historians of the professional theatre in London.

Appendix 1

Matthew Stokys on extraordinary commencement, 1564

Cambridge University Archives, Misc. Coll. 4, known as 'Stokys's Book', contains an account of Queen Elizabeth's visit to Cambridge in August 1564. Extensive citations are printed in John Nichols, *The Progresses and Public Processions of Queen Elizabeth*, 3 vols. (London, 1823), I, pp. 149–89. Citations concerning the stage in King's College Chapel are printed in REED, pp. 232–5. The following passage concerns the commencement stage in Great St Mary's church.

ff. 71v–72v

Agaynst one of the clocke was in St marie churche provided for disputacions a great and ample stage / from the hard wall of the belferye hard vnto the chauncell / In thest ende was made a spacious and hie Rome for the quenes maiestie which was by her owne servaunts Richelye hanged with arras and clothe of state and all other necessaries with a quoyshen to leane vpon All the disputacions were dryuen to that ende of the stage and by cause boothe the sydys were litle enough for the Lordes / and Ladies / new stages were divysed for the doctors vpon bothe the sydes fyxd to the syde postes and being some space above thoes that sat vpon the fourmes / & yet loer then the rayles of the hier stages. The dyvines sat vpon the sowthe syde / and with theim nexte to the quenes seete Mr Secretorie as Chauncelor havyng before hym | the vsuall clothe and a longe velvet quoishen / vpon thother syde sat the Lawyers / and phisicions nexte the quenes stage with whom sat Mr Doctor Haddon master of the requestes in his senioritie In the mydle almost stoode the responsall seate lookyng estward / Above that estward sat the bachiler of divinitie on bothe sydis with the non Regents benethe the master Regents and last of all westward stode the bachelors of arte./

...

... The proctors staull was set not far from the responsall vnder the doctors of divinitie / and vnder theim sat the proctors# of thuniuersitie of Oxford ['#Mr Marbacke, Mr Watkyns procuratori oxoniensis']...|...When all thynge was redye / and after the ryngyng of the vniuersitie bell The Quenes maiestie cam to the sayed place with Regall

pompe / at whoes entryng all the graduat*es* kneled / and cried modestlye / Viuat Regina
& she thanked theim / And after by mr Secretorie vnderstode thorder difference / and
placyng of every parson w*i*thin th*a*t theatre. ...

f. 73 (Monday 7 August)

... when the respondent had endyd his oration ffow*er* + m*aste*rs of arte standyng neere
vnto her stage and lokyng westward replied / w*i*th whom her ma*i*estie was so muche
pleasyd th*a*t she by divers gestures declared the same / and soundrie tymes stayed the
proctors for takyng theim vp/ ...

+ Mr Carterwright Tri*nitatis*   Mr Preston Regal*is*
  Mr Chatterton Xpi [= Christ's] Mr Clarke

f. 73v

... the doctors in their order disputed being .iij. but by cause their voices weare smalle
and not audible her ma*i*estie first sayed vnto theim loquimini altius / and when that
would not helpe she lefte her seate / and cam to the stage over their headd*es* but by cause
their voices were loe / and th*a*t she should not well heare theim her grace made not
muche of th*a*t disputac*i*on ...

Appendix 2

Nicholas Robinson on extraordinary commencement, 1564

Nicholas Robinson's Book, Folger Library, MS V.a.176 (described in REED, p. 796; copy in Baker MS 10 [British Library, MS Harley 7037], pp. 181–230), contains an account of Queen Elizabeth's visit to Cambridge in August 1564. Robinson's description of the stage in King's College Chapel is printed in REED, pp. 235–8. The following passage concerns the commencement stage in Great St Mary's church (translation by Abigail Young).

ff. [34v–35]

...Est iuxta forum ad Occidentem, Ecclesia Diuæ Mariæ dicata in qua Commitia maxima, tanquam in campo quodam martio ad designandos summos honores peraguntur, celebritates [= celebrationes?] absoluuntur frequentiores, reliquique omnes conuentus solennes fiunt, siue disputandum siue concionandum siue quid de Republica cum oppidanis sit aliquando agendum. Per totum huius corpus (quod nescio qua simultudine Nauis dicitur) extruitur siue circus quidam magnus siue Theatrum magnificum distinctum duabus tribusue ordinum differentijs. Ex eo capite quod Orientem spectat (vbi Regia sedes (quam honore quodam prosequimur) ponebatur) aulæis splendidissimis decorato et stragulis quam nitidis strato (regius enim erat omnis apparatus) ad octoque fere pedium altitudinem elevato, disputationis ac certaminis universum | cursum prospectabat Regina. In dextera quæ duobus gradibus dimittebatur stant consiliarij Regij: sinistram vero occupant Fœminæ nobilitate insignes. Reliquus locus, viros claros et ex comitatu Regio recepit. Secundam seriem utrinque ornabant Doctores Theologæ, Iuris, medicinæ coruscante amictu: inter eos duo Episcopi, Eliensis et Roffensis imam partem repleuerunt, alii ordines, quasi pedarij senatores, sed quæque turma seiunctim, viz Theologiæ Baccalaurei ac non Regentes primum sericis caputijs induti: tum Regentes Magistri, suis pelliceis albescentibus decorati: tandem Iuris Artium baccalaurei suis agminis bracceis conspicui. Hos omnes quaquam versum muniunt Satellites Regij ne extraneus quisquam vel oppidanus violato ordine temere ac insolenter irrueret. seque in Academiæ umbra obtegeret. atque etiam vt clementissima princeps vno veluti aspectu, ipsum Academiæ statum perlustraret.

Next to the marketplace on the west side is a church dedicated to St Mary in which very large meetings are held for elections to the highest offices, as if in some Campus Martius, fairly heavy crowds and other solemn gatherings take place [= celebrations are very frequently conducted?], whether for disputations, for sermons, or for matters concerning the state which must sometimes be dealt with together with the townspeople. Throughout the body of this church (which is called a nave because of some resemblance to a ship) is built a great circus or a magnificent theatre, divided by two or three differences in rank. From its head (decorated with very splendid hangings, strewn with such shining coverings – for all the gear was royal – and raised up to a height of nearly eight feet) which faces east [= at the east end], where the royal seat to which we do honour is placed, the queen looked out at the whole course of the disputation and debate. On the right side, which was let down two steps, the royal councillors stand, women of noble rank occupy the left side, and the remaining space holds celebrated men and those of the royal household. Doctors of theology, law, and medicine on either side decorate the second row with their gleaming robes; among them are two bishops, Ely and Rochester. The other orders, like lesser senators, fill the lowest part, but each group in turn, that is, first the bachelors of theology and the non-regent masters, wearing silken hoods, then the regent masters, adorned with their shining-white fur mantles, finally the bachelors of law and of arts, standing out in the two lines of their host [= in two rows]. The queen's guard surrounded them on every side lest any stranger or townsman burst in rashly or insolently, breaking the ranks, and conceal himself in the shadow of the university and also so that the most gracious queen with as it were a single glance might survey the very state of the university.

Appendix 3

Queens' College stage inventory, 1640

Queens' College Archives, MS 75, pp. 378–81. This inventory has been printed twice: in Smith, 'Academic', pp. 199–204; and in REED, pp. 688–93. To avoid printing yet another version, with a third set of page and line numbers, the REED transcription is reproduced here, by permission. The old-style date 18 February 1639 refers to 18 February 1640 new-style.

---

688   CAMBRIDGE 1639–40

Queens' College Inventory   QUA: Book 75   20
p 378*

The Colledge
stage.   The Colledge stage.   February 18. 1639.

February 18
1639   The Scaffold at the vpper end of the hall. aboue the stage markd all   25
              with red paint.
                              Vpright studs in the first face of the scaffold 4.
              The first markd on the East side with ♀ the second ₁ᴬ the third ₁ᴮ
              the fourth + these 3 last being all markd on their South side.
              Girts in those studs 3 first from ♀ to goe into ₁ᴬ at this ≈: the   30
West   second from ₁ᴬ to joyne with ₁ᴮ in this marke ☉ . the third fastend
ᴮEast   to   ₁ᴮ at this Mark ☰ is to goe into the East Wall.
              Two Railes ouer these. first 8 . second —ᵒ .

                              The second face of the scaffold.   35
                              5. Vpright studs.

West   First ♄ second ₂ᴬ Third ♄ Fourth ₂ᴮ fifth ♄ East.
              3 Girts.   Another stud with a staple fastened in
                                  it standing against ♄ Marked ♃   40

131

The first Girt from the West wall of the Hall, into the post $^A_2$ at this
mark —

West   The 2^d from $^A_2$ at this Mark = into the post $^B_2$ at this Mark Y

The 3^d from the post $^B_2$ at this Mark 8 into the East wall of the
hall ./.

    3. Vpper Railes.

West   The West Raile to goe into his post at this mark in Each ..

The next from this mark in each :: to this mark in his other end &
post ::

The 3^d from this mark in his end & post :: to the East wall.

    Vpon the Girts — = Y & 8 stand these 6 studs.

First K then $^A_2$ (comming from the ground) then L then $^B_2$

West   (comming from the ground) then M. then N.

A Board raile markd P some yard aboue the girts from K to $^A_2$.

Another from $^A_2$ to $^B_2$ markd Q. Another from $^B_2$ to M markd Y

Another some 16 inches lower from M to N markd S.

    3 Girts for the Vpper scaffold.

The first markd C : the second ◖ : the third Ɛ

West   3 Railes for the vpper scaffold.

The first F. the second G. the third H.

          The back of the scaffold.

Two vpright posts from the ground to the first gallery ye first markd

West $^A_3$ ye 2^d $^B_3$

Two ground peeces the first markd ≈ whereon stands $^A_3$ ye 2. ≋
whereon stands $^B_3$

Two braces the first markd Sp w belonging to $^A_3$ ye 2^d markd
Sp & belonging to $^B_3$

West   A Crosse girt ouer the 2 vpright posts from wall to wall marked W

Two vpright posts vpon that girt W. the first markd 11 the
second 12.

A Crosse girt ouer these 2 posts from wall to wall and marked 10.

Short Ieece in the first gallery marked in the extreme
ends 1.2.3.4.5.6.7.8.9.10.11.12.13.14.

West   Ieece in the 2^d gallery markd in ye extreme
ends 1.2.3.4.5.6.7.8.9.10.11.12.13.14.15.16.17.18.19. beside 2
binding-Ieece going into $^A_2$ the other into $^B_2$.

West   Ieece in the vpper gallery markd in ye side
ends 1.2.3.4.5.6.7.8.9.10.11.12.13.14.15.16.17.

    (line numbers in margin: 5, 10, 15, 20, 25, 30, 35, 40)

'Ŷ' in line 15 represents 'R'

690   CAMBRIDGE 1639–40

p 379*

West

Racks in this vpper Gallery markd in the Top ends
1.2.3.4.5.6.7.
Racks in the next Gallery below markd on the sides   5
1.2.3.4.5.6.7.8
      In the first gallery onely Matted formes.

The East side of the hall double scaffolded and the gallery before ye
Screene all markd with black paint.   10
The fore vpright post next the stage   A ⎱ both going up
The fore upright post next the ˏ'trap' dore   B ⎰ to the Top
A fore mid post betweene these two going up onely to the first girt H
         Vpright posts at the back of theis.
The first C at the back of A   15
The second K at the back of H
The third D at the back of B
An Vpright post to the girt standing about the middle of the screene
markd g
A Girt ouer this post markd 10.0.17 a back girt to it L.   20
Another vpright post standing next the west scaffold of the hall
markd M
A Spurre standing before the post g markd Sp = A little stud upon
yis spurre ˏmarkd *(blank)*ˏ
A back girt on the South side before the screene marked F.   25
A fore girt of the East gallery next the stage from A to B markd I.
Another girt from it to the end against the staires of the trap dore which
doth serue also for a Ieece markd on the side N.
Ieece for the first gallery markd from the stage to the screene in the ends
      1. 2. 3. 4. 5. 6. 7. 8. 9.   30
Ieece along before the screene markd soe 10. 11. 12. 13. 14. 15. 16. 17
Two Railes of board from A to B one 2 foote aboue the girt the other
2 foote aboue the former the first markd • the second ⁚
Two board Railes one at the end of the other two foote aboue ye girt
10.0.17 afore the screene markd = =   35
A stud Raile ouer them Crosse the hall, reaching from black B to
white B.
A slope board next the stage like a brace ◇
An vpright fore stud in the first gallery standing ouer H & markd Q
An vpright fore stud in that gallery next the screene X .   40
A back vpright stud ouer C marked Δ

A back upright stud ouer K marked Z
A back upright stud ouer D marked Y
Racks in this gallery markd from the stage 6. 7. 8. 9. 10.
A board nailed in the window next the stage for the ends of the rackes
to rest on marked ∘ Another for the same purpose next ye screene $\overset{\circ}{\circ}$ 5

In the upper Gallery

Two foregirts 18 R next the stage S next the screene
Two board railes aboue them V next the stage W next the screene.   10
The vppermost Raile aboue them T.

p 380

The Colledge   A Back girt answerable to R and S marked ✳   15
Stage   The Ieece in the vpper gallery markd in the ends from the stage
(Y next the stage first on the side) 18.19.20 21.22.23.24 25.26 27.
Racks in this gallery markd from the stage 1.2.3.4.5.
        The East Tyring house ouer the Bibleclarks table,
        Markd with black paint & this letter T.   20
Foure maine posts T_d and T_a back posts T_c and T_b foreposts.
North T_d and T_c North T_a and T_b South.
Betweene T_c and T_b foure fore studs T_f. T_g. T_h. T_j.
Betweene T_d and T_a one middle back stud T_e.
The fore girt T_m the back girt T_k.   25
The north end girt T_n. the south end girt T_l.

The second story.

Seauen Ieece from North to South markd T_1 T_2 T_3 T_4 T_5 T_6 T_7 30
North   Two middle fore studs T_p T_o.
Two middle back studs T_q. T_r.
One fore girt T_w. two back girts T_s. T_t.
North end girt T_x. South end girt T_u.

                                                  35

The 3^d story.

Seauen Ieece markd from North to South T_8 T_9 T_{10} T_{11} T_{12} T_{13} T_{14}
North   Two fore studs T_+ & T_Δ
Two Railes T_Y $T_\odot$ 40

692   CAMBRIDGE 1639–40

Additions to the North end of the Tyring house

Vpon the top of the [great] post in the great gallery markd with the
red letter N a backe girt ♎ .
A fore girt answering it ♍   5
Some eighteene Inches aboue this foregirt the board raile ♌
Some eighteene Inches aboue this last raile A stud raile ♋ .
Aboue this a fore girt going upon the top of the red M marked ♊
A back girt answering it markd ♀ .
The west Gallery haue all the same studs posts Girts Railes Ieece and   10
Racks with the 2 East Galleryes which haue all the same Marks saue
onely that the East are markd with black.
But the West with a whitish Russet paint.
The West Tyring house likewise hath euery thing answerable to the
East & is Marked with a light Russett paint in euery parcell as the East   15
is with black.

p 381

    ### Additions to the North end of the West Tyring house   20
          markd with light Russett.
The lowest stud next the Tyring house Y
The next stud from the Tyring house longer 8
A little short Ieece ouer Y markd in the extreme end ♊
A Parallell Ieece to it going at one end in 8 markd in the side ♋ .   25
A Raile from the Tyring house to 8 markd ♌
A Girt ouer it from the Tyring house to red K markd ♄
Three Ieece vpon this girt markd from the Tyring house a_1 a_2 and the
third at one end going into the red K is markd on the side ♍
A Board Raile ouer this girt ☉   30
Another Raile aboue it ♃
A Post Comming from the ground close by the stage side and making
with the corner of the Tyring house a dore way from of the stage to
the Doctors Gallery markd   ✡
Another against it grounded vpon that little fore gallery ♑   35
A slope board raile betweene them ♑
Another stud Raile ouer it ⊢→

The stage Frame.

                                                                      40
Fiue studs standing upon the ground on the North end of the stage

markd (from West to East for their order) where they are to bee
joynted to the North end Raising with black paint S1 S2 S3 S4 S5.
Fiue more vnder the middle of the stage so markd in order from west
to East. S6.S7.S8 S9 S10.

Fiue more such on the South side of the stage so markd for order from   5
West to East. S11.S12.S13.S14 S15. All these studs being markd on
their Northerne faces.

Three Raisings or Ieece peeced in their middles lying from west to East
ouer euery Row of studs where the studs be mortised in markd on their
North sides the first S1.S2.S3.S4 S5. The second S6.S7.S8 S9.S10.   10
The third S11 S12 S13 S14 S15.

Fourteene Ieece lying Crosse these former from North to South being
markd in their Extreme North ends in order from West to East with
theis markes S. S: S∵ S:: S∴: S∷ Sℏ S♃ S♂ S⊙ S+ S♀ S☿
S♄   15

Appendix 4

Comments on Queens' College stage inventory, 1640

A reconstruction of the 1640 Queens' College stage is attempted pp. 16–33, from the stage inventory printed in Appendix 3. The following points, many of which are not discussed in my text, remain problematic:

688/27–9: posts A and B presumably occupied the same relative place in each of the three faces. I assume that the three girts spanning the hall in the second face were approximately equal in length, but I have adjusted the posts so that they would receive the binding jeece between the second face and the third.

688/30: the girt extending west from A1 was evidently shortened to make way for the west addition (see 692/36). I have had to make the girt almost unreasonably short to accommodate the putative slope board leading from the stage to the first gallery.

688/31–3: the girt and the putative rail from B1 into the east wall risk interfering with the east addition.

688/39–40: I have not discovered a satisfactory role for the 'stud with a staple fastened in it'.

689/6–10: I assume that these three upper rails, identified by end markings, are the same as the '3 Railes for the vpper scaffold' marked F, G, and H (689/19–20).

689/12–13: Since rail Q from A2 to B2 is of one piece, I have stopped L at Q, though L may well have risen full height to support the girt above (Q passing through or around). K, M, and N too may have stopped before encountering the girts above (see 692/3–8).

689/15: on rail Q, see 698/12–13 above.

689/19–20: see 689/6–10 above.

689/33–4: I have made the fore gallery shallow: the jeece are characterized here as 'Short'; this 'Doctors Gallery' (692/34) is also called 'that little fore gallery' (692/35); and the three jeece in the western addition (assuming that they are spaced 16″ on centre) seem to define the distance from the tiring house to the second face as 42″ (see p. 30).

The principal posts in the first and second faces may have been connected by binding jeece, as were the second and third faces (689/37–8).

The disposition of the 14 jeece depends in part on the length of the girt extending west from A1 (see 688/30). I have followed Moxon (fig. 2) in his tendency (it is not his rule) to pair jeece on either side of a common girt.

I have set the first gallery at a height of 7′ on the assumption that it was the same height as the lower back gallery (see next comment).

689/36–8: I have set the height of this lower back platform at 7′ on the assumption that the third face backed directly against the upper-end wall and that the door at the north-west corner of the hall was usable. Even at 7′ headroom beneath may have been only 6′ because of the raised dais.

689/39–40: the upper platform had four fewer jeece than the lower back platform. The 'missing' jeece (two at either end?) may have enabled access by ladder.

690/3–4: racks at this level may have provided raised seating or standing to improve sight-lines for those at the rear.

690/5–6: racks at this level may have provided raised seating or standing: note that the fore platform was reserved for doctors, who might have obstructed the view but for the racks. Assuming that this gallery spanned the hall from wall to wall (approximately 27′), the eight racks averaged something over 3′ each in width.

690/20: the markings on this girt match the numbers on the jeece (690/29–30). The significance of the letter O (more doubtfully the number zero) between the numbers 10 and 17 is unclear: could it have been for a mid-platform binding jeece? (Note alphabetic sequence L-M-N-*x*.) Presumably the platform also had side girts (including N?: see 690/27–8).

690/23–4: the spur clearly carried the stud. Since stability could have been provided to the upper post merely by lashing a stud against both lower and upper post, perhaps the spur projected forward to provide triangulating support.

690/25: girt F apparently belonged to the side rather than the screens gallery (see p. 22).

690/27–8: since the disposition of the stair and trap-door cannot be known, the exact disposition of N cannot be known.

690/29–30: the nine jeece in the lower side-gallery platform sort oddly with the ten jeece in the upper platform. I have made the side platforms fairly deep on the assumption that racks indicate raised standing or seating in depth; also, side galleries projecting into the hall would accommodate the slope boards which served as braces. Deep galleries must, however, have interfered with sight-lines from the back corners.

690/38: this slope board/brace may have led from the hall floor at the north end of the side gallery (or galleries) up to the stage. Whether it provided access to the stage is unclear. Since reference is made at 692/36 to a slope rail, it seems possible that the slope board actually belongs at that location.

691/9: the first fore girt was probably designated as R rather than R18: the number 18 probably marked the position of the first jeece (see 691/15, 17).

691/17: Y must in fact have been a side girt rather than a jeece.

691/23: four fore studs seem extravagant, particularly when the back girt was supported by only a single stud; nevertheless, the description seems too clear for challenge.

691/33: how two back girts could have been disposed is unclear: I have placed one beneath the other with no claim to understand their respective roles.

691/39–40: I have designed the top rail as a stud rail to provide stiffening for the two top fore studs. Conceivably, however, the two rails were at the same level, each from a principal post to the adjoining stud, leaving an opening between.

692/3–4: the back girt described at 692/9 seems to be in exactly the same position as this girt, which I assume is the *lower* back girt going into N. I assume that all four girts and the two rails attach at their southern ends to the north principal posts of the east tiring house.

692/5: I assume that this fore girt attaches at one end to stud M (see next note).

692/8–9: I have not taken literally the direction that the girt should go 'upon the top of the red M' since this would seem to prevent M from reaching the girt above as would apparently be required for stability.

692/10–12: I assume (without full evidence) that the west side gallery had two platforms exactly answering 'the 2 East Galleryes'.

692/22: the height and purpose of this stud and associated jeece (692/24) are unclear. It is also unclear how this apparently free-standing stud was stabilized.

692/24–5: these two jeece are carried at one end by their associated studs; perhaps the other end of each was carried by the west wall. I assume (without real evidence) that the jeece carried a platform at the level of the tiring house floor.

692/28–9: see preceding note.

692/32–5: presumably this post stood in the same plane as the north principal posts of the tiring house. I have added a timber lintel with 7′ headroom.

692/36: I have placed this post directly behind the door post described in 692/32–5, although its exact placement is quite uncertain.

692/37: from this 'slope board raile' I infer a slope board leading *upward* from the stage to the fore gallery. See 689/33–4 for an argument that the fore gallery was higher and not lower than the stage platform.

693/12–15: the height of the stage platform is not given. I have assumed 5′ on the model of the 1564 stage in King's College Chapel.

Appendix 5

Security plans for royal visit, March 1615

Cambridge University Archives, U.Ac.1(3), 1617–18, under 'not found', tab 4 (misbound), contains the following list of assignments for guarding doors in Great St Mary's church (for commencement) and Trinity College hall ('at the Commodys'):

Saint Marys

At the north doore	of the garde – 6
	Mr Iohnson
	Mr Kydman
At the doore openinge into the body of the church	of the garde – 2
	Mr Norton
	Mr Ashton
	Mr Ienkes
At the head of the kings stayers	gentelmen vshers
For the Doctors seate	one of the garde
	Mr Tabor Registrary
At the entrance into the seate behynde the Doctors beinge a place for Knightes &c	one of the garde
	Mr Bembridge senior
At the stayers head agaynst the north doore	one of the garde
	[Mr Ienkes]
	Mr Warren
At the doore leadinge vpp the Deanes seates &c	one of the garde
	Mr Barcock
	Mr Clarke
At the head of the stayers for the Ladyes	one of the garde
	Mr Britton
	Mr Damforde
At the midle south stayers	one of the garde
	Mr Dereham Iunior

At the Belfry stayers   Mr Gibbon
                                                   one of the garde

                    At the Com[y]modys
For the Hall dore   of the garde – 6
                                                   Mr Tidswell
                                                   Mr Bambridg Iunior

For the doore entringe   Mr Pocklington
the Hall at the screene   Mr Clarke

For the doctors seates   Mr Tabor

For the Trapp doore   Mr Cecill
                                                   Mr Acroyd
                                                   Mr Goche

Appendix 6

Records of Trinity College drama, 1661–96

Records of Trinity College drama from 1661–2 to 1670–1 have been printed in Smith, 'Academic', pp. 174–82. While generally satisfactory, Smith's transcriptions are problematic in several respects.

Smith overlooked a set of entries for 1662–3 under the title, 'Worke about the Stage in the Parlour'; he left certain apparently insignificant details out of several records, faithfully recording the omissions with ellipses; he overlooked references to the Acting Room in 1671–2, a year in which a comedy was performed, and in 1695–6, when no play was performed.

Smith cited Junior Bursars' accounts bound into volumes, but overlooked a duplicate series of unbound notebooks. For the most part identical except for accidents of spelling and punctuation, the two series occasionally differ in significant ways, for example, the bound series refers to a 'Com:' chamber in 1669–70, which Smith expanded to 'Comedie' chamber whereas the duplicate entry reads 'Common' chamber (see pp. 52–4, 148–9).

Information in the headnotes concerning royal visits is derived from Cooper, and from Marion Colthorpe, *Royal Cambridge: Royal Visitors to Cambridge Queen Elizabeth I – Queen Elizabeth II* (Cambridge: Cambridge City Council, 1977). The following transcription generally follows rules set forth in REED, pp. 813–16, except that 'th' is substituted for 'y' or thorn.

Documents

I. Junior Bursars' Books 1648–93

In the following analysis, references are to the *concluding* year of an academic year: thus 1661–3 refers to the academic years from 1660–1 to 1662–3. Transcriptions from the Junior Bursars' Books which follow are from (A) unless otherwise noted.

Junior Bursars' Books from 1648 to 1693 survive in different formats; not cited here are books from 1638 to 1660 bound into a single volume (see REED, p. 777).

(A) Loose notebooks 1648–93 in two boxes
(B) Single volume dated on spine 1661–66, in fact 1661–3
(C) Notebooks 1664–93 bound into one volume

1648	A			1675	A	C
.				1676	A	C
1650	A			1677	A	C
.				1678	A	C
1658	A			1679	A	C
.				1680	A	C
1661		B		1681		C
1662		B		1682	A	C
1663		B		1683	A	C
1664	A*	C		1684	A	C
1665		C (2 copies)		1685	A	C
1666	A	C		1686	A	C
1667	A	C		1687	A	C
1668	A	C		1688		C (2 copies)
1669	A	C		1689	A	C
1670	A	C		1690		C
1671	A	C		1691	A	C
1672	A	C		1692	A	C
1673	A	C		1693	A	C
1674	A	C				

*One notebook with full year, one with first quarter only.

II. Junior Bursars' Accounts 1694–1726 (bound in one volume).
III. Senior Bursars' Audit Books.
IV. Stewards' Books 1649–1689.
V. Conclusion Book 2 (second in a series).

The records

1661–2

The college produced two comedies this year, evidently *The Silent Woman* by Ben Jonson, and the Latin *Adelphe* by Samuel Brook (Smith, *CP*, p. 15). The site of the production is unknown; if the hall, then this may have been the last performance in that location (see 1662–3). The sum of £8–0–0 authorized by the Conclusion Book is reflected in the final two entries cited from the Senior Bursar's Audit Book, for £6–7–10 and £1–12–2 respectively.

Conclusion Book 2, p. 62 (11 April)

Agreed then also by the Vicemaster & Seniors that eight pounds be issued out by the Senior Bursar toward the charges of a stage, & properties, & a Supper & for encouragement of the Actors of a Comœdy out of the Commencement moneys.

(*signed*) James Duport

Senior Bursar's Audit Book, f. 53v (Commencement expenses)

To the Bachelors Ashwednesday Feast & Priorum	16	5	0
Paid for the charge of a stage of the propertyes & other expences	6	7	10
To the Actors for a supper	1	12	2

f. 56v (Extraordinaries)

Paid for 10^{li} of wax Candles for the use of two Commodyes	0	16	8

Junior Bursar's Accounts (*B*), f. 39v (Extraordinaries; 3rd Quarter)

To Mr Hill senior for the expences of the Stage & other Charges for the Latine Comedie	20	0	0

1662–3

Plays this year were performed for James, Duke of Monmouth, who visited on 16 March 1663 (Cooper, III, p. 509). Records strongly suggest that the play was staged in the parlor, the apparent site for plays for the next decade.

Junior Bursar's Accounts (*B*), f. 45v (Smith for the College, 2nd Quarter)

[1]Worke about the Stage in the Parlour

For 11 paire of ioynts, 3 pounds of wire, for six hookes to hang up candles, for a bolt & a key for the Barre befor the Masters Porch as by Bill appears	0	19	1

f. 46 (Carpenters, Joyners etc.; 2nd Quarter)

To Silke for the Stage

(13 January)

For 26 slitt deales 1 s 8 d a piece, 145 wholl deales 14 d the foote	11	15	10
32 Standers 12 foote & $\frac{1}{2}$ long att 3 d the foote, 520 of quarters for bearers for the Scaffold att 1 d $\frac{1}{2}$ the foote	8	17	6
For 2 Posts & a raile att the Lodge doore, & for nailes	3	6	10
For turning ballasters, & paid to a carter, & for bread & beare	0	14	2
31 foote of railes about the Stage	0	5	7

[2]William Newling, Iohn Curde, Clifton Manners Silke for 8 dayes worke. Watts 6 dayes Peere 5 dayes Woodruf 6 dayes E. Neuling ⌜2 dayes $\frac{1}{2}$ day⌝

att 20 d per diem	4	19	2

(March)

21 deales used about the Stage when the Duke of Monmouth was here att 14 d the peece, 44 foot of peeces of timber, for bearers for the stage att 1 d $\frac{1}{2}$ the foote	1	10	0

For 28 ballasters turning at 2d a peece	0	4	8

Neuland [3]& Silke 4 dayes & ½ about the stage, Clifton 3 days Newland 2
days & $\frac{13}{2}$ taking downe & laying up the Scaffold & seates. [3]Silke 2 days

Cliffon 2 days, Curd 2 & ½ Peere 2 days	1	14	8[3]
[2]For nailes used about the stage	0	7	4

f. 53 (Extraordinaries; 2nd Quarter) (8 January)

To Iohn Piers 5 days Simson 6 days Phillips 5 days Jones 4 days Wisdome
& Knuckles 5 days Woodruffe 3 days for helping att the Stage, for painting,
haire cloths, Vizards, candles, & to the Porter & Brewers for keeping the

Gates as by Bill	4	9	5

(24 January)

Paid by the Masters Order to Mr Hill senior for the charges of two

Comedies [3]as by Bill of particulars[3]	29	4	10
[2]To Styles for Billetts & portage for the Dukes chamber[4]	0	19	0

(16 March)

Paid to Dominus Dove for charges of the Comedie before the Duke of

Monmouth as by Bill of particulars	8	18	6

To Mr Shuter for the use of his hangings, for a long cushion and for

curtaines, & for worke att the Comedie before the Duke	1	19	6

Paide then to Iohn Piers [3]for 4 dayes worke, Simpson 2 dayes Phillips 2
dayes ½ Iones 2 dayes Manners 1 day Andrews 1 day Gam ½ day Hooper 3
dayes[3] for helping the Carpenters. keeping the doores. paving the porch. for
wax & tallowe candles att the Comedie, for Lincks & Torches, hairecloth.

nailes and painting the Railes [3]as by Bill[3]	3	9	1

[1] Heading and entry overlooked by Smith.
[2] Entry overlooked by Smith.
[3] Text between pairs of this figure elided by Smith.
[4] Chamber: expansion uncertain.

Steward's Books (Extraordinaries)

To Mr Arrowsmith his Bill of expences att the Comedy before the Duke of

Monmouth	1	8	0

1663–4

Junior Bursar's Accounts (Expenses extraordinary, 2nd Quarter)

For the Comedie to Mr Craven upon his bils	11	17	7
To Mr Arrowsmith upon his bill for shapes, vizards &c	6	14	0
To Mistris Parker for jewels lost & broken & dressing the Actors	1	10	0
To Sir Dove 3s 7d & for candles, wax, & tallow 1[li] 12s 1d	1	15	8
To Silke & Peirce for worke & attendance as by bill	3	17	0
For a presse for the comedie cloaths, & carriage to the Audit Chamber	1	1	0
[1]Iron worke & a locke to the presse barre	0	3	6

[1] Entry overlooked by Smith.

Steward's Books (Extraordinaries)
[1]To him [= the Master's butler] for washing Linnen vsed at the
Declaration, Q*uar*ters Accounts and the Actors supper in the Lodgings   0 5 0

[1] Entry overlooked by Smith.

1664–5

Of the two copies of the Junior Bursar's Accounts bound in (C), Smith transcribes
from the second; the following transcription is from C(1).

Junior Bursar's Accounts (C) (preceding Extraordinaries)

Comedies

For a deaths-hed carved & painted	0	3	0
For the Inscription of the 2 Scenes	0	1	0
For wax to make Ticketts	0	0	4
For 6[li] of Tallow candles & 4 drinking cups	0	3	4
For 3 sackes of Sea-coale, 2 bushell of charkt Sea-coale, sedge, & carriage	0	5	3
To the woman[1] for making fires and attendance	0	2	0
To the Porter and his Assistants	0	5	0
For attending a Scholar prisoner in the Porters lodg	0	0	6
For watching & defending the walls	0	0	6
For 8 Tinne candlesticks	0	3	4
For linkes & broomes	0	1	0
To Fitch and 5 Labourers for work and attendance 2 dayes & $\frac{1}{2}$	0	17	2
To 5 more employed about the Coll*ege* avenewes	0	2	6
For wax candles, Linkes & Torches	1	14	2
To D*ominus* Seigniour upon his bill of expenses for the 2 Comedies	14	14	9
For wine spent at the Comedies	4	6	0
For deales, Nailes, & wages for the Scaffold work	3	19	0
For earthen candlesticks 6 d Drink to door-keepers		1	2
For new stuff, nailes, tacks, mending the Entrance hangings & work[2]	0	16	0
For a poinard bought in stead of one borrowed and lost	0	12	0
For 8[lb] of candles used at the comedies	0	4	0
For glass, solder, banding & nailes to the Low parlo*ur* windows taken down, & sett up again	1	8	1
Sum*ma*	29	18	11

[1] the woman: Goodw*ife* Smith (C(2)).
[2] work: the vpholsterers pains (C(2)).

Steward's Books (Extraordinaries)
[1]To the Master's Butteler for his paines at Barrington court 1st quarters
Accounts. Declaration. & the Actors suppers in the Lodge   0 10 0

[1] Entry overlooked by Smith.

1668–9

A play this year was performed for the visit of Cosimo de Medici ('Prince of Tuscany')
on 1 May 1669 (Cooper, III, pp. 532–7). Judging from the sign NOLA painted upon
the stage, the play was *Adelphe* by Samuel Brook (Smith, *CP*, p. 15).

Junior Bursar's Accounts (Glazier, 3rd Quarter)
... Upon the stage[1] lead quarrys 2s 8d ...
(Carpenters, 3rd Quarter)
For 17 deals & slitt deals in setting up the stage 1^1 17 s, a casement & pare
of ioints 1s 3d, nails 15s 6d, [2]three days worke of goodman Silke 5 s, of
Iohn Newland 5 [s], two days & ½ of Iohn Curd & Iames Barber 8s 4d
of William Bulkly 3 days 4s 6d   3 6 7[2]
(Bricklayers, 3rd Quarter)
... For mending the Pavement in the great court at the Prince of Tuscanys
coming 7s 6d ...
... for the hire of 4 hairclo^{r}a^{1}ths for the windows in the Comedy-room 8s[2]
a dozen of matts 6s mending them 1s skewers & broomes 7d packthread 4d
six hundred of nails 3d[2] ...
(Extraordinaries, 2nd Quarter)
To Mr Griffith ... for painting NOLA[3] upon the stage   0 1 0
For 4 pair of womens shoos at the Comedy   1 2 0
Payd to the Tapster at the Sun, for bear, pipes & bread & buttyr had by the
Actors   2 8 0
...
To Thomas Marshall for trimming powdering & dressing the actors,
wherein was spent 4 pound of powder 3 potts of Jessemin buttyr, &
attendance all the time of their acting   0 15 0
To young Chapman for running of Errands, making fires, keeping the dore
in the Acting chamber 3s to Iames for like service 2 s ...
To George Scarrow for keeping the gate in the time of the Comedy ...
Payd Robert Gill for Tobacco taken by the Actors   0 11 3
...
Payd to Thomas Williams for Oranges spent upon the Prince &
strangers at both the times the play was acted[4]   0 14 4
...
Payd to Mr Shuter for sixteen yards of green bays to cover the stage   2 18 0
To the Musick for 3 times attending the Comedy   2 0 0

To M*istri*s Frisby for things & service about the Comedy viz 13 yards
& ½ of 4 peny Ribbon[5] 3s 4d ½, 18 yards of pink't colour'd ribbon 4s 6d,
three yards of lemon colour 1s 6 d, a rowl, pins paint & patches 4s 3 peeces
of sattin ribbon 9 s. for the use of two pare of worsted hose, & for slee*ves*
6s 6d, for dressing & providing of cloaths 2[1], in all after her abating of 3s
10d ½   3   5   0

To Mr Moody for 17 pare of gloves for the actors.   1 14 0
For two pare of gloves more to Mr. Collins   0   3 10

[1] Relevance of this stage uncertain.
[2] Entries between pairs of this figure elided by Smith.
[3] NOLA: see headnote to this year.
[4] at both the tymes the play was acted: at the two times of public acting (C)
[5] Ribbon: Ribbon for the Comedy (C)

1669–70

An unknown play was performed this year for the Duke of Ormond, Chancellor of
Oxford, who visited on 21 April 1670, and again for the university (Cooper, III, p.
543).

Junior Bursar's Accounts (Extraordinaries, 2nd Quarter)

To Tho*mas* Cage for 28 pound of wax candles us'd at the Comedy[1] before
the Duke of Ormond & before the Uni*ve*rsity – in all   2   6   6

To Iohn Ivory his attendance 2 days upon the Actors & making them
Beards   0   5   0

To Gam for 2 sacks of coales for the Actors use   0   2   4
To Wisdome for Gilding the Sceptre[2]   0   2   6
To M*istri*s Powell for ale & pipes for the Actors   0 18 0

For wine at the Comedy before the Duke of Ormond 12 qts of Canary 12
qts of Claret 1[li] 18s 0d 6 qts of Canary & 6 qts of Claret for the Actors
themselves nineteen shill*ing*s 12 bottles lost 4s in all   3   1   0

For wine spent when it was Acted before the uni*ve*rsity 8 qts of Canary
& 6 qts of claret 1 3 4 a pottle of burnt claret 2s 8d & for the Actors 7 qts
of Canary & 12 qts of Claret in all   (blank)[3]

To Mr Moody for Kid Gloves for ninteen Actors & to Creighton Mr
Loosmore & S*ir* Manfeild 3 paire more 3 paire at 1s 10d the paire the rest
at 2s the paire in all   2   3   6

To Chapman for waiting upon the Actors 13 days   0   5   0

To Willi*a*m Caton the Ioyn*e*r for worke done in the acting roome to the
Smith 3s 3 sheperds staves 3s for stuffe Labour & nailes 3s 25 foot of
quart*e*rs for the Musicks Lattice 2s for a club 1s 2d for work 2s for work
done in the Com*m*on Chamber[4] about the Presses to hang the Act*or*s
cloathes in for sliting the boords 1s a lock 1s a row of pins 1s 2d [5]nailes 6d
2 men work 2s nailes for the windows & to hang the cloathes 1s seting up
S*ir* Babington's Portall 1s all is[5]   1   1 10

To Mistris Frisby for nine yards of Bloom colour'd ribband 3 s For 11
yards of Lemmon & red 2 s 9 d for 9 yards & $\frac{1}{4}$ of pink 3 d 4 yards of blew
Ribband 1 s 4 d 2 yards of 12 d ribband 1 s 8 2 yards of whit 6 d 7 yards of
4 d ribband 1 s 9 d 4 yards & $\frac{1}{2}$ 1 s 6 d a paire of whit Kid Gloves 2 s 2 yards
of white ribband 6 d 1 yard 3 d A Hat band 5 s[5]pins washing & a paire of
pendence 1 s 9 d for the use of 2 paire of Worsted stockins 2 s for dressing
& providing cloathes 1[li] 12 s 9 d in all[5]   3 0 0

To Thomas Marshall for Tobacco & pipes for the Actors   0 13 4

To Sir Holland for paper to writ out the Comedy for my Lord
Freschville & other Materealls   0 3 0

To Gam & Scarrow for keeping the doors at the Comedy   0 4 0

To Killingworth & Coolidge for keeping the Kings-gate & carrying
charcoale   0 2 0

To the University Musick for their attendance 2 days at the Comedy 2 0 0

To Matthew[6] Fitch for 500 of 6 d nailes spent ⌐about the Acting room⌐ 2 s
6 d 2 Matts 1 s The[7] hire of 3 haires 15 s[5]To him for 2 days attendance[5] 3 s
4 d Item for 18 yards of cloth for the Oakes trees & the Well 6 s 8 d For
the Oake-trees Painting & writing 2 names by Wisdome 12 s 2 d 2 Hoops
for the well 8 d in all   2 5 5

To Thomas Marshall for Trimming Powdering & dressing the Actors
3 potts of Gessima 4 pound of powder & 3 beards 15 s [in all]   0 15 0

To the Orang-man for Oranges spent the 2 days of the Comedy upon the
Spectators & Actors   2 12 0

To Ioshua Burton for making 2 green coates & 2 paire of Breeches 16
yards & $\frac{1}{2}$ of Green Se⌐a⌐rge etc. For making a light colour'd coat &
Breeches 8 yards & $\frac{1}{2}$ of searge etc: 3 round Caps 3 past-boards 4 scrips
&c in all   6 8 7

...

[8]To him [= Tym Cauerly] for a lock & 2 staples for the Acting roome
4 s 0 d ...

[1] the Comedy: a Comedy (C)
[2] This scepter may have appurtained to sculptures over the college gate.
[3] (blank): 1 8 2 (C)
[4] Common: Com' (C): Smith expands to Comedie.
[5] Entries between pairs of this figure elided by Smith.
[6] Matthew: (C) omits given name.
[7] The: Smith transcribes as ij d.
[8] Entry overlooked by Smith.

1670–1

The university was the object of two royal visits this year (Cooper, III, pp. 544–5).
The first, 2–3 October, was by the Duke of York (the future James II), accompanied
by his duchess and the Duchess of Cleveland (mistress of Charles II). The second
visit, 26 November, was by William Prince of Orange (the future William III): an
unknown play, for which the Prince declined to tarry, was played before the
university.

Junior Bursar's Accounts (Glazier)[1]

To William Key his bill ... in the Acting roome 82 quarries 6s 10d 46 foot leaded & soldered 7s 8d, nayles 8d ...

(Smith College)[1]

To Iames King ... 2 staples for the acting roome 4d ...

To Timothy Cauarla his bill for Iron worke Locks & keys in the Kitchin, Buttery & Acting-room   2 3 8

(Carpenters & Joiners)[1]

To him [= Thomas Silk] for a piece of 18 foot for the stage 3 s; 6 deales 8 s; 16 deales 12s 6d; 2 new doores into the Acting roome out of the Auditt Chamber 11 s; 100 double 10d nayles 1s 8d To William Newland 3 days worke 5s; to his son 2s 6d Buckly 4s 2d, Curd 3½ days 5s 10d, Babour 2½ dayes 4s 2d; 800 single 10d nayles 6s 4d; 500 8d nayles 3s 4d   3 7 6

(Extraordinaries, 1st Quarter)

To Thomas Marshall his bill, for powder, Iesimy, Trimming & attending the Actors   0 12 0

To Mr Shuter his bill, for nayles & tape for the Musick grate, setting on the green cloth & 18 candlesticks   1 16 0

To Mrs Friesby her bill for dressing the Actors at the comædy acted before the Vniversity, ribband, spoyling a necklace, for the vse of head-tire & of 3 paire of stockins, pinns, patches & gumme   3 17 11

For wine spent at the Comœdy[2] 8 quarts of canary & 6 quarts of clarett 1ˡⁱ 3s 4d, a potle of burnt claret 2s 3d for the Actors 7 quarts of Canary & 12 claret 1ˡⁱ 7s 2d   2 10 6

[3]For wine spent by the Actors when the prae pared for the Prince of Orange   · 1 10 0

For a lanterne for the Hall Staires   0 5 0

Spent at the comædy præpared for the Prince of Orange, tobacco & pipes 5s 2d; candles 3s; For Cooledge attendence 4 dayes 5s; to goodwife Lord 2s 6d; to Mrs Friesby 10 s   1 5 8

To the porters for keeping the gates when the comædy was acted before the vniuersity   0 5 0

To Mrs Powell for beare for the Actors   0 13 0

For the musick before the Vniuersity   1 0 0

To Caton for worke done at the Lodge when the Duke of yorke was here   0 14 0

...

To Chapman his attending the Actors   0 5 0

for hire of a wastcoat for an Actor   0 0 6

for a new scabbard for my Lord Asley's sword broake upon the stage   0 3 0

To Mrs powell for beare spent at the Comœdy[4] præpared for the Prince of Orange   0 14 0

To Thomas Mathews for a paire of laced shoes & slapps a paire of white shoes & slaps & whitning 2 paire   0 12 4

For candles, penns, inke, paper, broomes, sugar & nutmeggs for the Actors   0 8 0

To Goodwife Lord for attending & dressing the Acting roome   0 3 0

...

To Iosua Burton for 2 white calicoe habits[5]; canuas, thread buttons, ribband, taffety, Holland, binding, stammell sleeues   1 13 6

To Mr Moody his bill for gloues for the Actors   2 14 4

...

To Dr Wrag for tobaccho for the Actors[6]   0 9 6
(2nd Quarter)
To Thom*a*s Cage for 24 pound of wax candles præpar'd for the Comœdy
intended to haue bin acted before the Prince of Orange   2 0 0

...

[7]To Iohn Shuter his bill ... for tenternayles, leather, taking up & laying the
green cloth on the stage 10s; Flocks, matts & 2 staues 3 s, nayles & laying
againe the stage cloth 4s 6d, for taking downe & putting up Dr. Cudworths
hangings 12s 6d, tenternayles & packthread 2s 6d 3 yards of green bayse
for enlarging the stage cloth 12s 6d; 4 large tin-candlesticks 8s 2d fringe,
nayles, scouring & making 6 back-stooles 1^{li} 8 s ...
(3rd Quarter)
To Mr Shuter for 22 yards & $\frac{1}{2}$ of broad bayse for hangings for the Stage
& one yard added to the floore[8] 3^{li} 6s 9d, 7 skins & $\frac{1}{2}$ of gilt-leather 1^{li} 18 s;
thread, tape & coard for the hangings & making the hangings 1^{li} 6 14 9
To Ioh*n* Iuory for gilding 3 scepters[9]   10 0

[1] Entries under this heading overlooked by Smith.
[2] Comœdy: Comœdy acted before the vniuersity (C).
[3] For wine for the Actors spent at the comedy præpared for the Prince of Orange 10 qu*a*rts of canary & to quarts of claret (C).
[4] at the Comœdy: by the Actors that (C).
[5] habits: habits to dance in (C).
[6] tobaccho for the Actors: the Actors tobacco (C).
[7] Entry overlooked by Smith.
[8] one yard added to the floore: adding to the floore one yard (C).
[9] These scepters may have appurtained to sculptures over the college gate.

1671–2

Charles II visited Cambridge on 4 October 1671, dining at Trinity College, evidently
in the hall (Cooper, III, pp. 547–52). Alderman Newton and the *Gazette* both report
that the king witnessed a comedy at the college. This was apparently the last year of
play production in the college before modern times. Smith does not transcribe entries
from this year.

Junior Bursar's Accounts (Glazier, 1st Quarter)
To Willi*am* King his bill for ... a 110 quar*ries* in the Acting roome 9s 2d, 38 foot
leaded and soldered 6s 4d, nayles 2d
(3rd Quarter)
To him his bill ... in the Acting roome 4s 11d ...
(Extraordinaries)
To him [= John Wisdom] ... for whitning the Acting roome 4 s ...

1695–6

Apparently no plays were performed in the college this year; Smith does not transcribe these entries.

Junior Bursar's Accounts 1694–1726, f. 33 (Glazier)
For mending a window in the Acting Room   0 2 0
For 10 foot of glass soldered in the Audit Chamber 1s 8d …

Appendix 7

Tabor's search for the university theatre, c. 1620

Cambridge University Archives, CUR 18 (1(a)), contains an analysis in the hand of James Tabor, university Registrary, of the university's financial relationship to Great St Mary's (copy in Coll. Admin. 8, called 'Tabor's Book', pp. 586–7). The following passage concerns the commencement stage in the church. A date of c. 1620 is assigned by virtue of the fact that Tabor's valuation of the theatre at £4 holds up to 1621–2 but not thereafter.

Concerning the Stage. [In left margin]

[1] That the vniuersity had a Theatre, I find in the Auditt booke, about the yeere 1545. where the vicechancellor Doctor Parker, is allowed xx s 11 d for money, by him paid pro extruendo theatro.

[2] And so afterwards yeerely, till Anno domini 1552. there is 35 s 5 d allowed pro ædificando theatro, but where this theatre was, is not sett downe, but in all probability in this Church./

[3] Anno 1553. there is xvj s viij d allowed to the vicechancellor, for settinge vpp the stage for the Commencement.

[4] Anno 1555. Videlicet pro erigendo, et demoliendo theatro in Comitijs, and for stuffe to repayre the stage, there is 1 li 10 s 6 d allowed.

[5] Anno 1557. 1 li 16 s 8 d is allowed pro structura theatri in Comitijs.

[6] Anno 1560. there is allmost the like summe allowed.

[7] Anno 1561. there was about x li expended by the vniuersity, for buying timber for the Commencement stage, since which time, the ordinary charge for building, and taking downe the said stage, hath bein 4 li or thereabouts, besides such moneyes, as the Carpenter is allowed for new board, or timber, which he buyeth for the repayer of the same./

Endorsed: Mr Tabors brief About the building of St Maries & the Theater there.

[1] Matches accounts in U.Ac.2(1) for 1545–6

[2] Matches 1551–2

[3] Matches 1552–3

[4] 1554–5: £1–0–6 + 0–10–5 = £1–10–11

[5] 1556–7: £1–1–8

[6] 1559–60: £1–10–2 + £0–5–2 = £1–15–4

[7] 1560–1: total = £12–1–2½

Appendix 8

University graces for a theatre, 1673–5

Cambridge University Archives, CUR 46 (1–4), contains university graces (or resolutions) concerning the construction of a new building for the granting of higher degrees; of these, 1, 2, and 4 refer to the building as a 'theatre'. For another transcription of (1) and a partial translation of (2), see W&C, III, pp. 41–2.

(1) (Copy in Grace Book Theta, p. 85)

Cum locum Theatro Academico (si Deo visum fuerit) extruendo, parem et idoneum, inprimis desideremus; et novum, quod dicitur, Hospitium, conditione non gravi, nobis redimendum proponatur; Placet vobis ut Dr. Iacobus Fleetwood, Dr Robertus Mapletoft, Dr Theophilus Dillingham, Dr Radulphus Widdrington, Dr Iohannes Carr, Mr Thomas Page, et Mr David Morton, vel eorum quatuor aut quinque, una cum Domino Procancellario, huic negotio exequendo præficiantur; et quod illis, hac in re, expedire videtur, vos ratum acceptumque habeatis. Quo vero dicti Delegati authoritate vestra muniantur, Placet vobis ut literas vestras habeant syndicatas, sigillo vestro communi sigillatas.

Lecta 12 Novembris 1673

    Lecta et Concessa 2° Decembris 1673.

Endorsed: November 1673. Gratia de loco idoneo ad theatrum nouum extruendum parando.

(2) (Copy in Grace Book Theta, p. 87)

Cum magna spes subsit, Academiæ (modo ipsa non desit sibi) amicos non defuturos, Theatro, quod molimur, Academico manus auxiliatrices porrigere [soleant] ⌈paratissimos⌉ Cum etiam tanta molis opus aggredientibus, plurima evenire soleant, quæ duarum Congregationum (quibus Academiæ concensus peti possit) moras, et molestias ferre nequeant; Placet vobis ut negotij hujusce procuratio ad bienium demandetur curæ fideique Procancellarij qui pro tempore fuerit, Doctoris Duport, Doctoris Fletewood, Doctoris Breton, Doctoris Mapletoft, Doctoris Beaumont, Doctoris Dillingham, Doctoris Widdrington, Doctoris Turner, Doctoris Barrow, Doctoris Carr, Doctoris Paman, Magistri

Crouch, M*a*gis*t*ri Page, et M*a*gis*t*ri Morton; Ita ut quicquid illi (aut eorum quinq*ue*, [coram] quorum Procancel*larius* sit vnus) in pecunijs recipiendis, [literis] aut erogandis, Operarijs conducendis, domibus (si occasio fuerat) redimendis literis Academiæ nomine scribendis, aut re quavis alia huic operi promovendo inserviente fuerint, id ratum a vobis, et stabilitum, ad omnem juris effectum habeatur.

  Lect*a* 27 Martij 1674

Concess*a* eod*em* postmerid*ie*

Endorsed: 27 Ma{rtis} 1674 Grat*ia* pro synd*icato* statu*a*ndis de Theatro extru*e*ndo

(4)

April 6ᵗʰ 1675. at a metting of the Syndick appoynted for the [Theator] ⌜Museum⌝. at the Vice chanc*ellours* Lodgings In Iesus College pr*e*sent

Dr Boldero Procan*cellor* [and eleven others] ...

[It was then [ordered] ⌜declared as the sense of the major part⌝ That Rose should be the place where the Theater shallbe built.]

It was then declared, as the sense of the Major part from reasons on all parts alledg'd, that the Rose [and] ⌜with⌝ the houses thereunto adjoyning is the fittest place for the deccine [= design] aboue mentioned, And in perseuance thereof Doctors Dillingham, Dr Spencer, Mr Morton, and Mr Bainbrigg were desired to inquire into ⌜the⌝ Tene*n*ts, Rent, and prises of the said respective houses in order to the purchas.

Appendix 9

Commencement stage timber dimensions, 1528–1668

The following is a summary of known timber dimensions for the university commencement stage in Great St Mary's Church, gathered from CUCS. Measurements in board-feet are not included. Equals sign (=) between numbers signals my assumption that measurement is in running-feet, giving combined lengths.

1527–8 (Church of the Franciscan Friars)

Tabulae (= boards): $21 \times 18'$
Traba (= timber): $1 \times 9'$

1560–1

Timbers (verticals?):

$14 \times 3'' \times 6'' \times 12'$	$20 \times 3'' \times 6'' \times 4'\ 6''$
$10 \times 3'' \times 6'' \times 7'$	$4 \times 2'' \times 4'' \times 10'$

Girdings:

$6 \times 4'' \times 6'' \times 9'$
$6 \times 4'' \times 6'' \times 6'$
$10 \times 4'' \times 6'' \times 9'$

Rails:

$4 \times 4'' \times 5'' \times 12'$
$4 \times 4'' \times 5'' \times 9'$
$4 \times 4'' \times 4'' \times 6'$

1582–3

Studs: $3 \times 7'$

1591–2

Studs: 5 (pair?) × 9′

1651–2

Joists: 14 × 6′

1662–3

Timber: 9′
Studs: 3 = 21′ (c. 7′ each?)
Jeece:

4 = 28′ (7′ each?)	11 = 65′ (c. 6′ each?)
2 × 4″ × 6″ × 14′	7 = 40′ (c. 6′ each?)
2 × 4″ × 6″ × 15′	5 = 27′ (c. 5′ 6″ each?)
7 = 60′ (c. 9′ each?)	6 = 22′ (c. 3′ 6″ each?)

Rails: 2 = 38′ (19′ each?)
Deal boards:

100 × 10′ and 11′
110 × 11′ and 12′
12 × 14′

1667–8

Rails:

3 × 14′
1 × 10′
1 × 9′

Timber (for Oxford seat): 4′
Studs:

7 = 47′ (c. 7′ each?)	19 × 6′
3 = 15′ (5′ each?)	11 × 5′
2 × 8′	1 × 4′
11 × 7′	

Jeece: 12 × 5′
Girts: 2 × 11′

Appendix 10

Records of the university proctor's booth, 1597–1638

Cambridge University Archives, U.Ac.2(1), and vouchers in U.Ac.1(1–2), contain records concerning the proctor's booth from 1597–8 to 1637–8. The booth was rebuilt in 1604–5 after having burned down accidentally.

1597–8 U.Ac.2(1), p. 349 (Vice-Chancellor's accounts)

Item to Pryme for timber and stuffe to the Proctors boothe wherevpon reserved to the Vniuersitie a yearlie rent of xx s and the stuffe safe vt per billam xj li xvij s

1604–5 U.Ac.2(1), p. 398 (Vice-Chancellor's accounts)

Item pro booth timber &c for reedifiing the Proctors booth the former being casually burnt xl s

VCV.14(b.ii)

... the former tymber ...

1611–12 U.Ac.2(1), p. 438 (Senior Proctor's accounts)

Item for timber hayers and other furniture for the [the] newe booth vt patet per billam xix li xj s ix d

U.Ac.1(1), no. 1

Inprimis 12 studes of 8 ffot longe 5 & 3 Inches	0	9	0
Item 44 studes of 7 ffot longe 5 & 3 Inches	1	9	4

Item 7 peces of timber of 26 ffot longe 5 & 7 Inches	1	18	6
Item 4 beames of 21 fot longe 5 di [= half] square	0	10	0
Item 64 ffir deales at xij d *per* deale	3	4	0
Item 2 spruce deales of 27 ffot longe apec	0	16	0
Item for 90 pooles & 9 hardell*es*	1	4	0
Item for the Cariage of the pooles & hardell*es*	0	0	9
Item to 3 men ffor sewinge the hayres & ffor .l. packthred	0	4	8
Item to a laborer for 3 daies & di worke and ffor watchinge 3 night*es*	0	5	6
Item ffor 6 matt*es* & the Cariage	0	2	2
Item to the Carpenters for their worke	1	4	0
Item ffor nayles, trashes, & byndinge & for Corde	0	8	8
Item for 22 boult*es* of hare clothes[1]	7	6	8
Item for 3 payre of hauck*es* & hinges	0	2	0
Item ffor beere for the Carpenters	0	1	0
Item ffor Rent for 2 yeres for thould timber	0	5	0

seen & allowed by me

(*signed*) Bar*nabe* Goche Proca*ncellor*

[1] Cost: 6s 8d per bolt.

1614–15 U.Ac.2(1), p. 457 (Senior Proctor's accounts)

Item to a Timberman at Sturbridge ffayer for 130 foote of borde for the Proctors booth xv s

Item to the same for six hardles iij s

Item to the same for poles iiij s vij d

Item to the same for the hire of halfe a hundred of bord*es* to laye vnder the do*ct*ors feete xx d

Item for a locke, & a keye xiiij d

*U.Ac.1(3), no. 2, 2**

... 100′ of inchboard. 2 studs 8′ long & 2 peces of 12 apec...

1615–16 U.Ac.2(1), p. 465 (Vice-Chancellor's accounts)

Item for mending the Proctors boothe x s

U.Ac.1(3), no. 10

for the procters booth

Inprimis for the last yeare settinge vp the place for the Iudge to sit in & for nailes printes & bindinge	0	3	4
Item this yeare for my selfe & my men three dayes takin it downe and layinge it vp in the schooles	0	7	6
Item on to help vs lay vp the longe peces	0	0	6
Item one watchinge too nightes	0	0	8

Item to the carter caringe of it in	0 5	6
Item for settinge vp the Iudges seat this yeare	0 2	0

Sum is 19s 6d

no. 10xx (receipt by Nathaniel Bridges)

1630–1 U.Ac.2(1), p. 593 (Vice-Chancellor's accounts)

Item to Bridge Carpenter for the rent of the house for booth timber	0 13	4

1631–2 U.Ac.2(1), p. 607 (Vice-Chancellor's accounts)

Item paid for Timber & stuffe for the Vniuersity Booth in Sturbridge ffayer	0 11	8

U.Ac.1(3), tab 19, f. [1v] (under Henry Butts, Vice-Chancellor)

Item to Nathaniell Bridge for houserent for the booth timber & heares	0 13	4

no. 1 (under Thomas Comber, Vice-Chancellor)

Item to Bridge Carpenter for the rent of the house where the universitie booth tymber lyeth	0 13	4

1632–3 U.Ac.2(1), p. 618 (Senior Proctor's accounts)

Item for extraordinary expenses att the Proctores booth & hyring hayres and boordes in regard of the rainy and wett wether & for new timber	0 19	8

1633–4 U.Ac.2(1), p. 625 (Senior Proctor's accounts)

Item for diuers thinges done about the vniuersity booth	0 13	3

1634–5 U.Ac.2(1), p. 632 (Junior Proctor's accounts)

Item for a hairecloth for the Booth in Sturbridge faire	0 13	4

1635–6 U.Ac.2(1), p. 649 (Vice-Chancellor's accounts)

Item to Nathaniell Bridge for rent for Sturbridge faire booth timber	0 13	4

1636–7 U.Ac.2(1), p. 659 (Vice-Chancellor's accounts)

Item to Nathaniel Bridge for houserent for the booth timber and hares	0 13	4

1637–8 U.Ac.2(1), p. 661 (Junior Proctor's accounts)

Item for 2 Hareclothes, bought for the Proctors booth, and for poles and hardles for the same	2 6	10

Notes

Full bibliographical information for books cited frequently is given in Abbreviations and Select bibliography.

1. Introduction: London to Cambridge

1 For a history of the Rose and its rediscovery, see Eccles, *The Rose Theatre*. Pre-excavation conference reports and collaborative reconstructions include Hodges, Schoenbaum, and Leone (eds.), *The Third Globe*; and Gurr and Orrell (eds.), *Rebuilding Shakespeare's Globe*.

2 Eccles, *Rose Theatre*, pp. 85–189; Hildy (ed.), *New Issues in the Reconstruction of Shakespeare's Theatre*; and Blatherwick and Gurr, 'Shakespeare's Factory'. Cerasano, 'Shakespeare's Elusive Globe', queries the enterprise of reconstruction.

3 Construction of the first two bays of the new Globe was announced, with illustrations, in *The Independent*, 16 June 1992, p. 8. The most recent report is Gurr, Mulryne, and Shewring, *The Design of the Globe* (1993).

4 Joy Hancox, *The Byrom Collection: Renaissance Thought, the Royal Society and the Building of the Globe Theatre* (London, 1992), reveals that the approach to Shakespeare's Globe through geometry is not yet entirely dead. Reviewed by Alastair Fowler, 'The World's a Stage: Does the Globe Have a Cosmic Meaning?', *TLS* (28 August 1992), pp. 14–15.

5 *The Boar's Head Playhouse*; see also two volumes edited by Berry, *The First Public Playhouse: The Theatre in Shoreditch 1576–1598*; and *Shakespeare's Playhouses*; and an article, 'The First Public Playhouses, Especially the Red Lion'.

6 A list of playwrights emanating from Cambridge is given in REED, Appendix 16.

7 For broad coverage of Cambridge history, see Atkinson; Cooper; Mullinger; VCH; and Damian Reihl Leader, *A History of the University of Cambridge*, I: *The University to 1546* (Cambridge, 1988), and forthcoming volumes in this series. Principal authorities on Cambridge architecture are David Loggan, *Cantabrigia Illustrata* (London, 1688); W&C; and RCHM. For maps, see John Willis Clark, *Old Plans of Cambridge, 1574 to 1798*, text volume with portfolio (Cambridge, 1921); M. D. Lobel and W. H. Johns (eds.), *Cambridge*, Historic Towns Series (London, 1974); and REED, pp. 833–9.

8 On the establishment of the university, see VCH, pp. 150–1. Other foundation dates are given in the relevant chapters.

9 REED, Introduction (pp. 703–37), Appendixes 2–10.

10 REED, Appendix 8, identifies some 252 relevant entries before 1576; since many entries refer to plays in the plural, the total must easily exceed 300.

11 For the post-1660 history of Cambridge theatre generally, see REED, p. 714; Sybil Rosenfeld, 'The Players in Cambridge, 1662–1800', *Studies in English Theatre History*, Society for Theatre Research (1952), pp. 24–37; H. C. Porter, 'The Players Well Bestowed? Stourbridge and Barnwell Theatres 1740–1814', *Cambridge Review* (December, 1984), pp. 214–18; and the same author's 'The Professional Theatre in Victorian Cambridge', *Cambridge Review* (28 January 1983), pp. 27–31.

12 For analyses of the typical college hall, see W&C, III, pp. 354–72; and RCHM, pp. lxxx–lxxxii.

13 *OED* has no entry or sub-entry for 'minstrel(s')-gallery', but see *Webster's Third New International Dictionary of the English Language Unabridged* (Springfield, Mass., 1971). *OED* citations of indoor galleries are all relatively late: see 'gallery' 2c (architectural: 1756–7), 3 (interior: 1715), 3b (in churches: 1630), 3c (in a theatre: 1690), 4 (transferred sense: 1649). Leacroft's illustration of a play backed against hall screens in *Development of the English Playhouse*, p. 14, lacks historical warrant: see Nelson, 'Hall Screens and Elizabethan Playhouses'. Leacroft's illustration of a play away from the screens (p. 11) is more accurate, though the action should have been placed nearer the dais.

14 The first volume, printed in numbers (1678–9), is Wing M3013; the second volume, on printing (1683), is M3014. For an account of Moxon's life and career, see Joseph Moxon, *Mechanick Exercises on the Whole Art of Printing* (1683–4), ed. Herbert Davis and Harry Carter (London, 1958), pp. xix–lv (supersedes entry in *DNB*). Other useful contemporary documents are the 1598 contract for the Fortune Theatre, printed in Foakes and Rickert (eds.), *Henslowe's Diary*, pp. 306–15; the 1613 contract for the Hope Theatre, printed in Chambers, *ES*, II, pp. 466–8; and the plan of a theatre apparently erected at Christ Church, Oxford, 1605, analysed by Orrell in *HS*, pp. 119–29; also in *Shakespeare Survey*, 35 (1982), pp. 129–40; *Quest*, pp. 127–38, 168–70 (Appendix B); and *Theatres of Inigo Jones and John Webb*, pp. 24–38.

15 Eileen Harris, *British Architectural Books and Writers, 1556–1785* (Cambridge, 1990), pp. 38–40: Harris names Moxon elsewhere (see Index), but does not include him in this discussion of 'Carpenters' Manuals'. Regulatory statutes concerning house construction were issued from 1607 to 1630 (*STC* 8407, 8470–1, 8573–4, 8639, 8733, 8771, 8958, and 9341 [reprint of 8407]). Orrell, *HS*, pp. 152, 155, discusses surveyors' manuals (details in accompanying notes 8, 12, 13, 14). Useful modern authorities on timber construction include Joseph Gwilt, *An Encyclopaedia of Architecture, Historical, Theoretical, and Practical* (ed.) Wyatt Papworth (London, 1888), esp. pp. 615–49 ('Carpentry'); *Encyclopaedia Britannica*, 11th edn, 29 vols. (Cambridge, 1910–11), s.v. Carpentry; C. F. Innocent, *The Development of English Building Construction* (Cambridge, 1916); Francis B. Andrews, *The Medieval Builder and his Methods* (London, 1974, reprinted from *Transactions of the Birmingham Architectural Society*, 48, 1925); Martin S. Briggs, 'Building Construction, England', in Charles Singer *et al.* (eds.), *A History of Technology*, vol. III (Oxford, 1957), pp. 256–68 (with bibliography); Alec Clifton-Taylor, *The Pattern of English Building* (London, 1962), esp. pp. 36–52; L. F. Salzman, *Building in England Down to 1540: A Documentary History* (Oxford, 1967; rpt New York: Kraus, 1979), esp. chaps. XIII ('The Timber-Framed House') and XVI ('Timber'); and Richard Harris, *Discovering Timber-*

Framed Buildings (Princes Risborough, Buckinghamshire: Shire Publications, 1978) (with bibliography).

16 Moxon's name occurs in the index of only one of the studies listed in the Select bibliography, i.e., Hodges, Schoenbaum, and Leone (eds.), *The Third Globe*, relative to a discussion not of building construction but of turning large pillars.

17 Moxon printed Vignola at least five times between 1655 and 1694 (Wing B903–6).

18 Plate 7 (frontispiece to Part VI); text, pp. 105–6.

19 I discuss this topic at greater length pp. 119–22.

20 The joists of Queens' College stage platform, which lie over the raisings, are an exception to this generalization (see Moxon, p. 141, and my figs. 18, 19).

21 Moxon refers to scantlings throughout, but see particularly pp. 142–5, where he cites building codes for London after the Great Fire of 1666.

22 Graham Chainey, 'Royal Visits to Cambridge: Henry VI to Henry VIII', *Proceedings of the Cambridge Antiquarian Society*, 80 (1991), pp. 30–7. For royal visits from 1564 onward, see Marion Colthorpe, *Royal Cambridge* (Cambridge, 1977).

23 Cooper, I, p. 305 to II, p. 178; Mullinger, I, p. 553 to II, p. 165; VCH, pp. 172–80; and H. C. Porter, *Reformation and Reaction in Tudor Cambridge* (Cambridge, 1958). See also Patrick Collinson, 'Andrew Perne and his Times', *Andrew Perne: Quatercentenary Studies*, Cambridge Bibliographical Society Monographs, 11 (Cambridge, 1991), pp. 1–34.

24 John Nichols, *The Progresses and Public Processions of Queen Elizabeth*, 3 vols. (London, 1823), I, pp. 149–89.

25 Stanley M. Leathes (ed.), *Grace Book A: Containing the Proctors' Accounts and Other Records of the University of Cambridge for the Years 1454–1488* (Cambridge, 1897), p. xxv. See *The Historical Register of the University of Cambridge … to the year 1910*, ed. R. J. Tanner (Cambridge, 1917), pp. 180–8, for more recent traditions.

26 RCHM, pp. 99–117, 154–6; photographs, plates 149, 152 (exterior), 150–1 (interior), 161 (side chapel); plan opp. p. 102, and in map of college in box; on screen, pp. 105, 128–30; photographs, plates 182–7.

27 'Stokys' Book'; 'Robinson's Book'; Cambridge University Library MS Ff.5.14; and Abraham Hartwell, *Regina Literata* (1565). Excerpts from these and other documents are printed in REED, pp. 227–44. For summaries, see F. S. Boas, *University Drama in the Tudor Age* (Oxford, 1914), pp. 89–99; and Chambers, *ES*, I, p. 227.

28 REED, p. 234: it is just conceivable that by two chapels Stokys meant a single chapel on each side of the antechapel, yielding a stage 25′ deep (see Hotson's analysis cited in note 31 below).

29 A 5′ stage would leave 5′ of headroom through a 10′ door. For a photo of a typical tall, narrow side-chapel door, see RCHM, plate 192.

30 RCHM, p. 112. On the cutting of doorways for royal visits, see Wickham, 'Plays for Queen Elizabeth I at Oxford, 1566', in *Early English Stages*, I, pp. 356, 358; and this volume, p. 51 (Trinity College hall, 1614–15).

31 Wickham, *Early English Stages*, I, pp. 248–50; Leacroft, *Development of the English Playhouse*, pp. 12–13 (illustration p. 13; apart from the problem with the side houses, Leacroft's reconstruction is excellent); Chambers, *ES*, I, pp. 226–7 (see also Boas, *University Drama*, pp. 89–98); Hotson, *Shakespeare's Wooden O*, pp. 161–3 (illustration p. 162).

32 James I was unhappy with the proposal to place him at the focal point of the perspective set

at Oxford in 1605, complaining that the audience would see 'his cheek only' (Orrell, *Quest*, p. 132).

33 RCHM, pp. 275–80; plan p. 276; photos plates 286–7. For further discussion of Great St Mary's, see Chapter 5.

34 REED, pp. 1217 (note to p. 244), 1029.

35 See reference to rails, p. 127.

36 Wickham, *Early English Stages*, I, p. 250, appreciates the quasi-theatrical character of this stage.

2. Queens' College

1 Appendix 3.

2 Other useful documents are noted p. 162, note 14.

3 See pp. 169–72; Hotson gives date as 1638, p. 169.

4 For records of the original construction, see REED, pp. 144–6, 149–52, 156–81. Relevant entries between 1550–1 and 1639–40 are sparse (pp. 35–6); nevertheless, the college account books are complete, and would presumably have reflected another such campaign of stage construction.

5 RCHM, pp. 172–3; plan opp. p. 168; photo of hall roof plate 226. W&C, II, 44–8. The hall was extensively altered by James Burrough 1732–4; roof restored 1845–6.

6 Compare *OED* 'rack' (sb. 2(5d)): 'an inclined frame or table on which tin-ore is washed' (see also 'wreck' following 'wreck' [sb. 3]; and 'rake' [sb. 4(2)]): 'the inclination of any object from the perpendicular or to the horizontal; slope' (earliest use 1802; for a stage, 1893; but see nautical use under (1), dated 1626).

7 REED, p. 145, lines 20–1 (see also translation). Moxon, p. 145, states that girders must go into masonry at least 10″, but the temporary nature of this structure would lessen the requirement.

8 Hotson, pp. 171–2, places the trap-door on the stage platform. The original screen was removed and the current screen installed during the reconstruction of 1732–4 (RCHM, pp. 172–3), so there is no hope of finding evidence in the surviving structure for an earlier trap-door.

9 Compare to the 'slopp scaffold' in the '1605 Christ Church Oxford drawing': see Orrell, *Quest*, p. 169 (note J).

10 The distance between jeece is essentially independent of the thickness of the individual jeece. As with other repetitive members of a frame construction, the distance from one jeece to the next is measured not as the space between the timbers, but as the distance between centres. Granted that it is possible to space thicker and stronger jeece more widely than lighter jeece and carry the same load, nevertheless if it is known how many jeece spanned a given distance it is possible to calculate their spacing (on the assumption that the spacing was regular) even if their individual dimensions are not known.

11 Moxon, *Mechanick Exercises*, p. 145, declares that the maximum centring for jeece is 12″ (on p. 142 he gives 10″), but he allows jeece to bear over a distance of 10′.

12 Assuming a side girt of the tiring house and three evenly spaced jeece all 16″ on centre, the distance from the centre of the girt to the centre of the third jeece would come to $3 \times 16″ = 48″$. I have subtracted 3″ each for the width of the vertical posts into which the girt and the third jeece are mortised.

13 Noted p. 13.

14 Berry, 'The First Public Playhouses', p. 47; Orrell, *Quest*, p. 168 (note G: '7 foote at least vnder'). Even granted that the average height of males in Renaissance Europe was less than today's, consideration nevertheless had to be given to more elaborate head-coverings.

15 The mark represented by a Greek gamma in REED 689/15 is in fact an R.

16 On the college's plays, see REED, pp. 766–7. Keyle is known to have worked on the university's commencement stage: see p. 113.

17 Spelled 'sutwytche' in the original (REED, pp. 122, 1111)

18 REED, pp. 1204–5, note to pp. 121–2.

19 Smith, *CP*, proposed (p. 31) that this chest is 'still in existence' (1923): he probably had in mind an early chest now in the college library (see black and white plate 7 in John Twigg, *A History of Queens' College, Cambridge 1448–1986*, Woodbridge: Boydell, 1987); it is by no means certain, however, that this is the chest supplied by Burwell in 1547–8.

20 D. F. McKenzie argues that the stagehouse was preserved largely intact and incorporated within the New Printing House: see his *Cambridge University Press, 1696–1712*, 2 vols. (Cambridge: University Press, 1966), I, pp. 17–18; and 'A Cambridge Playhouse of 1638', *Renaissance Drama*, 3 (1970), pp. 263–6. Smith, *CP*, pp. 10, 24, also accepts the proposal that the stagehouse was a playhouse. See, however, REED, p. 994; and Nelson and Wright, 'A Queens' College Playhouse of 1638?' Queens' College Archives, Item 328 ('Map Portfolio'), no. 4, a plan executed by Robert Grumbold on 14 June 1683, discovered after the publication of this article, confirms that the stagehouse was a small, rectangular building with a groundplan 29' by 18'.

21 Nelson and Wright, 'A Queens' College Playhouse of 1638?' p. 185.

22 Ibid., p. 180.

3. Trinity College from 1605

1 REED, pp. 538–9. On the royal visit, see REED, pp. 529–45, Appendixes 4–5; and John Nichols, *The Progresses, Processions, and Magnificent Festivities of King James the First*, 4 vols. (London, 1828), III, pp. 39–76, 82–91; IV, pp. 192–3.

2 REED, pp. 889–90. *Albumazar* (1615; *STC* 24100), Act I, Scene iii; the dialogue carries on further in the same vein.

3 RCHM, pp. 62, 224–8; plan in box which accompanies the volumes; section, p. 225; photos plates 253 (exterior), 256–7 (interior). W&C, II, pp. 489–94.

4 Chambers, *ES*, II, p. 466: '... Tyre house and a stage to be carryed or taken away ...'

5 Berry, 'The Stage and Boxes at Blackfriars', in *Shakespeare's Playhouses*, pp. 47–73.

6 For royal visits to Oxford, see REED, *Oxford*, ed. John R. Elliott, Jr (forthcoming). See also VCH, *A History of Oxfordshire*, vol. III: *The University of Oxford*, ed. H. E. Salter and Mary D. Lobel (Oxford, 1954), pp. 235 (1566, 1592), 24 (1636); Wickham, 'Plays for Queen Elizabeth I at Oxford, 1566' (full citation in note 21 below); John R. Elliott, Jr, 'Queen Elizabeth at Oxford: New Light on the Royal Plays of 1566', *English Literary Renaissance*, 18 (1988), pp. 218–29; and Orrell's analysis of the theatre apparently erected at Christ Church, Oxford, in 1605 (see p. 162, note 14). For the 1578 visit to Audley End, see REED, p. 281 (esp. endnote).

7 Royal and noble visitors generally dined in the great dining room in the master's lodge of

Trinity College (parentheses give REED page and line numbers): 1612–13 (princes in the Great Chamber: 507/11–13; nobility in Mr Hall's Chamber: 509/29); 1614–15 (not established); 1622–3 (588/32, 589/23); 1627–8 (not established); 1628–9 (621/36–622/2); 1631–2 (640/34–6); 1635–6 (not established); 1641–2 (700/28–9). By way of exception, in December 1624 part of the king's 'retinue dined in the great hall at Trinitie college' (598/23); a scheduled play had been cancelled because of the king's illness. College documents confirm that dining and plays were mutually exclusive hall activities: in 1612–13 members of the college were recompensed for dining out 'during the time of our being out of the hall for the Comedyes' (Trinity College Archives, Old Conclusion Book, 1612–13, p. 39); in 1631–2 fifteen poor scholars were given extra commons over six weeks 'in the time of the Comedye'. For the royal visit to Oxford in 1636, see preceding note; see also John R. Elliott, Jr, 'Mr. Moore's Revels: A "Lost" Oxford Masque', *Renaissance Quarterly*, 37 (1984), pp. 411–20.

8 REED, pp. 620–1 (the orders for this year are unusually elaborate, perhaps because the king was not in attendance and adjustments were required for the smaller retinue).

9 Revised orders for 1635–6, Cambridge University Archives, Collect. Admin. 8 (Tabor's Book), p. 534: 'the non Regents sitting vpon the formes beyond the stage ... reservinge the scaffolds beyond the stage for the Courtiers and doctors' (not in REED).

10 Two sets of orders were issued in 1612–13, one set each in 1614–15, 1622–3, 1624–5, 1628–9, 1631–2, and 1635–6 (with revisions: see preceding note).

11 I have made the side scaffolds 'reach to the stage' by bringing them as far forward as the stage, though not down to the level of the stage (to preserve standing-room beneath). That the main scaffold above the stage was raked seems certain from the reference to 'the lowest seat of the said scaffold'.

12 See REED 569/33 for a correction in the original which seems to confirm the hypothesis that the tiring chamber had doors both to the master's lodge and to the hall.

13 Although RCHM, p. 224, asserts, 'The cellars below the Hall were dug in 1751–2', the Loggan print of 1688 (fig. 22) shows cellar windows; apparently the cellars were extended in 1751–2.

14 Photograph in the series described below, note 16.

15 Openings from masters' lodges into halls, chapels, and other areas are discussed by W&C, III, p. 335.

16 Five photographs of this construction are held in the office of the Junior Bursar; of these, three show the back of the upper-end wall. Rooms which since Bentley's time had been in the possession of the Master were transformed into a passageway and fellows' parlour on the ground level and a combination room above: see RCHM, pp. 229–30.

17 W&C, II, pp. 475–86. Willis and Clark give the date of the plan as 1595 in the caption to their fig. 10, but Philip Gaskell, *Trinity College Library; The First 150 Years* (Cambridge, 1980), p. 61, corrects this to 1555.

18 Plan in box which accompanies the volumes.

19 W&C, II, p. 609; original in Junior Bursar's Accounts, 1614–15, f. 352v (Tilers, Bricklayers, Slaters and Paviors): 'Item to Abraham 5 dayes diging of a dore out of the lodging into the Hall & carring rubbish at 8d – iij s iiij d'. W&C, IV, fig. 9, designate the north-west door as 'Door to Lodge 1614–15'.

20 Odd inferences follow from Willis and Clark's discursive argument and drawing: for the first ten years of its life, the new hall was not directly accessible from the master's lodge; or,

if the north-west door was not cut until 1614–15, then the hall originally had a functional door at the north-east corner but no door at the north-west corner, and over time this situation reversed itself exactly.

21 'Plays for Queen Elizabeth I at Oxford, 1566', in Wickham, *Early English Stages*, I, pp. 355–9 (Appendix H); entrance cut, pp. 356, 358.

22 Under 'Extraordinaries'; cited by W&C, II, p. 610, note 1.

23 Cooper, IV, pp. 10 (1689), 71–2 (1705), 197 (1728). See also Marion Colthorpe, *Royal Cambridge* (Cambridge, 1977), under appropriate dates. Payment of £27 to the carpenter Abraham Silk 'For Making the scafoulds in the Hall and ye Musick Gallery & the seats ouer the screen and the worke in the Kitching and all other workes in the severall Offices belongin to the said Entertainment' is recorded in Cambridge University Archives, CUR 27* (A18).

24 On the original installation of the panelling, see W&C, III, p. 358. RCHM, p. 226, identifies the panelling as original, but see also p. 224: 'In 1955 the dais panelling and the Royal arms were taken down, restored, redecorated and regilded ...' In fact, the panelling seems not to have been seriously disturbed in 1955.

25 Smith, *CP*, pp. 10, 24; Trevelyan, *Trinity College: An Historical Sketch* (Cambridge, 1943), pp. 29–30, 33; RCHM, plan in box which accompanies the volumes. For a comment of my own which the present analysis aims in some part to correct, see REED, p. 991.

26 W&C, II, p. 624 (citing from Alderman Newton's diary). See J. E. Foster (ed.), *The Diary of Samuel Newton, Alderman of Cambridge (1662–1717)* (Cambridge, 1890).

27 CUCS: in addition to 1610–11, see 1626–7, 1630–1, etc.

28 Robert Stewart (ed.), *The Travels of Cosmo the Third, Grand Duke of Tuscany, in England in the Reign of Charles II., With A Memorie of his Life* (London, 1821), p. 229; cited by Cooper, III, p. 533; and W&C, II, p. 624. The account continues, 'The comedy concluded, in the midst of rejoicings, with a ball, which was managed with great elegance'. The original Italian is printed by Anna Maria Crinò, *Un Principe di Toscano in Inghilterra e in Irlanda nel 1669* (Rome, 1968), p. 85: 'nella stanza del teatro piuttosto angusto che spazioso'.

29 W&C, II, p. 625, note 1. Cited by Smith, *CP*, p. 178; also in Appendix 6. For a doubtful reference to the comedy room, see p. 54.

30 W&C, II, p. 615; cited from *A True Copy of the Articles against Dr Bentley* (London, 1710); in *The Present State of Trinity College in Cambridge, in a Letter from Dr Bentley ...*, six tracts in one volume; 2nd edn (London, 1710), p. 60.

31 *Some Remarks* (one of the six tracts mentioned in the preceding note), p. 56.

32 W&C, II, p. 624; cited from 'MSS Parne II. 165' (original not traced).

33 W&C, II, p. 625, conclude with an elaborate but probably unwarranted description: 'there was space for a room about 75 feet long by 25 feet wide, lighted, as we learn from the Accounts, by four windows, ventilated by a louvre, and sufficiently remote to be called "the Comedy House" and "the theatre"'. Their evidence for four windows is the use of four haircloths in 1668–9, but one window may have required more than one haircloth, and the windows may not have been those in a remote room.

34 Less certain in its relevance is a payment among expenses for a comedy of 1670–1 'for worke done at the Lodge when the Duke of Yorke was here'.

35 W&C, II, p. 619, cite many archival references to bow windows, most of which concern the dining room and drawing room within the west range. See also RCHM, pp. 230 (dining room, ground floor), 231 (master's drawing room, upper floor). The Loggan print of 1688 (fig. 22) shows no bow windows in the range leading to the river.

36 II, p. 264; W&C cite only one occurrence of 'Acting-Room' (1670–1) out of some dozen in the Junior Bursar' Accounts: see Appendix 6, 1668–9 (× 1), 1669–70 (× 3), 1670–1 (× 5), 1671–2 (× 3), 1695–6 (× 1).

37 W&C, II, p. 624, propose that 'it was the practice in other Colleges to use one of the best rooms in the Lodge for the double purpose of Dining-Room and Audit-Room', and they conclude: 'if such was the practice here, we may identify a portion of the Gallery with the Acting-Room or Comedy-Room'. We have no separate evidence, however, and it seems unlikely, that the best rooms in the lodge were those in the gallery.

38 Smith, 'Academic', p. 179. See Appendix 6, 1669–70, note 4.

39 On the college's plays, see REED, pp. 774–5.

40 Lobel and Johns (eds.), *Cambridge*, Map 2. For an amusing episode in which George I was left to cool his heels in this 'most dirty, filthy place', see Colthorpe, *Royal Cambridge*, p. 40.

41 Augur is named as a witness who would depose to this effect, but no deposition survives.

42 Trinity College Archives, Old Conclusion Book, p. 39. For another example of payments in lieu of meals, see REED, p. 634.

43 G. P. V. Akrigg, *Shakespeare and the Earl of Southampton* (London, 1968), p. 187.

44 Identified by Mary Edmond, 'Limners and Picturemakers', *The Walpole Society*, 47 (1980), pp. 152–3. I am grateful to William P. Williams for supplying this information.

45 Alan H. Nelson, 'Women in the Audiences of Cambridge Plays', *Shakespeare Quarterly*, 41 (1990), pp. 333–6; Smith, *CP*, p. 26. Women are specifically addressed in the prologue to *Albumazar* (REED, pp. 889–90).

46 Trinity College Archives, Old Conclusion Book, p. 62. The two comedies were apparently *The Silent Woman* by Ben Jonson, and *Adelphe* by Samuel Brook: see Appendix 6, 1661–2, headnote. Hill senior was evidently either Thomas (Venn, fifteenth of this name, adm. 1652), or Richard (Venn, ninth of this name, adm. 1654); Hill junior was evidently John (Venn, thirtieth of this name, adm. 1659).

47 On the implications of 'Comedy House', see p. 52.

48 Sixteen yards of fabric to cover the stage, assuming standard widths of 6′, implies a playing area of 864 sq. ft.; if the stage were square, it would have been almost 30′ on a side! Conceivably the fabric was used not only for a floor-covering, but for skirting and perhaps for spectator scaffolds.

49 The play was apparently a revival of *Adelphe* by Samuel Brook: see Appendix 6, 1668–9, headnote.

4. Other colleges

1 REED, pp. 918–19, 944–6; see also p. 847.

2 Ed. Robert Lordi (New York, 1979), Part II, Act V, Scene i, following line 87; and Part III, Act V, Scene iii, following line 43.

3 REED, p. 286.

4 W&C, III, pp. 354–72; RCHM, pp. lxxx–lxxxii.

5 The hall of Emmanuel College is 26′ 3″ wide, originally 58′ in length to the screen; it was wainscoted in 1694 and refitted with an eighteenth-century interior in 1760–4: RCHM, pp. 66–8; photo plate 125; plan opp. p. 64; section p. 67 showing the medieval roof timbers still *in situ* above the flat ceiling. W&C, II, pp. 687, 690–1, 694, 714, 717. On the question of whether Emmanuel supported plays, see REED, p. 753.

6 REED, pp. 199, 731, 736. See also Parne's account, cited p. 53.

7 Alan B. Cobban, *The King's Hall Within the University of Cambridge in the Later Middle Ages*, Cambridge Studies in Medieval Life and Thought, 3rd series, 1 (Cambridge, 1969). On the college's plays, see REED, pp. 759–60.

8 W&C, II, pp. 431–3, 436–40, 455–6.

9 See p. 67.

10 On the college's plays, see REED, pp. 755–6. On the plays of Eton College, its sister institution, see David W. Blewitt, 'Records of Drama at Winchester and Eton, 1397–1576', *Theatre Notebook*, 38 (1984), pp. 88–95, 135–43; and the Buckinghamshire collection in the REED series (in preparation). For a possible 1550–1 reference to the college stage, see p. 175, note 3.

11 W&C, I, pp. 374, 536–7; III, p. 84; see also RCHM, p. 17; plan p. 13 ('Old Schools', 'Old Court of King's College'). The present hall was built 1824–8: RCHM, pp. 132–3.

12 RCHM, plate 46; see also late fifteenth-century cupboard in side chapel 'C', plate 192.

13 A Hillary Cluxton played a prominent role in the maintenance of the university commencement stage from 1560–1 to 1574–5 (CUCS).

14 On the college's plays, see REED, pp. 748–9.

15 RCHM, pp. 26, 32–3; plan opp. p. 28. W&C, II, pp. 200, 219–21; see p. 216 (figs. 6–7) for details of the ends of the hall. Loggan print in W&C, II, p. 191.

16 W&C, II, pp. 216–17; RCHM, p. 34.

17 On the college's plays, see REED, pp. 769–70. For evidence that plays were not performed in the college's Long Gallery (as has been supposed), see REED, pp. 989–90.

18 REED, p. 1194 (original Latin p. 845). For a discussion of yet another letter by Ascham, see p. 175, note 3.

19 RCHM, pp. 187–8, 193; plan in accompanying box; photo plate 239. Original full length was 68′. W&C, II, pp. 308–11.

20 In addition to the dated inventories, see undated inventories, REED, pp. 842–3.

21 W&C, II, pp. 389–430; 463. No plays are recorded for King's Hall after 1516–17, and neither of the other institutions is known to have had a playing tradition (on Michaelhouse, see REED, p. 988).

22 On the college's plays, see REED, pp. 774–5.

23 See discussion of the commencement stage in Great St Mary's, Chapter 5.

24 See discussion of trash nails, pp. 109–10.

25 *CP*, p. 27. The phenomenon occurs not in all MSS as Smith implies, but only in Douce 315, and in Lambeth Palace 838, Art. 5 (see REED, p. 905, for a full list of known MSS).

26 On the college's plays, see REED, p. 751.

27 RCHM, pp. 48–9, 57; plan opp. p. 50. W&C, I, pp. 263–5; section p. 264.

28 Cited by W&C, I, p. 265.

29 On the college's plays, see REED, p. 755.

30 W&C, II, pp. 160–4; plan of stair entrance at lower end of hall, p. 163. RCHM, pp. 83, 92–4; plan of college opp. p. 84; plans of hall pp. lxxxi, 93; photo plate 239.

31 W&C, II, pp. 122–60. RCHM, pp. 82, 86–91; plates 138–9.

32 The entry (REED, p. 254) points ambiguously to two and to three breakages.

33 On the college's plays, see REED, pp. 764–5.

34 W&C, I, pp. 19, 62–3. RCHM, p. 160; plan opp. p. 158; plan of hall p. lxxxi.

35 On the college's plays, see REED, p. 750.

36 W&C, I, p. 84: their 'fig. 2', a reduced copy of the plan drawn up during the reign of Charles I discussed pp. 81–2, is printed in vol. IV (not included in the 1988 reprint).

37 REED, pp. 377–8 (see endnote for date).

38 On the college's plays, see REED, p. 754.

39 W&C, I, pp. 196–7. RCHM, pp. 74, 77–8; plan p. 75. Loggan print in W&C, I, opp. p. 164.

40 On the college's plays, see REED, pp. 763–4.

41 W&C, I, pp. 121, 129, 151–3. Loggan print W&C, I, opp. p. 128. RCHM, plan p. 150 (new hall only).

42 On Clare college plays, see p. 74. Smith, *CP*, p. 16, reasonably considers *Ignoramus* a university play because its cast was drawn from many colleges (REED, pp. 954–5).

5. The university commencement stage, 1464–1720

1 Appendix 8; W&C, III, p. 41.

2 Cited by W&C, III, p. 42, note 2. See also CUCS.

3 All Soul's College, Oxford, Wren MSS, vol. I, numbers 52–5; reproduced and analysed by John Olly, 'Classical Masters' Plans for Cambridge', *The Architect's Journal*, 188 (1988), pp. 36–49, 52–7.

4 Original not traced; copy by Thomas Baker in Cambridge University Library MS Mm.1.45, pp. 127–8; printed in *Correspondence of John Cousin, D.D., Part II*, Surtees Society, 55 (1872), p. 383; whence cited by W&C, III, pp. 37–8. This undated letter is generally assigned to c. 1664–5, when Sparrow served as Vice-Chancellor, but a date following the announcement of a benefaction on 2 February 1669, referred to in the letter, may seem more appropriate. On the history of the Senate House, see Dorothy M. Owen and Elisabeth Leedham-Green, *The Senate House Inside Out: Catalogue of an Exhibition of University Archives Held in Association with the Cambridge Festival in the Senate House 20–26 July 1983* (Cambridge: Cambridge University Library, [1983]); copy in Cambridge University Library, Cam.c.983.41.

5 On early degree ceremonies, see Stanley M. Leathes (ed.), *Grace Book A: Containing the Proctors' Accounts and Other Records of the University of Cambridge for the Years 1454–1488* (Cambridge, 1897), pp. xx–xxx.

6 Oxford: Royal Commission on Historical Monuments, England, *City of Oxford* (London, 1939), pp. 10–12; plan p. 11; photos plates 59 (ceiling), 60 (exterior). Noted by Orrell, *HS*, pp. 202–3. Cambridge: W&C, III, pp. 34–55. RCHM, pp. 9–11; plan p. 10; photos plates 69–70, 72. On the Senate House and the Banqueting House in Whitehall, see Olly, 'Classical Masters' Plans for Cambridge', p. 49.

7 Cooper, III, p. 280; citing from MS Baker 6 (BL Harley 7033), 152. Original not traced.

8 Records of the commencement stage are transcribed in CUCS. Early records are printed in Leathes, *Grace Book A* (1454–1488); and Mary Bateson (ed.), *Grace Book B*, in 2 parts (1488–1511, 1511–1544, Cambridge, 1903–5).

9 Cambridge university archival documents of this period refer to the Senate House under various names, including the New Building, the Public Building(s), the Commencement House, the New Commencement House, the New Regent-House, the New Senate House, and simply the Senate House. In the Vice-Chancellors' vouchers VCV 12–14, the Senate House is often called a 'theatre' as follows (spelling varies). 1721–2: 12(5), F, nos. 29v, 36. 1727–8: 14(1), B, no. 22; C, nos. 3–5, 7. 1728–9: 14(2), C, no. 13. 1729–30: 14(3), C, nos.

5, 7[d], 7[f], 8–9, 13[d], 19. 1730–1: 14(4), A, no. 4; B, no. 27; one of two unnumbered documents ('the Theater' 5 times). U.Ac.2(2) contains similar uses under several Vice-Chancellor's Accounts: 1728–9 (p. 557); 1730–1 (p. 580); 1731–2 (pp. 590–1).

10 VCH, *History of the County of Cambridge and the Isle of Ely*, vol. II: *The City and University of Cambridge*, ed. L. F. Salzman (London, 1948), pp. 280 (Franciscan Friars), 288 (Austin Friars). Willis and Clark, III, p. 35, remark that Great St Mary's 'could not have been particularly convenient for such a purpose', but the persistence of the tradition suggests that the arrangement was felt by most participants to be generally satisfactory.

11 REED, pp. 507; full description pp. 507–11.

12 Cooper, I, p. 288. William Done Bushell, *The Church of St Mary the Great, the University Church at Cambridge* (Cambridge: Bowes and Bowes, 1948), p. 127. RCHM, pp. 275–80; plan p. 276; photos plates 286–7. VCH, pp. 129–30.

13 London, 1714; 2nd edition the same year. The verses were addressed to the 'British Fair Ones, Who in Silence sit', that is, to the female guests, who were confined behind a screen in the chancel.

14 See pp. 10–15.

15 Called 'Tymbers', but since other pieces are identified as girts, joists, and rails, the horizontal pieces seem to be accounted for.

16 See pp. 81–2.

17 The deans were probably Thomas Nevile, master of Trinity and dean of Canterbury; and Humphrey Tyndall, President of Queens' and dean of Ely (compare REED, pp. 505–6).

18 The accounts for 1553–4 reveal that lumber was purchased that year on 25 June, about a week before the 2 July commencement. Other acounts (1558–9, 1559–60, 1593–4, 1602–3) reveal that the occasion of the purchase was St John the Baptist or Midsummer Fair, held on Midsummer Common on 22–5 June (REED, p. 1037).

19 See discussion of trash nails, pp. 109–10.

20 Cambridge University Archives, Collect. Admin. 6a (Buckle Book), p. 635 (second series of pagination), 18 January 1582 (copy Collect. Admin. 6b, f 33): '1 key of the store howse'; flyleaf contains an entry dated 16 October 1587 concerning an inventory of lead which 'there remayned in the storehowse'. Records for 1582–3 and 1634–5 in CUCS.

21 CUCS; previously cited in J. E. Foster (ed.), *Churchwardens' Accounts of St Mary the Great Cambridge from 1504 to 1635*, Cambridge Antiquarian Society, Octavo Series, 35 (Cambridge, 1905); see Index, s.v. Commencement.

22 Continuation of passage cited p. 78. Cooper, III, p. 280, cites yet another negatively biased but still useful description of church services from 1636.

23 Mentioned in record dated 1662–3 (CUCS).

24 Cambridge University Archives, V. C.Ct. 32 (118).

6. Secular playing sites

1 REED, pp. 403–4 and endnote.

2 J. Milner Gray, *Biographical Notes on the Mayors of Cambridge* (Cambridge, 1922), pp. 30, 32; and Charles Henry Cooper and Thompson Cooper, *Athenae Cantabrigienses*, 3 vols. (Cambridge, 1906), II, pp. 426–8. Edmunds was buried 15 September 1606, less than two months after this incident.

3 Venn; *DNB*.

4 John Tucker Murray, *English Dramatic Companies 1558–1642*, 2 vols. (London, 1910), I, p. 202 and II, p. 294, records a payment to the company at Ipswich 25 July 1606.

5 Chambers, *ES*, I, pp. 331–40; and John Wasson, 'Professional Actors in the Middle Ages and Early Renaissance', in *Medieval and Renaissance Drama of England*, I, ed. J. Leeds Barroll (New York, 1984), pp. 4–5.

6 Atkinson, pp. 81–7, 91–4; VCH, pp. 119–20.

7 Cited by Atkinson, p. 85.

8 Reproduced after British Library MS Cole, vol. 12 (= Add. 5813), fols. 129v, 130v, in Atkinson, p. 83; and from thence in REED, p. 724. That the hall had a distinct upper (and lower) end is clear from Cambridge University Archives, Grace Book Theta, p. 519 (5 October 1705) 'in the joint seat at the upper end of the Guild Hall'. The new hall of 1782, which covered an area of 72′ by 28′, apparently comprehended the overall groundplan of the older structure.

9 Maps (*STC* 12734.7, Wing L2836–7) printed in John Willis Clark, *Old Plans of Cambridge, 1574 to 1798*, text volume with portfolio (Cambridge, 1921).

10 On Norwich, see D. F. Rowan, 'The Players and Playing Places of Norwich', in *The Development of Shakespeare's Theater*, ed. John H. Astington (New York, 1992), esp. pp. 92–3. Other towns known or thought to have had temporary demountable stages were Gloucester, Maidstone (Kent), Nottingham, Plymouth, and Stafford (Chambers, *ES*, I, pp. 331–40, particularly p. 333, note 3).

11 Mullinger, II, pp. 156–7.

12 REED, p. 1278 (this was Thomas Howard, ninth Duke of Norfolk and fifteenth earl of Suffolk since 25 August 1554).

13 F. A. Reeve, *Victorian and Edwardian Cambridge, From Old Photographs* (London: Batsford, 1971), caption to fig. 41: 'Queen Mary saw "a play at the Fawcon Inn" in 1557.' Henry Bosanquet, *Walks Round Vanished Cambridge: Petty Cury* (Cambridge: Cambridge History Agency, 1974), caption to plate 12: 'Elizabeth I stayed in a suite of rooms along the gallery on the right, probably watching Shakespeare or Marlowe acting in the yard, for such galleries were the earliest theatres.' Sara Payne, *Down Your Street: Cambridge Past and Present*, vol. I: *Central Cambridge* (Cambridge: Pevensey Press, 1983), p. 165: 'Queen Elizabeth I is said to have stayed in a suite of rooms in the gallery of what was Cambridge's largest galleried inn – The Falcon.' The story concerning Elizabeth is repeated in a caption of a coloured drawing of the Falcon from 1902 in the Kettle's Yard Museum of Folklore (Item 584/74). A more reliable analysis of the Falcon is given by M. J. Petty, *Cambridge in Pictures 1888–1988* (Cambridge: Cambridge Newspapers Ltd, 1988), p. 14.

14 RCHM, p. 324; photo, plate 304. On Cambridge inns generally, see Enid Porter, 'Old Cambridge Inns', *Cambridge, Huntingdon, and Peterborough Life* (September, 1968), pp. 17–19.

15 Palmer, *Cambridge Borough Documents* (Cambridge, 1931), I, pp. 63 (1483), 87 (1561). Palmer reasonably suggests (p. 140) that the Saracen's Head may have been an alternate name for the Blackamore, also recorded as a contemporary Cambridge surname (p. 47). See also W&C, IV, Magdalene College, fig. 1, for the site of the Black Boy.

16 Palmer, *Cambridge Borough Documents*, I, pp. 46 (1513–14, from Cambridgeshire Record Office roll PB/XVII/24A), 85 (1561), 138 (comment).

17 On the recent destruction of the Falcon, see Bosanquet, *Walks Round Vanished Cambridge: Petty Cury*; and Cambridgeshire Collection, Cutting File, O.Fal.

18 A painting of 1875 in the Fitzwilliam Museum showing the same view as the photograph is reproduced in REED, p. 726. The Cambridgeshire Collection contains a number of late nineteenth- and twentieth-century illustrations of the Falcon: illustrations file, O.Fal. See also the coloured drawing of 1902 in the Kettle's Yard Museum of Folklore (Item 584/74).

19 Noted in the course of a useful description of the Falcon by RCHM, p. 329.

20 See the plan in the Cambridgeshire Collection by the lithographers Foister and Jagg, published for a sale of the Falcon at auction; and another by G. J. Smith, 'Collection of Plans of Properties in Cambridge 1688–1886', iii. By the middle of the nineteenth century the Falcon had become a slum: see Payne, *Down Your Street*, pp. 165–6.

21 Atkinson, p. 74, gives a colourful but unverifiable word-picture of the event: the galleries surrounding the innyard 'gave accommodation to the Quality when a dramatic performance was being given in the inn yard; their inferiors meanwhile stood about in the yard or pit, in the centre of which the stage was erected'. I assume with Atkinson that play performances at inns were normally held out of doors; indoor entertainment, however, particularly musical, was common in Cambridge inns in the eighteenth and nineteenth centuries: see VCH, p. 115.

22 RCHM, p. 115; location at No. 4 Bridge street shown in Enid Porter, *Victorian Cambridge: Josiah Carter's Diaries 1844–1884* (London: Phillimore & Co., 1975), map opp. p. 14; and discussed by Porter, 'Old Cambridge Inns', p. 17: 'Inside the house was a large room in which, on occasion, plays were performed as, for example, on March 19th, 1830 when a university amateur performance of *Much Ado about Nothing* was given.'

23 REED, pp. 740–1. See also *The New Grove Dictionary of Music and Musicians*, ed. Stanley Sadie, 20 vols. (London, 1980), s.v. Cambridge (reproduces a programme for a concert in the Black Bear, 1790).

24 See REED, Index, for references to Cambridge problems with Chesterton. A recent history is VCH, *History of the County of Cambridge and the Isle of Ely*, vol. IX: *Chesterton, Northstowe, and Papworth Hundreds*, ed. A. P. M. Wright and C. P. Lewis (London, 1989), pp. 5–39 (see p. 11 for inns).

25 On the Cambridge bullring in the market, see REED, pp. 395, 407, 409, 412, 457, 593, 651.

26 B. R. Hartley, 'The Wandlebury Iron Age Hill-Fort, Excavations of 1955–6', *Proceedings of the Cambridgeshire Archaeological Society*, 50 (1957), pp. 1–27. VCH, *History of the County of Cambridge and the Isle of Ely*, vol. VIII: *Armingford and Thriplow Hundreds*, ed. A. P. M. Wright (London, 1982), pp. 227–8. Photo in REED, p. 728.

27 Richard Southern, *Medieval Theatre in the Round: A Study of the Staging of 'The Castle of Perseverance' and Related Matters* (London, 1957; 2nd edn 1975); Natalie Crohn Schmitt, 'Was There a Medieval Theater in the Round? A Re-examination of the Evidence', pp. 292–315, and Alan H. Nelson, 'Some Configurations of Staging in Medieval English Drama', pp. 116–47, both in *Medieval English Drama: Essays Critical and Contextual*, ed. Jerome Taylor and Alan H. Nelson (Chicago, 1972); K. M. Dodd, 'Another Elizabethan Theater in the Round', *Shakespeare Quarterly*, 21 (1970), pp. 125–56; and David P. Dymond, 'A Lost Social Institution: The Camping Place', *Rural History*, 1 (1990), pp. 165–92.

7. Cambridge staging practices

1 Information concerning the commencement stage not given in Chapter 5 may found in CUCS.

2 Palmer, *Cambridge Borough Documents*, I, pp. 47, 50.

3 Cambridge practices are described by John Bowtell, in Downing College MS Bowtell Bequest 63.4, pp. 922, 928.

4 Demountable structures are usefully discussed by Orrell, *HS*, pp. 42–3.

5 RCHM, p. 110 (King's College Chapel roof timbers); Richard Harris, *Discovering Timber-Framed Buildings* (Princes Risborough, Buckinghamshire, 1978), p. 93.

6 Buck's Book, c. 1665 (Queens' College, Book 89), cited in CUCS.

7 Tripods are recorded at Queens' in 1546–7 and at Peterhouse in 1575–6, but these may have been stools rather than supports for platforms. The *sustentacula mensarum* are recorded at King's College in 1578–9.

8 Discussed pp. 40–2.

9 REED, p. 1038; discussed by Hodges, 'What is Possible: The Art and Science of Mistakes', in Hildy, *New Issues*, p. 48.

10 Joseph Wright (ed.), *English Dialect Dictionary* (Oxford, 1898–1905), s.v. Trace (sb3); and J. O. Halliwell, *A Dictionary of Archaic and Provincial Words*, 3rd edn (London, 1855), s.v. trash (sense 2). William G. Cooke, 'Lexicographic gleanings from the Cambridge records', *REEDN* 13, number 1 (1988), p. 5, notes the failure of REED, p. 1385, to have come up with a satisfactory definition by the time of its publication.

11 William Campbell (ed.), *Materials for a History of the Reign of Henry VII*, 2 vols. (London, 1877), pp. 15, 18, 26. See also J. E. Foster (ed.), *Churchwardens' Accounts of St Mary the Great Cambridge from 1504 to 1635*, Cambridge Antiquarian Society, Octavo Series, 35 (Cambridge, 1905), p. 333 (1614).

12 Downing College MS Bowtell Bequest 63.4, p. 928; cited by Palmer, *Cambridge Borough Documents*, I, p. 166. On the use of leather in conjunction with nails, see also Trinity College accounts for 1670–1, John Shuter's bill (p. 151).

13 REED pp. 230–41 (1563–4), 388–9 (1601–2), 425–7 etc. (1610–11), 491 (1611–12), 509 (1612–13), 540–2 (1614–15). A performance on 4 February 1636 which lasted from 4 p.m. to 8 p.m. (REED, p. 667) would have been mostly in the dark. William Soone, writing in 1575 (REED, p. 846), implies that performances were at night. See also Smith, *CP*, pp. 25, 33.

14 REED, pp. 356, 588–9, 610, 622, 640–1, 667, 700, 912. In 1635–6, under exceptional circumstances, one of two plays was given in the morning (pp. 667–8).

15 See pp. 109–10.

16 Cambridge University Archives, U.Ac.1(3), no. 10 (bill of Thomas Brook, Esquire Bedell).

17 Hardwick received 6s 6d 'settyng vpp & pullyng downe the Raile', whereas Richard Bell received 2s 6d 'setting vpp the stage & Raile': I am assuming that Hardwick, like Bell, worked on both the stage and the rail.

18 Owen and Leedham-Green, *The Senate House Inside Out* (full citation above, p. 170, note 4), pp. 4, 12, observe that the first public commencement at the new Senate House was also its last. The word 'Last' in Laurence Eusden's *Verses at the Last Publick Commencement at Cambridge* (1714) means 'most recent', not 'final'.

8. Postscript: Cambridge to London

1 Conference proceedings published in Hildy, *New Issues*. This Postscript focuses on this and two other recent publications: Orrell, *HS*; and Blatherwick and Gurr (with an added note by Orrell), 'Shakespeare's Factory'. If in this chapter I seem to take issue with Professor Orrell more than with any other scholar, it is because he more than any other scholar has had the industry and courage to express bold opinions on numerous topics.

2 *OED*, s.v. theatre, sb. 2: 'In modern use, An edifice specially adapted to dramatic representations; a playhouse'; first citation 1577. John M. Wasson (ed.), *Devon*, REED (Toronto, 1986), cites Latin 'in teatro' from Exeter, 1348 (discussed p. 439).

3 See pp. 77–8; Chapter 5; figs. 6, 29–30; Appendixes 1, 2, 5, 7–9. On 5 October 1551 Roger Ascham wrote to his friend Edward Raven from Brussels (REED, p. 845):

> the Chirches be mad like theatra, *videlicet* one seat hiher than a nother and round about be stages above as is at the Kinges Colledg buttrey dore *videlicet* in Chirstenmas[;] the pulpet in the middes[,] the table of the lord standes commonlie in the hiher end…

I have not included this reference in my discussion of King's College stage because Ascham may be referring to shelves in the college buttery arranged for displaying food and plate (note 'buttrey dore' rather than 'hall'): see *OED*, s.v. stage (sb. 1.f).

4 I discuss animal baiting rings at greater length pp. 122–3. Orrell, *HS*, p. 44–5, 47, 59–60, agrees that Burbage and Brayne aimed at functionality, but believes that in the case of polygonal theatres functionality was compatible with architectural sophistication.

5 Martin S. Briggs, 'Building Construction, England', in Charles Singer *et al.* (eds.), *A History of Technology*, vol. 3 (Oxford, 1957), p. 256.

6 See p. 7. Gurr, *Playgoing in Shakespeare's London*, p. 86, notes Ben Jonson's quarrel with Inigo Jones for 'reducing the secrets of universal harmony to mathematical tables'.

7 See my discussion of the 'original' form of Queens' College stage, and subsequent alterations and additions, pp. 26–9, 32–3.

8 The *ad quadratum* principle was by no means unknown: it was described in detail by Serlio, with illustrations, and in a treatise on laying out gardens (Orrell, *HS*, pp. 130–49, 155). For an argument that the square Fortune was also *ad quadratum*, see Orrell, *HS*, pp. 150–8.

9 Orrell, *HS*, pp. 43–4, 152, 157. Orrell's argument (p. 29) that alterations or expansions were 'entirely precluded by the highly integrated design of the original structure' has been undercut by excavations at the Rose.

10 An additional complication concerns possible jettying of successive stories, giving a different gallery depth at each level: at which level does *ad quadratum* pertain? Cerasano, 'Shakespeare's Elusive Globe', p. 267, protests against unwarranted claims to precision in attempted reconstructions of Renaissance theatres. Note Orrell's claim, *HS*, p. 154, to have established the inner diameter of the Globe at 69'.

11 Blatherwick and Bowsher, 'The Structure of the Rose', p. 59, assert that the foundations of the first Rose reveal *ad quadratum* proportions. Orrell, 'Beyond the Rose', pp. 102–7, agrees, although he presents a thoroughly revised argument for the logic of a fourteen-sided *ad quadratum* polygon. Hodges, 'Reconsidering the Rose', pp. 87–93, describing the Rose as 'squiffy', makes no mention of *ad quadratum*, rejects 'ideal models' (p. 88), and (in his more recent drawings) takes the disclosed foundations rather than imputed geometric regularity as the irreducible given. Hodges makes a similar point in 'What is Possible?' pp. 45–6.

12 Orrell, 'Beyond the Rose', pp. 100, 109, concedes that the Globe was probably not designed *ad quadratum*. Blatherwick and Gurr, 'Shakespeare's Factory', pp. 321, 323–4, project an 80′ Globe on *ad quadratum* principles, but are answered by Orrell in an appendix to the same article, pp. 329–33.

13 Moxon, *Mechanick Exercises*, pp. 85–90, explains the use of a bevel and of a mitre box, taking as his example a frame for an octagonal picture or mirror (illustrated in his frontispiece). The mathematician Gauss demonstrated the impossibility of constructing a regular polygon of 7 (also 9, 13, 14, 19, 21, etc.) sides by geometrical means: see *Encyclopaedia Britannica*, 11th edn, 29 vols. (Cambridge, 1910–11), XI, p. 682, col. 2.

14 A brief experiment will show that a high degree of precision can be reached for a regular polygon of any reasonable number of sides in three tries at the very most.

15 See pp. 129–30. Fortune contract in Foakes and Rickert (eds.), *Henslowe's Diary*: 'in suche sorte as is prefigured in a Plott thereof drawen' (p. 308). Orrell, *HS*, p. 159, mentions the Fortune 'Plott', but accords it no role in the building's laying out. He also notes (p. 153) a 'platt' for a gatehouse which Henslowe and Alleyn agreed to build at the Bear Garden in 1606. Note various contemporary plans for theatres, reproduced in *HS*, pp. 121, 170–1, 174–7, 180–3, 227.

16 On the Red Lion, see Orrell, *HS*, pp. 20–8. On the Boar's Head, see *HS*, pp. 10–12 (documents thoroughly analysed and theatre reconstructed by Berry, *Boar's Head*).

17 Orrell, *HS*, pp. 22–3. Orrell asserts (p. 22): 'nor indeed was the Red Lion an inn at all'. A more recent analysis is Berry, 'The First Public Playhouses, Especially the Red Lion'. See *OED*, s.v. 'sign', sb. 6: 'A characteristic device attached to, or placed in front of, an inn (house) or shop'; see also 6b. Certainly nothing precludes the possibility that the Red Lion was an inn, and its sign remains suggestive.

18 Orrell, *HS*, p. 8; as Orrell notes, in a subsequent edition of 1596 Lambarde added the Theatre to this list of show places.

19 Orrell, *HS*, pp. 8–9. Orrell, p. 10, follows Wickham in dismissing the apparent significance of a London ordinance of 1574 attempting to control or forestall crowds gathered 'In great Innes, haveinge chambers and secrete places adioyninge to their open stages and gallyries', arguing that 'open' in respect to both stages and galleries means 'public' rather than 'open to the sky'. It is almost impossible to imagine, however, that any inn was so capacious as to have had stages plus accompanying galleries indoors. The galleries of the Falcon, a typical inn (figs. 33–5), afforded a view of the yard on the one hand and access to chambers on the other. Note also a reported abortive plan by John Brayne in 1580 to lease the George Inn, Whitechapel, 'to build a playhouse therein': Orrell (*HS*, p. 260, note 13) argues, 'the word "therein" might equally well apply to an enclosed auditorium in one of the inn's larger rooms'. But in the absence of evidence that internal rooms of inns were ever converted to theatres (much less playhouses), 'therein' must be taken to refer to the innyard.

20 Berry, *Boar's Head*, p. 16; cited by Orrell, *HS*, pp. 259–60, note 8.

21 Nelson, 'Hall Screens and Elizabethan Playhouses'.

22 Berry, 'The Stage and Boxes at Blackfriars', pp. 64–6.

23 For Cambridge instances of sitting on the stage, see pp. 13, 42, 109. For London instances, see Orrell, *HS*, pp. 89–90.

24 Hotson, *Shakespeare's Wooden O*, pp. 152–4, makes a similar argument for two opposed audiences; clearly, however, a strict bifurcation of the audience is more likely in hall theatres than in open-air playhouses, where the audience was disposed more nearly in the round.

25 Blatherwick and Bowsher, 'The Structure of the Rose', p. 66; Gurr, 'The Rose Repertory', p. 124.

26 Orrell, *HS*, pp. 186–7. Orrell himself attempts a reconstruction, pp. 186–203. For a more conservative analysis, see Berry, 'The Stage and Boxes at Blackfriars'.

27 Berry, 'The Stage and Boxes at Blackfriars', pp. 52–66.

28 Orrell, *HS*, p. 267, note 25, cites early references to tiring houses/rooms. He suggests that the 'tyringe house' between the hall and the master's lodge at Trinity College was used for academic rather than for theatrical purposes, but see above, pp. 43–4.

29 Thomas Lodge and Robert Greene, *A Looking glass for London and England*, ed. Russell Fraser and Norman Rabkin, in *Drama of the English Renaissance*, I (New York, 1976), p. 383: this play is 'a spectacular resume of the state of the theater in 1590', and includes 'lightning that burns up Remilia, a flame from the earth that swallows up Radagon, and a serpent that eats the vine that shelters Jonas'.

30 Orrell, *HS*, pp. 61–5, 89 (and notes). The most complete article on this subject is John Astington, 'Descent Machinery in the Playhouses'.

31 Thomas Legge's *Solymitana Clades* (= *Destruction of Jerusalem*) contains a concluding note on 'The attire of such as be in the Show in the beginning of the Third Action'. Various explicit details are given, including some cited from Josephus, Legge's source. Legge adds: 'this attire is pictured out in the King of Spaines great bible and the capps which they vse. note in the showe they are all bare headed sauing the Sadduces'. The reference is apparently to the large folio Latin Bible (Antwerp, 1583), sig. f1, plate illustrating the sacred vestments of the Hebrews. A copy of the bible is Cambridge University Library, Bible Society Collection, 1.7.15. Further on *Solymitana Clades*, see REED, p. 938.

Select bibliography

This bibliography of articles and books is strictly limited to recent publications of peculiar relevance to my subject, and to a very few older publications cited frequently in the notes (see also the List of abbreviations). A more comprehensive bibliography of the subject may be found in Hildy, *New Issues*, pp. 35–7.

Astington, John, 'Descent Machinery in the Playhouses', *Medieval and Renaissance Drama in England*, 2 (New York, 1985), pp. 119–33.

Berry, Herbert (illustrations by C. Walter Hodges), *The Boar's Head Playhouse* (Washington D.C., 1986).

(ed.), *The First Public Playhouse: The Theatre in Shoreditch 1576–1598* (Montreal, 1979).

'The First Public Playhouses, Especially the Red Lion', *Shakespeare Quarterly*, 40 (1989), pp. 133–48.

Shakespeare's Playhouses, AMS Studies in the Renaissance (New York, 1987).

'The Stage and Boxes at Blackfriars', *Studies in Philology*, 63 (1966), pp. 163–86; reprinted in his *Shakespeare's Playhouses*, pp. 47–73 (citations from reprint).

Blatherwick, Simon, and Julian M. C. Bowsher, 'The Structure of the Rose', in Hildy, *New Issues*, pp. 55–78.

Blatherwick, Simon, and Andrew Gurr, 'Shakespeare's Factory: Archaeological Evaluations of the Site of the Globe Theatre at 1/15 Anchor Terrace, Southwark Bridge, Southwark', *Antiquity*, 66 (1992), pp. 315–33.

Cerasano, S. P., 'Shakespeare's Elusive Globe: Review Article', *Medieval and Renaissance Drama in England*, 3 (New York, 1986), pp. 265–75.

Eccles, Christine, *The Rose Theatre* (London, 1990).

Foakes, Reginald, *Illustrations of the English Stage 1580–1642* (London, 1985).

Foakes, R. A., and R. T. Rickert (eds.), *Henslowe's Diary* (Cambridge, 1961).

Gurr, Andrew, *Playgoing in Shakespeare's London* (Cambridge, 1987).

'The Rose Repertory: What the Plays Might Tell Us About the Stage', in Hildy, *New Issues*, pp. 119–34.

Gurr, Andrew, Ronnie Mulryne and Margaret Shewring, *The Design of the Globe* ([London]: The International Shakespeare Globe Centre, 1993).

Gurr, Andrew, and John Orrell, *Rebuilding Shakespeare's Globe* (London, 1989).

Hildy, Franklin J. (ed.), *New Issues in the Reconstruction of Shakespeare's Theatre: Proceedings of the Conference Held at the University of Georgia, February 16–18, 1990*, Artists and Issues in the Theatre, 1 (New York, 1990).

Hodges, C. Walter, 'Reconstructing the Rose', in Hildy, *New Issues*, pp. 79–94.

Hodges, C. Walter, S. Schoenbaum, and Leonard Leone (eds.), *The Third Globe: Symposium for the Reconstruction of the Globe Playhouse, Wayne State University, 1979* (Detroit, 1981).

Hotson, Leslie, *Shakespeare's Wooden O* (London, 1959).

Leacroft, Andrew, *The Development of the English Playhouse* (London, 1973).

Nelson, Alan H., 'Hall Screens and Elizabethan Playhouses: Counter-Evidence from Cambridge', in *The Development of Shakespeare's Theater*, ed. John Astington (New York, 1992), pp. 57–76.

Nelson, Alan H., and Iain Wright, 'A Queens' College Playhouse of 1638?: Reconsiderations', *Renaissance Drama*, n.s. 22 (1991), pp. 175–89.

Orrell, John, 'Beyond the Rose: Design Problems for the Globe Reconstruction', in Hildy, *New Issues*, pp. 95–118.

The Human Stage: see List of abbreviations.

The Quest for Shakespeare's Globe (Cambridge, 1983).

'Shakespeare's Factory: Appendix', in Blatherwick and Gurr, 'Shakespeare's Factory', pp. 329–33.

The Theatres of Inigo Jones and John Webb (Cambridge, 1985).

Smith, George Charles Moore, *College Plays*: see List of abbreviations.

Wickham, Glynne, *Early English Stages 1300–1660*, vol. I: *1300–1576* (London, 1959).

Index

Such permanent fixtures of colleges or ecclesiastical institutions as halls, kitchens, staircases, galleries, and chapels are listed below under the appropriate institution. Strictly theatrical items such as costumes, partitions, seats and seating galleries, stage doors, stage platforms, and stairs for stages are listed individually. Also listed individually are such theatre-oriented college appurtenances as acting chambers, a comedy room, tiring chambers, upper-end walls, and such windows as were subject to breakage during ceremonies or performances. Appendixes are indexed, but not endnotes. Members of the university whose names appear only in Appendixes 6, 8, and 10 are not indexed. Many individuals, including workmen, are identified in the records and in this Index by surname only (first name given as blank); a handful are identified by first name only.

acting chamber/room (Trinity) 47, 54, 57–9, 142, 147–52; *see also* comedy room
acting chambers 34–7 (Queens'), 74 (Clare)
acting companies, *see* players (professional)
acting clothes, *see* costumes
actors/acting (college) 29, 37, 43, 57–61, 64–5, 68–9, 74, 76, 78, 107–8, 113, 124, 144–51; *see also* players, professional; plays
acts (of plays) 55; *see also* Oxford (act), music act
ad quadratum, *see* geometrical constructions
Adams, John (carpenter) 114–15
Adamson, John 100
additions to hall stage (Queens') 18, 26–30, 32–3, 107, 124–5, 135–9
Adelphe 116–17, 143, 147
Æmelia 45, 116
Albumazar 38–9
Alcock, John 71–2
aldermen (of Cambridge) 52, 57, 89, 92, 102, 114, 151
ale, *see* beer
All Saints Day 76
Allen, John J. 118
altar (as prop) 35
ambassadors, *see* dignitaries
Ames (Hames), John (cooper) 64
amphitheatre (London) 126
Andrews, — 145
Anne, Queen 51; *see also* Queen Anne's Company
answerer 84

Antwerp 66
apothecary 64
apparatus (for stage) 64, 112
archaeology 1–2, 52, 118, 121, 124, 126
architects (architecture) 1–2, 7, 35, 68, 77, 89, 118–22, 124
Aristippus 116
Aristophanes 70
arras 14, 108, 127; *see also* cloth
Arrowsmith, Mr 145
ascends 51, 79–80, 82–3; *see also* seating, scaffolds
ascents (descents, flying, heavens) 35–6, 70, 113, 126
Ascham, Roger 66
ash (wood) 16, 104–5
Ash Wednesday 16, 144
Asley (Ashley), Lord 150
assistants (men, servants) 14, 34, 36, 56, 64–5, 67–70, 73, 76, 78, 84–7, 108, 113–15, 146, 149, 159; *see also* labourers
Atkinson, T. D. 89–92, 94–5
Atkinson, — 33
attiring chamber, *see* tiring chamber (Trinity)
audiences (playgoers, spectators) 16, 30, 36, 38, 42–3, 55, 57, 59–61, 70, 95, 97–8, 100, 107–8, 116, 119–20, 124, 149
Audley End 39, 76
Auger, Nicholas 55
Aulularia 76
Austin Friars (church of) 78, 86, 103
Avesse, Martin 34, 103

Babington, Sir 149
Babour, *see* Barber, James
bachelors of arts (B.A.) 12, 15, 53, 77, 98, 103,
    113, 127, 129–30, 144; *see also* doctors,
    masters of arts, students
back-stools 151
backdrops, *see* scenes
baiting rings 120, 122–3; *see also* bearbaiting,
    bull-baiting
baize 58–9, 148, 151; *see also* cloth
balconies, *see* galleries
ballasters 57, 144–5
Banks, — (blacksmith) 64
Bankside (London) 1–2
Banqueting House (Whitehall, London) 39, 77,
    119
banquets, *see* dining
Barber (Babour), James 147, 150
Barber, Thomas 34
Bargar, Mr 74
Barnes, William(?) 66
Barnwell 3
Barrington Court 147
bars (of iron) 54, 58, 67, 145
bars (rails) 40–3, 109, 144–5; *see also* rails
Basil, Simon 126
basket (as prop) 70
Baxter, John 100
bay windows, *see* bow windows
beams 159; *see also* timber
Bear Inn 4, 93, 97–8
Bear-garden (London) 122–3
bearbaiting 39, 97–100, 123
beards (for actors) 148–9
bearers 57, 144
bearwards 98
beer (ale) 147–8, 150, 159
Bel Sauvage Inn and Fair (London) 123
Bell Inn (London) 123
Bell, Richard (carpenter) 68, 113
Bell, Robert (carpenter) 64, 67
benches (forms) 15, 18, 20, 34, 36–7, 41, 59–60,
    67–9, 73, 82, 86–7, 103–4, 127
Bende, Anthony 98
Bene't College, *see* Corpus Christi College
Bene't Street 78
Bentley, Richard 52–3
Berry, Herbert 2, 125
bibleclerks 134, 137–9
billets 145
bills (for plays) 99
bills (of carpenters) 42, 58, 82–3, 85, 104, 115,
    145–6, 150–2
binding 151, 159
binding-jeece 10, 18, 20–1, 29

Bissell, — 87
Black Bull Inn 92
Blackfriars hall/theatre (London) 2, 39, 125–6
blacksmiths, *see* smiths
Blatherwick, Simon 118
Bloom, Hans 7
Boar's Head Inn (London) 2, 123
boards (planks) 10, 18, 20, 24–6, 28–32, 34, 36,
    54, 56, 58, 64–5, 67–8, 82–3, 103–7, 115,
    137–9, 149, 153, 156, 159–60; *see also*
    deals, inch-boards, slope boards
boats (for carriage) 67, 103, 105
bolts 44, 144
booths 99–103, 110, 113; *see also* proctor's
    booth
Botes, — (?) 68
Botman, — 35
bow windows (bay windows, oriels) 5; *see also*
    under individual colleges
Bowsher, Julian M. C. 118
Bowtell, John 110, 113
boxes (theatrical) 82, 84, 125
braces 10, 18–19, 25, 30
brass (funeral) 14
Brayne, John 119, 121–3
bread, *see* dining
breakage 34–6, 60, 64, 66–7, 70, 73–6, 79, 87,
    103, 105, 110, 113, 146, 150; *see also*
    disorders, repairs
Brewer, Matthew 68
brewers 145
Brewers, — 57
bricklayers 147
bridals 89
bridges 1, 11, 13, 51, 91, 107
Bridges, Nathaniel (carpenter) 114, 160
broadcloth 59, 86, 106, 151; *see also* cloth
Brook, Samuel 143, 147
brooms 146–7, 151
Buck, Thomas 108
Buckler drawings 96
Buckly (Bulkly), — 147, 150
buckram 76; *see also* cloth
Bull Inn (London) 123
bull-baiting 100
bullring 65, 100
Burbage, James 16, 119, 121–2
Burghley, Lord, *see* Cecil, William
burnt claret 148, 150; *see also* wine
Burros, Baron 70
Burton, Joshua (tailor) 149, 151
Burton, — (carpenter) 74
Burwell, John (apothecary) 34, 64
Butcher, D. and William 68
butlers 146–7

Button, William 70
buttons 151

Cage, Thomas 148, 151
Caiton, *see* Caton
Caius College, *see* Gonville and Caius College
calico 151; *see also* cloth
Cam (river) 3–4, 52, 56, 67
Cambridge Evening News 52
Cambridge town 1–15, 88–101, 118–26; *see also*
    aldermen, council, Guildhall, market,
    mayors, townspeople
    maps 4, 91, 93
    treasurers 89
Cambridgeshire Collection 94–5
Cambridge University, *see* university
Cambyses 14
canary 148, 150–1; *see also* wine
candelabra 74, 112
Candlemas 65
candles 33–5, 57–9, 64–5, 67, 69, 73–4, 111–12,
    144–6, 148, 150–1; *see also* wax
candlesticks 33, 35, 56, 58–9, 64, 66–7, 69, 76,
    111–12, 146, 150–1
canvas 33–4, 108, 111, 151; *see also* cloth
carpenters 2, 5, 7, 10, 16, 33–7, 56, 58–60,
    64–9, 71, 74, 78, 82–5, 88, 100, 102, 105,
    108, 113–15, 119–22, 144–5, 147, 150, 153,
    159–60
carpenters' marks, *see* marking of timbers
carpenters' tasks and charges (summaries) 84–5,
    114–15
carpentry 5, 7, 9, 58, 120
carriages, *see* carts
carriers 64, 100, 103–4
carrying (carriage) 34, 36, 51, 54, 56, 58, 64, 69,
    86–7, 102–6, 145, 149, 159–60
Carter, Edmund 71
carters 56, 69, 144, 160
carts (cartloads, carriages, waggons) 34, 56, 92,
    95, 103–4
Cartwright, Mr 128
carving (of props) 146
casements, *see* windows
castle (as prop) 70
Castle of Perseverance, The 100
Caton (Caiton), William (joiner) 58–9, 148, 150
Cavarly, Timothy 58, 149–50
Cecil, William (Lord Burghley) 12–15, 78, 99,
    127
Cecill, Thomas 45, 141
celures (sayleirs) 56, 111; *see also* cloth
centaur (as prop) 56, 111
ceremonies (academic) 13–14, 39, 77–8, 84, 103,
    108, 110; *see also* commencement

chairs 60, 82; *see also* seats
chamber of presence (royal) 108
Chamberlain, John 43
Chambers, E. K. 14
chambers, *see* acting chamber, comedy chamber,
    and under individual colleges
Chancellors (university) 15, 40–1, 127, 148
chapels 100; *see also* Jesus, King's, Great St
    Mary's
Chapman, Mr 90
Chapman, — 54, 58, 147–8, 150
Chapple, — 56
charcoal, *see* coals
Charles I, King 38, 51, 56, 74, 79–80, 83, 109,
    113, 117
Charles II, King 54, 149, 151
Chatherton (Chatterton), Mr 65, 128
Chesterton 3, 98–9
chests (coffers, trunks) 34–5, 56, 64–5, 67, 69,
    104, 111–12
Childermas Day 111
Christ Church, *see* Oxford
Christ's College 3–4, 10, 42, 62, 64–6, 108,
    111–12, 128
    chimney, fireplace, interior window, louvre,
    master's lodge, oriel, screens 65
    hall 62, 65–6
    windows 65–6
Christmas 13, 53, 66–7, 71, 73; *see also* lords of
    Christmas
Christus Triumphans 68
churchwardens 86
circus magnus 119, 129–30
Civil War 36, 40, 55
Clare College 3–4, 56, 62, 64, 74, 76, 99, 104,
    111–12, 117; *see also* acting chambers
    hall 62, 74
    Master 99
    plan, screens, windows 74
Clark, George (victualler) 100
Clark, John Willis, *see* Willis and Clark
Clarke, Mr 128
Clarke, Thomas 89
classical plays (architecture, theatres) 2–3, 13,
    70, 77, 119–20; *see also* Latin plays
Clayton, Richard 88
cleaning (sweeping, washing) 35, 37, 86, 146,
    149, 151
Cleveland, Duchess of 149
Clifton, — 144–5
cloth of state 14, 127
cloth (fabrics) 15, 33–4, 56, 58–60, 66, 70, 76,
    78, 85–7, 108–10, 114–15, 127, 149–51; *see
    also* broadcloth, costumes, green cloth,
    pastoral cloth

Club Law 74, 117
clubs 55, 71, 113, 148; *see also* weapons
Cluxton, Hillary 65, 115
coals (charcoal) 34, 56, 58, 64, 66, 69, 74, 76,
    112, 146, 148–9; *see also* fires
Cochey, *see* Cutchie
coffers, *see* chests
Cole, Richard 65, 114
Cole, William 90
colliers 64
Collins, Mr 148
colours, *see* marking of timbers, paint
columns, *see* pillars
comedies 3, 13, 33–5, 40, 42–5, 48, 52–3, 55–8,
    64–5, 67, 70–1, 73, 76, 89, 104, 108, 111,
    113–14, 116–17, 140–51
comedy chamber/room/house (Trinity) 44, 47,
    52–4, 57–60, 113, 142, 147; *see also* acting
    chamber
comedy-cloths 54, 58; *see also* costumes
commencement 10, 13, 57, 77, 87, 105, 109, 113
    (bachelors'), 115–16, 127–30, 140–1, 144,
    154–5; *see also* ceremonies
commencement stage (house, scaffold) 12,
    14–15, 52, 77–87, 102–7, 109–11, 113–15,
    119–20, 125, 153–7; *see also* stages
Compton, Baron 70
constables 98–9
contracts 39 (Hope), 122 (Fortune)
control of access 58, 60, 84, 100, 107–8, 112,
    124
control of conduct 40, 55, 60, 100, 115
Cook, George (victualler) 100
Coolidge, — 58, 149–50
cooper 64
Cooper, Charles Henry 142
cord 59, 64, 67, 69, 112, 151, 159; *see also*
    packthread, ropes, string, thread, whipcord
coronation (as play action) 61
Corpus Christi College 3–4, 34, 61–2, 64, 71,
    76, 103, 106, 108, 112, 116; *see also* upper-
    end walls
  bow windows, brazier, chimney, doors,
    kitchens, lantern, master's lodge, screens,
    windows 71
  hall 62, 65–6, 71, 116
corrales de comedias 118
Cosby, Theo 118
costumes 33–7, 54–6, 58–60, 64–5, 67, 69, 92,
    104, 111, 115, 125–6, 145, 148–9, 151
  breeches, caps, coats 149
  gloves 148–9, 151
  hose 148
  jewels, shapes, vizards 145
  patches 148, 150

sleeves 148, 151
slops, waistcoat 150
stockings 149–50
costume materials and techniques: *see also*
    guilding
  pendants 149
  pinking 148–9
  skins 151
  trimming 147, 149–50
cotton 86; *see also* cloth
council, town 89–90
courtiers, *see* dignitaries
courts (college) 100; *see under individual colleges*;
    see also yards
Craven, Mr 145
Creighton, — 148
cressets 69, 74, 112
Cromwell (Crumwell), Baron 70
Cross Keys Inn (London) 123
Crowfoot, John 97, 107
Croyland, Robert de 63
Cudworth, Dr 59, 151
cupboards 86
Curculio 73
Curd, John 144–5, 147, 150
curtains 57, 107, 124, 145; *see also* cloth
cushions 14–15, 57, 87, 127, 145
Custance map of Cambridge 92
Cutchie (Cochey, Cutchey: family of carriers)
    64, 104
  John 100

D'Ewes, Simonds 66, 99–100
damage, *see* breakage, disorders
dancing 151
Daniel, John 98
Dant, William 98
dart (as prop) 74
de Medici, Cosimo 52–3, 58, 117, 147
deals (deal-boards, slit deals) 58, 79, 144, 146–7,
    149–50, 157, 159; *see also* boards
deans 70, 77, 81, 84, 108
death's head 58, 111, 146
decorations (theatrical) 33, 66, 85–6, 110
Dee, John 70, 116
della Porta, Giambattista 38
demountable stages 39, 78, 91, 101–3, 125; *see*
    also stages
descents, *see* ascents
desks 103
Destruction of Jerusalem 66
dialogue 73
diases 5; *see also under individual colleges*
digging of doorway 51; *see also* archaeology
dignitaries (nobility) 12–15, 35–6, 38, 40–1,

51–3, 57–60, 65, 68, 70, 74, 80, 82, 89, 107, 109, 116–17, 119, 124–5, 127, 129–30, 140, 147, 148–51; *see also* doctors, knights' eldest sons, royal visits

dining (banquets, dinners, food) 5, 34, 36–40, 51, 53, 56–7, 59, 70, 74, 76–7, 89, 110, 144, 146–7, 151; *see also* drink

disguisings 63–4, 110

disorders 36, 40, 52, 55, 57, 59–60, 64–5, 69, 71, 74–6, 78, 87, 97–100, 107, 114–16, 125; *see also* breakage, riots

disputations (orations) 14–15, 39, 127–30

Ditterlin (Wendel Dietterlein) 7

doctors/bachelors of divinity, law, medicine 12, 14–15, 29, 36, 39–41, 59, 65, 70, 77, 79–80, 83, 108–9, 127–30, 159; *see also* dignitaries

doctors' gallery (Queens') 29, 36–7, 124

doctors' seats 44, 51, 81, 109, 140–1; *see also* galleries, seats

dogs 64, 98

doorkeepers (door-keeping) 54, 58, 84, 87, 145–7, 149; *see also* watching

doors (openings, passages) 5, 115, 124, 140–1, 145–7, 149–50; *see also* doorkeepers, stage doors, Great St Mary's, *and under individual colleges*

Dorrell, Edward 68

Dove, Sir 145

Dowsey (family of carpenters) 56, 113
    John the elder 33–5, 113
    John the younger, Nicholas, Thomas 113
    William 64, 68, 83–5, 113, 115

drafts, *see* plans

dramatis personae 70, 108–9

dressing (of actors) 146–50; *see also* costumes

dressing (of parlour) 53, 56

drinking cups 146

drums (drummers) 51, 53, 62

dry vats 64, 86 (non-theatrical)

Dudley, Robert 13–14

Duke, John 88–9, 91

Durdon, — 56

Dutton, — 99

Eagle Inn 4, 92

earthenware 58, 112, 146

East Anglian plays 100

Edmunds, John 88

Edward VI, King 10

Eirene, see Pax

Elarye, *see* Cluxton, Hillary

Elephant Inn 4, 92, 97

Elizabeth, Queen 10–15, 39–40, 51, 64, 76, 78–9, 83–4, 92, 106–9, 112, 127–30; *see also* Queen's Men, royal visits

elm 83

Ely, Bishop of 52, 129–30

Emmanuel College 62
    hall 62

emperor, *see* lords of Christmas

Esquire Bedells 33, 88, 91, 97–8, 100

Essex, Earl of 70

Essex, James 90–1

Essex, Sir Charles and Lady 125

Eusden, Laurence 79

Evans, Thomas 71

examinees 55, 57

excavations, *see* archaeology

exits from stages, *see* stage doors

fabrica 78

fabrics, *see* cloth

faggots 35, 66

fairs 92; *see also* Midsummer, Sturbridge, Bel Sauvage fairs

Falcon Inn 3–4, 89, 91–6, 124, 126

farce 3

Fardell, John (carpenter) 100

Farr, Henry and Samuel 98

Fastingham 66

feasts, *see* dining

feet (for trestles) 68, 106

fellow commoners 5, 40, 79

fellows/members (of colleges) 16, 36, 52–4, 59, 67, 71, 73–6, 115–16; *see also* Senior Fellows

fencing, *see* games

fir (wood) 56, 67, 83, 159

fires 74, 158

fires/heating (for plays) 33, 35, 38, 54, 58, 66, 69, 74–6, 112, 146–7; *see also* coal, wood, *and under individual colleges (fireplaces)*

fireworks, *see* squibs

Fisher, John 10, 65

Fitch, Matthew 146, 149

flax 85; *see also* cloth

flocks 59, 151

floor (of stage), *see* platforms

floorboards, *see* boards, platforms

floors (as accommodation for spectators) 31, 41–3

flowers 86, 110; *see also* rushes

flying, *see* ascents

foods; *see also* dining
    nutmeg, sugar 151
    oranges 147, 149

forms, *see* benches

Forrest, John 68

Fortune theatre (London) 120, 122

frales 69, 112

frames 18, 25, 34, 69, 78, 110, 115
  for painters 74, 111
Franciscan Friars (church of) 78, 84, 86–7, 103,
  156
frankincense 110; *see also* rushes
Freschville, Lord 149
fringe (for stage cloth?) 151
Frisby (Friesby), — 148–50
frons scenae 124
Frost, John 34–5, 103–4
Fucus or *Histriomastix* (play title) 116
Fuller, Thomas 74

galleries 1, 5, 10, 15–24, 26, 28–33, 36–7, 39,
  41–3, 45, 51, 59–60, 69, 77–80, 82–3,
  106–7, 109, 120–1, 124–5, 127, 132–9; *see
  also* Great St Mary's, seats, seating
  platforms, Trinity
galleries (of inns) 92–7, 124, 126
gallows (as prop) 68
Gam, — 58, 145, 148–9
games (fencing, sports) 39, 98–101, 123, 126
Gammer Gurton's Needle 3, 65
gardens 34, 92
garments, *see* costumes, stagekeepers' garments
Gascoigne, George 123
gatekeepers (gate-keeping) 57–9, 145, 147,
  149–50; *see also* watching
gates (of colleges) 99; *see also* Great St Mary's
  and under individual colleges,
Gayttes, John 34, 103
geometrical constructions 1–2, 7, 105, 119–22,
  124–5
George II, King 51
Georgia, University of 118
gessima, *see* jasmine
Gibbons, Mary and Orlando 97
Gibbons, William 90, 97
Gibbs, James 77
gilding (gilt-leather) 148, 151
Gill, Robert 147
girt-jeece 23
girts (girders) 6, 8–10, 18–33, 37, 48, 82–3, 104,
  106, 131–9, 156–7
glass (quarries) 34–5, 56, 58, 67, 69–71, 73–4,
  87–8, 91, 113, 146–7, 150, 152; *see also*
  windows
glaziers 56, 66, 87, 147, 150–2
Globe theatre (London) 1–2, 39, 118, 120–1,
  124; *see also* Theatre
glue 56
Gog Magog Hills 3, 99–102, 126
Gonville and Caius College 3–4, 61–5, 75–7,
  116
  brazier 75–6

butteries, cellars, chambers, court, doors,
  kitchen, members, screens, windows 75
hall, library 62, 75
Master 61, 75
Gorge, Arthur 57
graces 77, 154–5
graduates, *see* students
grates, *see* music lattices
Graves, John 34–5, 104
Great Shelford 56
Great St Mary's Church 3–4, 10, 12, 14–15, 52,
  69, 77–87, 102–3, 106–11, 119, 125,
  127–30, 140–1, 153, 156; *see also* pillars
asiles 10, 14, 73, 82, 121
belfry 12, 14, 80–3, 106, 127, 140
chancel 10, 12, 14–15, 80–1, 109, 127
chapels, churchyard gates 87
doors, stairs 82, 84
galleries 10, 12, 79, 82–4
steeple 79, 83
windows 59, 87, 111
Greek plays, theatres, *see* classical plays
green cloth 58–9, 66, 85, 148–51; *see also* cloth
Green, Mistress 56
Green, Robert 2
Green, Thomas 88–9, 91
Grene, John (carpenter) 64
Griffith, Mr 147
Griffith, — (painter) 58, 111
grocer 119
ground-pieces 19
Grumbold, Robert 77
Gryme, Christopher 98
guards (royal) 129–30, 140–1; *see also* watching
Guildhall 3–4, 88–93, 100, 102
  door, pantry 89
  kitchen, parlour, stairs 89, 91
  plan 90
  windows 90–1
gum 150
guns, gunpowder 61, 64, 71

habits, *see* costumes
Haddon, Walter (Master of Requests) 12, 15,
  127
haircloths 52, 56–8, 64, 110, 113, 145, 147,
  149, 158–60; *see also* nets
halls 2, 5, 61–2, 100, 104, 107, 109, 113, 117,
  124–6; *see also under individual colleges*
Hames, *see* Ames
Hamond map of Cambridge 91
hangings 57–9, 70, 109, 111, 127, 129–30,
  145–6, 151; *see also* cloth
Hardwick, William 33, 68, 108, 113
Harsnett, Samuel 42, 109

Hartwell, Abraham 13
hasp 35
hats (hat band, head-tire) 149–150
Hawkesworth, Walter 70
headroom 31–2, 42–3, 106; *see also* stage heights
heads of colleges 99; *see also under individual
    colleges (Master, President)*
heating, *see* fires
heavens, *see* ascents
Henry (painter) 67
Henry VI, King 63
Henry VII, King 110
herbs 86, 110; *see also* rushes
Hill senior 57, 144–5
Hillary, *see* Cluxton, Hillary
Hinde, Sir Francis 100
hinges 84, 107, 159
Hippolytus 64
Hobson, Thomas 104
Hock Tuesday 90
Hodges, C. Walter 118
holes (in masonry) 19–20, 34; *see also* digging
Holland 149, 151; *see also* cloth
holly 56; *see also* rushes
hooks (hookpins) 34, 57, 122, 144, 159
Hoop Inn 97
Hooper, — 145
hoops 58, 64, 69, 149
Hope theatre (London) 39
horizontals 10, 83; *see also* girts
horseraces 100
horses (horse-hire) 35, 100, 103
Hotson, Leslie 14, 16
houses 5–9, 24, 63, 68, 70–1, 86, 91, 103, 123,
    155, 160; *see also* comedy house,
    commencement house, inns, stagehouses
Howes 100
Hudson, Juda 100
Huntingdon 56
hurdles 159–60
Hutchinson, John 98
Hynde, Mr 115
Hypocrises 34

Ignoramus 57, 74, 76
illumination, *see* lighting
inch-boards 18, 64, 83, 105–6, 159
ink 151
innkeeper 97
inns 89, 91–99, 107, 123–4, 126
innyards 92–5, 97–100, 123–4; *see also* yards
inscriptions (painted) 58, 111, 146–9
interior windows, *see* Christ's, Trinity
interludes 88, 97–9, 123
International Shakespeare Globe Centre 118

inventories 3, 9–10, 16–34, 42, 64, 67, 69, 82,
    91, 105–8, 112, 116, 125, 131–9
Ipswich 88
iron (iron-work) 33, 56, 58, 67, 69, 75, 104, 107,
    112, 145, 150
Italian comedy 3
ivory 148, 151
ivy 56; *see also* rushes

Jackson, — (innkeeper) 98
jail, 98; *see also* prisons, Tolbooth
James I, King 38, 40, 42–3, 56–7, 64, 74, 81–2,
    109, 116, 150–1
jasmine (gessamin, jessemin butter) 147, 149–50
jeece (joists) 6, 9–10, 18, 20–32, 36, 48, 56,
    82–3, 104, 131–9, 157
Jenks, William 73
Jesus College 3–4, 62, 71–3, 112, 116, 119, 155
    chapel 71–3
    clock 73
    hall 62, 71–3, 116
    master's lodge 155
    oriel, panelling, plan, stairs 72
    screens, windows 72–3
Johnson, William 35
joiners (joinery) 5, 58–9, 74, 119–20, 144, 148,
    150
joints (iron?) 144
joints (mortise-and-tenon) 5, 7, 9–10, 21, 25–6,
    28, 36, 79, 84, 102, 104–5, 115, 122, 131–9,
    147
joists, *see* jeece
Jones, Inigo 7, 39, 77, 119–20, 122, 126
Jones, — 145
Jonson, Ben 5, 143
judge (at Sturbridge Fair) 159–60
Jupiter's palace 70

keeping of passages 87; *see also* watching
Kelly, Theodore 57
Kemp, — (glazier) 56
Keyle, John (carpenter) 33, 113
keys, *see* locks
Killingworth, — 58, 149
King's College 3–4, 10, 62–5, 71, 76, 83, 97,
    104, 106, 108, 110–14, 116, 126
    bay windows, buttery, cellar, court, door,
        kitchens, oriel, plan of 1635, screens 63
    gate 65, 114
    great post, porter's lodge 65
    hall 10, 62–4, 76
    windows 63–5
King's College Chapel 4, 10–15, 32, 40, 51,
    62–4, 68, 71, 76, 79, 83, 106–9, 112, 114,
    127–30

antechapel, 10, 13, 40
  doors, rood screen, stairs 11, 13
  high altar 15
  organ 13
  side chapels 11, 13–14, 107–8
King's Hall 3–4, 62–3, 67
  door, kitchen, screens 63
  hall 62–3
King, John (carpenter) 34, 67, 113
King, William 152
knights, *see* dignitaries
knights' eldest sons 40–1, 43
Knights, Thomas (innkeeper) 97
Knuckles, — 145

L'Astrologo 38
labour, *see* carpenters' tasks and charges
labourers 1, 35, 42, 52, 56, 58, 64, 66, 68, 78,
    85, 87, 103–4, 113–15, 146, 148, 159; *see*
    also assistants
Labyrinthus 70, 108–9
ladders 68, 83–4, 107; *see also* stairs
Laelia 35
Lamb, — (carpenter) 71, 108
Lambarde, William 122–3
Lame, — (painter) 68, 111
lamps, *see* lights
Lane, John 76
lanterns 112, 150; *see also* lights
lanterns (of halls) 59, 69, 71
Lany, Benjamin 87
lashings 24–5
lath 34, 108
Latin plays 3, 52, 57; *see also* classical plays
lattice, *see* music grate
Laud, William 78, 86
Laurence (carpenter) 115
law, doctors of, *see* doctors
Layfield, Thomas 55
Le Orm, Philip 7
Leacroft, Richard 14
lead (leading) 147, 150, 152; *see also* plumbers,
    solder
leather 59, 110, 151
lecturers 53
Legge, Thomas 61, 66, 75
Lent 13, 57, 77
Lewyn, 'Mother' 34–5
lights (lighting) 5, 33–5, 37, 55–6, 58, 60, 69,
    74–6, 111–13; *see also* lanterns
lightning 64
lignarium 33–4, 103; *see also* lumber houses,
    storehouses
linen 67, 78, 85, 146; *see also* cloth
links, *see* torches

linsey-woolsey 85–6; *see also* cloth
Lion Yard 93–4
liturgical vestments 64, 69
locks (keys, padlocks) 35, 44, 51, 54, 58, 64–5,
    67–70, 84, 88, 91, 98, 103, 107, 144–5,
    149–50, 159
locksmiths, *see* smiths
locus (as theatrical term) 78
Loggan, David 43–4, 72, 91
London 1–3, 5, 14, 38–9, 56, 74, 99, 118–26
Looking Glass for London, A 126
Loosmore, — 148
lords of Christmas (masters of revels) 53, 62, 65,
    111, 113
Lords' Room 124
lucernae 112; *see also* torches
lumber-houses 86, 103; *see also* lignarium,
    storehouses

machina 35, 78
machines, *see* heavens
Madingley (village and Road) 100
Magdalene College hall 62
man-days (carpenters'; summary) 114–15
mandates, *see* orders
Manfeild, — 148
Manners, — 144–5
Manutius, James (painter) 56, 107, 111
Marbacke, Mr 127
market (Cambridge) 3, 88–9, 91, 100, 102,
    129–30
Market Passage 93
marketplace (Trinity stage) 70
marking of timbers 16, 18–20, 22–4, 28, 36,
    78–9, 105, 131–9
Marlois (Samuel Marolois) 7
Marlowe, Christopher 2, 92
Marshall, Thomas 147, 149–50
Mary Magdalene 100
Mary, Queen 10, 91–2
masks (visors) 60, 75, 115–16
Mason, Robert 55
Mason, — 90
masonry walls 19, 21, 48–9, 51
masons 70, 77
masques 77
masters of arts (regents and non-regents) 10,
    12–13, 15, 40–1, 43, 76–9, 97–8, 127–30
masters/heads of colleges 5; *see also under*
    individual colleges
materials (summary) 114–15
mathematics, *see* geometrical construction
Mathews, Thomas 150
mats (matting, padding) 18, 20, 36, 56, 58–9,
    82, 109, 147, 149, 151, 159

mayors (of Cambridge) 88–92, 102, 117
Mechanick Exercises, see Moxon, Joseph
medicine, bachelors and doctors of, *see* doctors
members/fellows of colleges, *see* fellows, *and under individual colleges*
men, *see* assistants
mending, *see* repairs
merchants 64, 102
Mere, Joan 33
Mere, John 33–4, 62, 70, 89, 91–2
Michaelhouse 48, 62–3, 67–8, 103, 105
    hall 62
Michaelmas 105
Midsummer Fair 105
minstrels' galleries 5, 124
mockado 76; *see also* cloth
Monmouth, Duke of 53, 144–5
Moody, Mr 148, 151
mortises and tenons, *see* joints
Moses, Miles 76
Mountjoy, Baron 70
Moxon, Joseph, *Mechanick Exercises* 5–10, 18, 24, 120–2, 137
musaeum 77, 155
Museum of London 1
music act 79, 83, 114
music lattice/grate 58–9, 148, 150
music room/scaffold/stage 79, 83, 106, 114
musicians (music, waits) 56, 61–2, 64, 70, 74, 76, 90, 148–50

N-Town cycle 100
nails (nailing) 18, 24, 31, 33, 35–6, 56, 58–9, 64–5, 67, 69, 73, 76, 79, 83–4, 86, 109–10, 112–13, 145–53, 159; *see also* spikes, tacks, tenterhooks, trash nails
names, *see* inscriptions, nomenclature
Nashe, Thomas 2
Naze, — (joiner) 74
necklace 150
nets 67, 113; *see also* haircloths
Nevile, Thomas 39–40, 48, 55, 61, 71, 98
New Inn 86, 103, 114, 154
New Printing House 36; *see also* University Press
New Year's Day 70, 91
Newling/Newland (family of carpenters) 114, 145
    Edward 114, 144
    John 114, 147
    William 114, 144, 150
Newmarket 116
Newton, Samuel (alderman) 52, 57, 89, 151
Nicholls, Arthur (photographer) 95
Nichols, John 127

night-watchmen, *see* watching
nightcap 116
noble men and women, *see* dignitaries, women
NOLA 58, 111, 147–8; *see also* inscriptions
nomenclature 7; *see also Oxford English Dictionary*, theatre (nomenclature)
non-regents, *see* masters of arts
Norfolk's players 89, 92
North, Lord 98
Norwich 91, 123
nozzle (for candles) 69, 112

oak 13, 58, 83, 104, 111
oak trees (as props) 149
Odam, Nicholas 68
Office of the Works 10
oil-lamps 33–4, 111–12
Old Schools, *see* Schools
Olympic games 100; *see also* games
open-air performance sites 99–101, 124–5; *see also* innyards, playhouses
openings, *see* doors
Orange, Prince/Duke of 58, 149–51
orders (mandates, statutes) 35, 40–3, 48, 53, 66–7, 75, 87–8, 91, 98, 102, 116
oriels 5; *see also under individual colleges*
Ormond, Duke of 58, 148
ornamentation, *see* decorations
ornaments, *see* costumes
Orrell, John 118–19
Ott, Nicholas 33
outdoor/indoor performances 2, 38, 69, 89, 91, 97, 111–13, 123–6; *see also* open-air performance sites
Oxford English Dictionary 83, 105, 110, 116, 119
Oxford University 3, 12, 39–40, 51, 77–9, 82, 126
    act 77
    Chancellor 148
    Christ Church hall/theatre 39–40, 51, 126
    Proctors 15, 127
    seat 157
    Sheldonian Theatre 77
Oxford, Earl of 89
Oxley, Robert 55

packthread 67, 69, 147, 151, 159; *see also* cord
padding, *see* mats
padlock, *see* locks
paint (painting) 56–8, 60, 76, 105, 107–11, 145–9; *see also* marking of timbers
painters 33, 35, 56–8, 60, 64, 67, 74, 76, 110–11
palace (as scene) 70
Palatine, Prince 51, 56, 79–80, 83, 109, 113
Palladio, Andrea 7

Palmer, John 61
panelling (wainscoting) 7, 48, 52, 66, 71–5, 87, 107
papaly stag (?), *see* stag
paper 149, 151
paper boards, *see* pasteboard
Paris Garden (London) 122–3
Parker, Matthew 153
Parker, Mistress 145
Parkin, William 68
parlours, *see* Queens', Trinity
Parnassus plays 3, 116
Parne, Thomas 53–4
Parris, Richard and Thomas 98–9
partitions 42, 70, 79, 82, 84, 108
passages, *see* doors
pasteboard (paper boards) 34, 64, 108, 149
pastoral cloth 56, 109, 111; *see also* cloth
paving 66
Pax (Eirene) 70
Peare/Peere, — (carpenter) 56, 64–5, 114,
    144–5
pegs 21, 36, 83, 104–5, 122; *see also* pins
Peirce, — (carpenter) 114, 145
Pembroke College 3–4, 42, 55, 62, 71–2, 76, 112
    combination room, doors, hall, parlour,
    screens 76
pens 151
Pepper, — (scholar) 97–8
Pereson, Roger 65
Perrin, — (scholar) 42, 55
perspective glass (as prop) 38
perspective set 126
Pestill, Thomas 35
Peterborough, Bishop of 61
Peterhouse 3–4, 62, 73–4, 111–13
    doors, fireplace, oriel, windows 73
    hall 62, 73–4
Petty Cury 91, 95
phanum, *see* shrines
Phillips, — 145
physicians (physic), *see* doctors
Physwick Hostel 67, 69, 103, 107
Piers, John 114, 145
pillars (columns) 7, 13–15, 82, 87, 120
pins 54, 58, 69, 104–5, 148–50; *see also* hooks,
    pegs
pinwood 105
pipes, *see* tobacco
Piss Pot Lane, *see* Trinity Lane
pitch 69, 112
place (as theatrical term) 78
plague 91
planks (planking), *see* boards
plans (drafts, platts) 120, 122; *see also under*
    individual colleges

platforms 5, 151; *see also* seating platforms,
    stage platforms
platts, *see* plans
Plautus 33, 76
play books (play texts) 2–3, 5, 13, 61, 108
players (professional) 2–3, 63, 88–92, 99, 124;
    see also actors
playhouses 1–2, 52, 118–25; *see also* theatres
playing gear, *see* costumes
plays (college) 3, 5, 10, 13–14, 33–40, 42–3, 45,
    53–71, 73–6, 78, 100, 104, 107–13, 115–17,
    125, 142, 147–8, 150–2
plays (professional) 2–3, 5, 7, 88–92, 97–101,
    119, 123–6
playwrights 2, 45, 61, 65–6, 75
plumbers 87; *see also* lead, solder
poles 67, 104, 159–60
polygonal geometry, *see* geometrical
    constructions
Popler (Pople), John 34, 36, 113
portals 67, 107, 149; *see also* shrines
Porter, — (carpenter) 57, 71, 108
porters, *see* Trinity
posts 5, 8–10, 18–29, 31–3, 37, 97, 107, 125,
    132–9; *see also* King's
powder (powdering) 147, 149–50
Powell, Mistress 148, 150
presses (for costumes) 35–6, 54, 58, 111, 145,
    148
Preston, Mr 128
Preston, Thomas 14
Prevaricator's stage 78
Prime, Benjamin 87, 97, 115, 158
prints (?) 159
prisons (prisoners) 71, 98, 146; *see also*
    Tolbooth
private performances, *see* public/private
    performances
Privy Council 99
Proctor's booth/stall 86, 103, 113, 127, 158–60
Proctors 12, 15, 82, 98, 128, 158–60
props 35–7, 56, 58–60, 68, 70, 74, 104, 126
Pryce, Robert 103
public/private commencement 79, 116
public/private performances 10, 33–5, 58–9, 68,
    71, 75, 113, 116–17, 148
public/private theatres 123, 125
pulleys 56, 70
Punter, — (scholar) 75, 116

quarries, *see* glass
quarters, *see* timbers
Queen Anne's Company 88
Queen's Men 90, 99
Queens' College 3–4, 9, 16–37, 42–3, 53, 61–6,

68, 70–7, 91, 95, 102–13, 115–17, 119,
124–6, 128, 131–9; *see also* acting room,
stagehouse
bibleclerks' table 24, 32
chimney, dais 32
doors 17, 24, 28–9, 32–3, 37
fireplace 17, 32, 34
hall 16–24, 29–37, 53, 62–4, 116, 131–9
hall dimensions 29–32, 62, 64–6, 68, 71–6,
91, 95
master's chamber, parlour 34
oriel 17, 30
President 16, 34, 36, 77
president's lodge/chamber 34, 117
screens 16–18, 21–4, 29–32, 34, 36, 43, 62,
133, 137–9
stairs, trap door 23–4, 30–1
tower/treasury 33–7
windows 17–18, 24, 31–2, 137–9

racks 18, 20, 24, 29, 31, 36, 109, 137–9
rails 9–10, 15, 18–29, 31–3, 40–2, 56–7, 59, 68,
82–3, 104, 107, 109, 111, 121, 127, 131–9,
156–7; *see also* bar
raisings 25
raked seating 18, 79, 82, 100
ramps, *see* slope boards
rank (academic, hierarchy) 70, 109
Ray, George (smith) 34
Red Lion Inn 93
Red Lion playhouse (London) 123–4
Regent House 103
Regent Walk 40, 77
regents, *see* masters of arts
Registrary 44, 78, 91, 99, 153
rehearsal stages 74, 104
rehearsals 33, 35–6, 43, 59, 61, 66, 76; *see also*
tiring chamber (Trinity)
removing, *see* carrying, setting up
repairs 35, 56, 58, 64–8, 70, 73, 79, 84, 87,
146–7, 152–3, 159; *see also* breakage
responsal seat (respondant) 12, 15, 127–8
revels, *see* lords of Christmas
ribbons 148–51
Rich, Baron 70
Richardson, Rowland 68, 76
Richardus Tertius 61, 66, 75
Ridding, Richard 97
riots 55, 65, 69, 74, 112–14, 117; *see also*
disorders
river, *see* boats, Cam
Robert (carpenter) 78, 105
Robinson, Nicholas 13–14, 32, 119, 129–30
Robinson, — 100
Robyns, Richard (carpenter) 33

Rochester, Bishop of 129–30
Roger (glazier) 66
Roman comedy, *see* classical plays
Roman theatres 119–20
ropes 33, 70; *see also* cord
Rose Crescent 93
Rose Inn 93, 155
Rose theatre (London) 1–2, 118, 121, 124
Round Church, *see* St Sepulchre Church
round, *see* Wandlebury Round
Rowland, *see* Richardson, Rowland
Roxana 107
Royal Commission on Historical Monuments
48–9, 51–2
royal treasury 10, 119
royal visits (royalty) 10–15, 39–40, 42, 44, 51,
54, 56, 59, 64, 71, 74, 76, 78–9, 82, 92,
106, 109, 112, 116–17, 119, 129–30, 142,
144, 147, 149–51; *see also* dignitaries, *and
individual monarchs*
Royston 42, 56, 108
Ruggle, George 57, 76
rushes (sedge, strewing) 53, 55–6, 65, 86, 110, 146
Rust, Mr 90
Rutland, Earl of 70

St Catharine's College 34, 93, 106
St John's College 3–4, 10, 34, 45, 55–6, 61–2,
64, 66–7, 75, 88, 103–8, 111–13, 116–17
buttery 67, 108, 112
door, kitchen, screens 66
hall 61–2, 66
Master 88
master's chambers/lodge, windows 67
members 117
wainscoting 66–7
St Michael's Church 103
St Radegund (nunnery of) 71, 73
St Sepulchre (Round) Church 97
Sancroft, William 77
Saracen's Head Inn 91–2, 124, 126
satin 148; *see also* cloth
satire 3, 74
satyrs (as decorations) 120
sawyers 56, 84
say 66; *see also* cloth
sayleirs, *see* celures
scaena, *see* scenes
scaffolds 20, 23, 33–4, 36, 40–3, 51, 55–8, 60–1,
65, 79, 86–7, 101, 103, 106–7, 114, 122–3,
125, 131–9, 144–6; *see also* commencement
stage
scantlings 10, 32, 82, 104
Scamotzi (Giovanni Domenico Scamozzi) 7
Scarabeus (character in play) 70

Scarlett, John 42, 55

Scarrow, George 58, 147, 149

scenes (*scaena*) 58, 78, 111, 109, 146; *see also frons scenae*

scholars, *see* students

schoolkeeper 86

Schools 63, 77, 86, 103, 159

Scott, Robert 99–100

screens 5, 107, 124; *see also* King's College Chapel, Great St Mary's, *and under individual colleges*

scrips (?) 149

seating platforms 13–15, 18–22, 24–6, 28–32, 51–2, 68, 78, 82–6, 104, 106, 108–9; *see also* galleries

seats (seating) 13–15, 18, 20, 29–30, 36, 40–4, 51, 56, 59, 68, 70–1, 78–9, 82, 84–5, 87, 100, 105, 107, 109, 121, 124, 145, 160; *see also* chairs, thrones

Secretary, Mr, *see* Cecil, William

security plan of 1615 44, 82, 84

security, *see* watching

sedge, *see* rushes

Seigniour, Sir 146

Senate House 77–8, 86

Senile Odium 116

Senior Fellows 5, 48, 57; *see also* fellows

sepulchre, *see* shrines

serge 149; *see also* cloth

Serlio, Sebastiano 7, 119

servants (of the queen) 127, 129–30; *see also* guards (royal)

servants, *see* assistants

setting up and taking down stages 33–4, 42, 57, 64–9, 74, 79, 84–5, 103, 113–14, 145, 153, 159

sewing 159

Shakespeare, William 1, 5, 16, 39, 92, 118

Sheffield, Baron 70

Sheldonian Theatre, *see* Oxford

shepherds (as characters) 148

shoes 147, 150

shopkeeper's house (Moxon) 6–8, 24

Shoreditch (London) 16

shows (college) 34–5, 62, 66, 68–70, 73, 105, 111, 116

shows/showmen (professional) 91, 102

Shrewsbury, Earl of 70

shrines (*phanum*, temples, sepulchre) 33–5, 67, 108–9, 111; *see also* portals

Shuter, John 57–9, 114, 145, 148, 150–1

Sicelides 116

Sidney Sussex College 78

signatures (personal) 36–7

Silcock, James (carpenter) 73, 113

Silent Woman, The 143

Silk (family of carpenters) 114, 144–5, 147, 150
  Abraham 114
  Thomas 114, 150

silver (silver-plate) 33, 112

Simpson (Simson), Rowland and Samuel 114

Simson, — 114, 145

singers 61; *see also* musicians

skewers 147

skirting (for stages) 78, 85–6, 106, 109; *see also* cloth

slope boards/rails 18, 23, 25, 28–30, 107, 137–9

Smith, Edward 97

Smith, Goodwife 146

Smith, George Charles Moore 52, 54, 70, 108, 131, 142, 146–49, 151–2

Smith, Samuel 56, 113

smiths (blacksmiths, locksmiths) 33–4, 51, 56–7, 64, 69, 76, 112, 120, 148, 150

Smyth, Mr 42, 55

sockets (for candles) 66, 112

solder (soldering) 146, 150, 152; *see also* lead, plumbers

soldiers (as characters) 61

Solymitana Clades, *see Destruction of Jerusalem*

Some, Robert 99

sophisters, *see* students

soutage 33; *see also* canvas, cloth

South Bank (London) 118

Southampton, Earl of 56

Southwark 1, 99

Spanish theatres 118

Sparrow, Anthony 77

spars 56; *see also* timbers

spectators, *see* audiences

spikes 33, 107; *see also* nails

sports, *see* games

spruce 83, 159

spur 22–3; *see also* timbers

squibs (fireworks) 71

stability (of scaffold stages) 10, 19, 21–2, 24–6

stables 86, 92, 95, 103; *see also* New Inn

stag, papaly (?) 111

stage doors 28–9, 37, 43–52, 58–60, 86–7, 107–8, 124–5

stage heights 13–14, 32, 82–3, 86, 104, 106; *see also* headroom

stage platforms 1–2, 6, 11–18, 23–6, 28–32, 39, 41–3, 45, 51, 58–60, 67–8, 73, 78, 80–1, 83, 86–7, 106–7, 109–10, 120, 126

stagehouse (Queens' College storehouse) 16, 35–6, 103, 115

stagehouses 11, 13–14, 25, 33, 37, 41–3, 45, 56, 60–1, 65, 68, 70–1, 106–9, 111, 113, 124–5; *see also* tiring houses

stagekeepers 55, 59–60, 64–5, 67, 69, 71, 74–5,
      84, 87, 112, 115–16
   garments 55, 60, 115
stages (college) 3, 5, 9–11, 13–14, 16–37, 39–43,
      45, 48, 51–3, 56–62, 64–71, 73–4, 76,
      102–17, 120, 124, 127–39, 142, 144–5,
      147–8, 150–1; *see also* commencement stage
stages (commercial) 1–2, 78, 106, 120–1, 124–5
stages (enlarging of) 59, 79, 85, 113
stair-keeping 84, 87
stairs (steps) 6, 14, 23, 33, 51, 79, 81–4, 87, 97
      (Elephant), 106–7, 115, 129–30, 140–1; *see
      also* ladders, churches, chapels, inns, *and
      under individual colleges*
stammell 151; *see also* cloth
standers 57, 144; *see also* timbers
Standish, John 98
Stanley, Lord 61
staples 19, 28, 58, 69, 112, 131–9, 149–50
Star Chamber 57
statutes, *see* orders
staves (shepherds' staves) 148, 151
Steeple Bumpstead 34, 103, 106
steps, *see* stairs
Sterne, George 68
Stevannage, — 64
Stevenson, William 65
Stocket, Lewis 10
stocks 65
Stokys, Matthew 13–15, 76, 78, 119, 127–8
stones (stonethrowing) 64–5, 71, 113; *see also*
      disorders, breakage
storage (storehouses, store-rooms) 16, 33–6, 48,
      59–60, 67, 69, 78, 86, 102–8, 111, 114–15,
      125, 158–60; *see also* stagehouse
straps 33
strewing, *see* rushes
string 34; *see also* cord
students (graduates) 14, 36, 40, 53, 55, 59, 61–2,
      64–5, 74, 76, 87, 97–8, 107, 116, 119, 128,
      146
studs 10, 18–19, 21–2, 24–6, 28–30, 32, 64, 83,
      86, 104, 106, 131–9, 156–8; *see also* timbers
Sturbridge Fair 3, 92, 102, 105, 113, 159–60
Styles, — 145
sugar chest 65, 111
Sun Inn 147
suppers, *see* dining
surveyors 40, 77
Suttell, — 73
Swan theatre (London) 120, 124
sweeping, *see* cleaning

tables 5, 11, 13, 24, 32, 35–7, 51, 59–60, 64–5,
      72, 106, 134, 137–9

Tabor, James 44, 78, 99–100, 140–1, 153
tacks 58, 146; *see also* nails
taffeta 151; *see also* cloth
tailors 36; *see also* Burton (Joshua)
taking down (stages, etc.), *see* setting up
tallow, *see* wax
tape 59, 150–1
tapestries 73, 82; *see also* cloth
tapster 147; *see also* innkeeper
targets (as props) 104
Tayler, Lawrence 34
temples, *see* shrines
tenons, *see* joints
tent 64
tenterhooks (tenternails) 33, 59, 69, 151; *see also*
      nails
textiles 85; *see also* cloth
Thaxted, John 68
theatre (nomenclature) 14, 71, 77–8, 119, 125
Theatre, the (London) 16, 39, 118–23; *see also*
      Globe theatre
theatres 1–2, 5, 7, 13–16, 19, 32, 34–5, 39–40,
      52–3, 55–6, 59, 64, 66, 70, 73–4, 77–8,
      86–7, 102, 107–8, 110, 118–21, 123–6,
      128–30, 153–5; *see also* boxes, playhouses,
      stages
Thexton, Robert 76
Thomas (first name? painter) 33, 110
thread 59, 151; *see also* cord
thrones 10, 13–14, 51, 106, 109, 128–30
thunder (thunder-barrel) 64, 67, 108
Thurles, Lord 125
tickets 58, 60, 117, 146
timber merchants 64, 82, 159
timbers 2–3, 5, 7, 9–10, 16, 18, 24–6, 29–30,
      32–3, 35–6, 43, 48, 56–9, 64, 68–9, 74,
      78–9, 82–3, 86, 94–5, 102–6, 114–15,
      120–2, 125, 144, 153, 156–60; *see also*
      marking of timbers
time of day (for performances) 13–14, 35, 38,
      52, 55–6, 61, 65, 69, 75, 111–13; *see also*
      lights, watchmen
time required for stage construction (summary)
      114–15
tin 58–9, 146, 151
tiring houses (Queens') 16–18, 24–32, 36–7,
      106, 108, 124–5, 134–9
tiring/repeating chamber/room/house (Trinity)
      39–45, 48–9, 51, 56, 59–60, 74, 124; *see
      also* stagehouses
tiring houses (other) 39, 124–5
tobacco (tobacco pipes) 40, 147–51
Tolbooth 89, 97; *see also* prisons
Tomkis, Thomas 38–9
torch-holders 112

torches (links) 14, 33–5, 55–8, 60, 64, 67, 69, 71, 73–4, 76, 112, 115, 145–6; *see also* lights
towers, *see* Queens', Trinity
Town Hall, *see* Guildhall
townspeople 36, 38, 40, 55–6, 59, 74, 97, 115, 129–30; *see also* aldermen
tragedies 3, 33–4, 66–7, 70, 103–4
transportation, *see* carrying
trap-doors 107–8, 126; *see also* Queens', Trinity
trash nails 69, 86, 109–10, 113, 159
treasury, *see* Queens', royal treasury
treatises, 119, 121
trees (as source of timber) 35, 115
trees (as props) 56, 58, 111, 149
trestles 64, 66–9, 103, 106
Trevelyan, G. M. 52
Trinity (Piss-Pot) Lane 55
Trinity College 3–4, 38–60, 67–71, 82, 84, 91, 102–17, 124–6, 128, 140–52; *see also* acting chamber, bars, comedy room, tiring chamber
  audit chamber/room 54, 58, 60, 111, 145, 150, 152
  bow windows 41, 44, 47, 53–4
  Bursars 44, 57, 142–52
  buttery 150
  cellars 45, 69, 103
  chambers (miscellaneous) 56
  chapel 69
  common chamber 54, 58, 60, 111, 142, 148–9
  conclave magistri 46, 49
  court 43–4, 46–7, 49, 60, 62, 70–1, 91, 147
  dais 45, 48–52
  Declaration Feast 146–7
  dining room 47
  doors, openings 40–1, 43–5, 47–52, 54–5, 58–9, 68, 145–7, 149; *see also* keeping
  drawing room 47, 53–4
  fireplace 56
  galleries 41–2, 51, 59–60
  gallery (long) 44, 47, 52–3
  gates 55, 57–60, 145, 147, 149–51; *see also* keeping
  hall dimensions 43, 68
  halls *frontispiece*, 38–53, 55, 68–71, 74, 104, 112, 141, 143, 150–1
  interior window 48, 52
  kitchens 48, 51, 150
  louvre 68
  Master 39–40, 48, 52, 54, 57, 59, 105, 144–5
  master's lodge 40–1, 44–5, 47–9, 51–3, 59–60, 146–7, 150
  members 55, 59, 61
  orders 48
  oriels 68; *see also* bow windows
  panelling 48, 52
  parlour 53–4, 56–60, 111, 117
  pavement 147
  plan of 1555 46, 48, 51, 68, 71
  porch 51, 144–5
  porters 145–6, 150
  posts, rails 144
  sceptres 148–9, 151
  screens 41, 43–4, 51, 55, 59–60, 68, 141
  sculptures 149, 151
  Senior Fellows 48, 52, 57, 144
  stairs 43, 45, 51, 55, 59–60, 150
  tower 69
  trap-door 39, 43–5, 141
  Vice-Master 144
  walls 146
  wicket 70
  windows 41, 44, 47, 52–3, 56
Trinity Hall 3–4, 14, 62
  chapel 14
  hall 62
Trinity Street 60
tripods 34, 74, 106
trumpets (trumpeters) 51, 53, 61–3, 71
trunks, *see* chests
Twelfth Night 67
Tysetone, Leonard (locksmith) 112

university 3, 76, 129–30, 148–51, 153, 158; *see also* ceremonies, Chancellors, commencement stage, graces, orders, Proctors, Vice-Chancellors
  press 61; *see also* New Printing House
  senate, syndics 77, 154–5
upholsterers 56, 58, 146
upper-end walls, doors 18, 30, 32, 39, 41, 43, 45, 47–51, 59, 62, 65–6, 68, 73, 103, 107, 125

Valetudinarium 35
vandalism, *see* damage
Vaux, Lord 98
velvet 15, 127; *see also* cloth
Venus (temple/shrine of) 35, 108
Verses at the Last Publick Commencement, see Eusden, Lawrence
verticals 10, 82–3, 104, 156; *see also* posts, studs, timbers
vestments, *see* liturgical vestments
Vetule, Margaret 34, 103
Vice-Chancellors (university) 82, 84, 87–8, 97, 99–100, 102, 109, 153–5, 158–60
victuallers 100
victuals, *see* dining

Vignola (Giacomo Barozzi) 7
violence, *see* disorders
visors, *see* masks
Vitruvius (Marcus Vitruvius Pollio) 7, 119

Wade, John (carpenter) 86–7, 105, 114–15
waggons, *see* carts
wainscoting, *see* panelling
waits, *see* musicians
Wanamaker, Sam 1–2, 118
Wandlebury Round 3, 99–101
Ware 56, 100
warrant (for arrest) 98–9
washing, *see* cleaning
watching (watchmen) 36, 44–5, 56, 58–9, 65, 69,
    76, 82, 84, 86–7, 92, 95, 108, 112, 124, 146,
    159; *see also* doorkeepers, gate-keepers,
    guards (royal), keepers of passages, stair-
    keeping, stagekeepers
Watkins, Mr 127
Watson, Thomas 68
Watts, — 144
wax (tallow) 35, 57–9, 74, 76, 111–12, 144–6,
    148, 151; *see also* candles
weapons 55, 57, 112, 115, 125, 146, 150; *see also*
    clubs
Webster, John 55
well (as prop) 58, 149
Westminster 98
Whaley, Thomas 100
Wharton, — 64
whipcord 69; *see also* cord
Whitehall, *see* Banqueting House
whitening (of slops) 150
whitewashing 51, 54, 59, 67, 152
Whitgift, John 100
Whyrte, Christopher 34

Wickham, Glynne 14
wigs 64
William III, King 51
Williams, Thomas 147
Willis, Robert, and John Willis Clark 43, 49,
    51–4, 63, 68, 71–2, 75–6
Wilshaw, Thomas 71
windows (breakage of, care for) 34–5, 53, 64–7,
    69, 73–5, 87–8, 91, 113, 146–7, 149, 152;
    see also glass
windows (interior) *see* Christ's, Trinity
wine 56, 146, 148, 150–1
velvet 127; *see also* cloth
Winning of an Holde 70
wire 144
Wisdom, — (family of painters) 58, 111, 145,
    148–9, 152
    John 111, 152
women 12–15, 51, 57, 82, 117, 127, 129–30,
    140, 146–7
wood 5, 33–4, 36, 67, 69, 76, 101–2, 104–5, 107,
    110, 112; *see also* boards, elm, fir, oak,
    spruce, timber
Woodruffe, — 144–5
wool 85; *see also* cloth
workmen, *see* labourers
worsted 148–9; *see also* cloth
Wotton, Henry 7
Wrag, Dr 151
Wren, Christopher 77, 120
writing, *see* inscriptions
Wylliams, Martin (vicar) 98

yards (of playhouses) 1–2, 120–1, 123; *see also*
    innyards
Yeoman Bedell 87, 115
York, Duke of 59, 149–50